W9-CLD-228

CROSSING CUSTOMS

GARLAND STUDIES IN HIGHER EDUCATION
VOLUME 18
GARLAND REFERENCE LIBRARY OF SOCIAL SCIENCE
VOLUME 1193

GARLAND STUDIES IN HIGHER EDUCATION

This series is published in cooperation with the Program in Higher Education, School of Education, Boston College, Chestnut Hill, Massachusetts.

PHILIP G. ALTBACH, *Series Editor*

CROSSING CUSTOMS

INTERNATIONAL STUDENTS WRITE ON U.S. COLLEGE LIFE AND CULTURE

EDITED BY
ANDREW GARROD
JAY DAVIS

FALMER PRESS
A MEMBER OF THE TAYLOR & FRANCIS GROUP
NEW YORK AND LONDON
1999

Library of Congress Cataloging-in-Publication Data

Crossing customs : international students write on U.S. college life and culture /
   by Andrew Garrod and Jay Davis.
            p.   cm. — (Garland reference library of social science ;
   v. 1193. Garland studies in higher education ; v. 18)
         Includes bibliographical references.
         ISBN 0–8153–3162–2 (hardcover : alk. paper). —
      ISBN 0–8153–3395–1 (pbk.)
         1. Students, Foreign—United States—Diaries. 2. Foreign study—
United States. 3. Dartmouth College—Students.   I. Garrod, Andrew,
1937– . II. Davis, Jay. III. Series: Garland reference library of social
science ; v. 1193. IV. Series: Garland reference library of social science.
Garland studies in higher education ; vol. 18.
LB2376.4.C76   1999   99–11643
370. 116'2—DC21
   CIP

Printed on acid-free, 250-year-life paper
Manufactured in the United States of America

For
Langley Keyes
Geoff Fox
Mervyn Morris

    A.G.

For
my mother, father, and brother,
and my wife, Julie

    J.D.

SERIES EDITOR'S PREFACE

Higher education is a multifaceted phenomenon in modern society, combining a variety of institutions and an increasing diversity of students, a range of purposes and functions, and different orientations. The series combines research-based monographs, analyses, and discussions of broader issues and reference books related to all aspects of higher education. It is concerned with policy as well as practice from a global perspective. The series is dedicated to illuminating the reality of higher and postsecondary education in contemporary society.

Philip G. Altbach
Boston College

Contents

Re-Viewing Identity

Foreword

Marianne Hirsch

In the United States, the experience of going to college is most often associated with leaving home, joining other age mates on a residential college campus and living and learning in a campus setting. Postsecondary education is, for many, an education not only in the humanities, the social sciences, and the sciences, but also an education in living with peers, in a temporary and transient environment that constitutes a formative influence on individual development. Residential learning acknowledges that postsecondary studies are not only intellectual, but also bear potential for emotional, psychological, and interpersonal growth, in addition to providing an opportunity to learn how to live with those who are like us and with those who are different, distant, unfamiliar.

This was not my experience. When I was ready to go to college, I applied to the excellent university in my town and agreed, without much protest, to live at home throughout my four college years. Having emigrated from Europe with my family only four years before, I did not yet understand this essential element of college experience and, without misgivings, I followed the European model with which I had grown up. There, young people live at home throughout their university education if they can, and define their education along narrower, strictly academic grounds, for reasons as much economic as philosophical.

I got to know my peers in classes, I talked to them in the library, and joined some extracurricular activities, but I missed, entirely, the pleasures and perils of dormitory life and institutional food, as well as the quality of companionship that comes from constructing a living environment with one's peers. What I did not miss, however, was the shift in perspective and outlook, the healthy dislocation that going to college entails. I did not miss it because I had actually already left "home" five years earlier, when I immigrated to the United States from Rumania with my family at the age of thirteen. Throughout my high school years and then in college I maintained a double vision: Sometimes illuminating, sometimes blinding, this is the classic sense of alienation that college tends to cultivate when students confront the values they learned at home with a new set of beliefs and perspectives. I had already done some of that work by the time I arrived at Brown University, and throughout college I continued to experience this sense of dislocation and cultural relativism in my studies and relationships.

Living at home for the duration of my college years allowed me to live out and even to cultivate the ambivalence I felt about assimilating to American culture, extending the feelings of displacement that I had first experienced as strangely creative in early adolescence. As I studied French and comparative literature, immersing myself in European literature and culture, I secretly planned to move back to Europe when I graduated, or at least to visit, in order to see whether I might be—as I suspected—more European than American. I certainly did not aim to be a typical American college student. Still, I often experienced my difference as painfully humiliating, for I wanted to belong. Paradoxically, I both valued my double outlook and wanted desperately for it to disappear.

Reading the personal narratives of international students in this volume has brought such memories back to me in a rush of autobiographical identification with the writers. But while I left "home" as an adolescent to emigrate with my family, these young people left their homes on their own, to come to a distant and foreign place for their education. Most are here for that purpose alone, fully intending, at least initially, to return to their home after graduation. While American students travel several hundred or thousand miles to relocate to a university campus, these students travel across countries and continents to encounter a strange culture and an education system based on premises that can diverge widely from their own. And while American students can usefully absorb some cultural relativism as they compare home with school, these international students must bridge significant gaps in values, beliefs and practices in ways that call for complex skills of adaptation and flexibility. Can we then say that their education is the same as that of their American peers?

I identify most with the perspectives of Stephen Kobourov and Maria Popova who grew up under Bulgarian communism, close to my Rumanian upbringing. The fear, suspicion and hatred that marked Stephen's relationships with neighbors and peers also marked mine, making the openness of American interactions a difficult adjustment even though friendship and trust are absolutely life-sustaining. Like Maria, I was stunned by the loneliness one can feel as an outsider in a group of people who are familiar with one another's customs. Her roommate Melanie, focusing on Maria's 'hilarious' accent, is not otherwise curious to know more about her, and the relationship soon devalues to silence. This happened with many of my classmates, who seemed to find me too difficult to take on as a foreigner with an accent, unfamiliar with their rituals and frames of reference.

This volume is the first to confront the relationship between education, adolescent development and cultural displacement, and as such it offers much more than a set of developmental stories. In recent years, diasporic studies of refugeehood, emigration and cultural displacement have received a great deal of critical and theoretical attention. As the myth of the American melting pot has been revealed as both untrue and inadequate as a model, American identities have been seen as hyphenated, and personal identification has become more precise. We all need labels and categories by which to define ourselves—e.g., female and male, African-American or Asian-American, straight, gay or bisexual, urban or rural. The insistence on diversity has often emphasized difference rather than commonalities. Identity politics have encouraged an intense categorization that has even led to separatism on some college campuses. But as the widespread realities of twentieth-century diasporic experiences are increasingly acknowledged and discussed—experiences of emigration, exile, migration, expatriation and the effects of war and de-colonization—scholars are focusing more and more on the hybrid identities that are no longer the exception. Like myself, growing up in Rumania as part of a German-speaking Jewish minority, many of the students writing here bring to the experience of displacement an already culturally hybrid bi- or multi-lingual identity which is further expanded and complicated by the move to the United States. As Lai Heng Foong says in her essay in this book: "Borders between foreign and familial became blurred and undefined. . . . I believe that one's identity can be formed and reformed and that who I am is constantly in flux." This is an expression of a conception of identity as hybrid, and formed in the experience of the diaspora that has become quite common in recent theory that relativizes the power of national definition, revealing the concept of nation as no more than a contingent construct. These students, like theorists of exile and emigration, highlight the strengths that come from these multiple perspectives, positioning mobility rather than rootedness as the cachet of identity.

What has rarely been studied, and what this volume beautifully illuminates, is the developmental trajectory of the hybrid, multicultural self. What psychological processes go into the formation of the diasporic subject? What kind of adaptation is required? What type of resistance emerges? How are conflicting allegiances and contradictory visions negotiated? What elements of the culturally hybrid's adolescent development are geographic and cultural, and which are psychological? How does the international student mediate between home and school, when these realities are so widely divergent? And how can a consciousness of the multiplicity of diasporic identity serve as a response to the virulent angers and misunderstandings among the separate and often uncompromising student groups that have emerged with identity politics? Many of the essays in this volume suggest that the easiest and strongest community for them to inhabit is that of international students themselves. As Georgina Gemmill writes, "I also find many Americans apathetic about attempting to meet and understand international students. At the same time, I find many international students, like myself, largely critical of American society and thus choosing to mix primarily within the international organizations at Dartmouth." Although links across cultural boundaries are reportedly difficult to forge, every essay, nonetheless, points to at least one moment of illumination and connection, whether among women classmates in the context of Women's Studies, as for Yu Chen, or on a foreign study trip for Maria Popova. These moments are where we might focus to find the possibilities and hopes that each essay contains.

A diasporic model of selfhood can respond to, complicate and broaden a simple identity politics that assumes the self as static and rooted in community. In their college experiences, these international students have themselves forged identities that can reflect and negotiate the diversity we hold up as a model. This does not mean that they are not often lonely, frustrated or unhappy in their new surroundings, or that they do not profoundly miss their homes. But the cultural relativism that results from their displacement opens up new worlds for them, both interior and exterior, and this is what I find so inspiring in their moving and painful narratives.

Personal narratives constitute a welcome genre for this kind of story. The narratives of adaptation contained in this volume show that identity is a process, fluid and evolving, never static. The reminiscences of home—sometimes nostalgic, often painful—combine with the impressions of school—sometimes incredulous, at times admiring—to create a unique lens through which to view the adolescent moment. The struggle of adaptation focuses not just on the journey to adulthood, but on difficult cultural choices that complicate that trajectory and which are largely left unresolved. And yet the solutions to personal struggle— friendship, allegiance to home (however conflicted), self-reliance, choice of community—will not be unfamiliar to any reader. For each of us can find a way to enter these essays, savoring the points of connection and identification they offer and marveling at the courage of these students as they sustain the intense cultural, intellectual and emotional work required of adaptation.

To see this process from the inside, honestly articulated in admirable and elegant prose, is a privilege indeed. Readers cannot fail to be moved and inspired.

Preface

Crossing Customs: International Students Write on U.S. College Life and Culture contains the personal narratives of international students who have studied at Dartmouth College in New Hampshire. Over the past five years, the editors approached approximately forty such students (men and women in equal numbers), inviting them to write about their earlier years in their mother countries and their college experiences in the U.S. with a particular focus on the challenges of adapting to American college life and mores.

The results will speak to both the particularity and the commonalities of this experience as it was shaped through independent studies with Andrew Garrod, who was himself an international student later in life at Harvard, and whose choice to leave Britain as a young adult (still, technically, an adolescent himself) to work and study in Canada and the U.S. must surely have a bearing on this project. Jay Davis became involved with the book because of his interest in language and expression, and his position as Assistant Director of the Dartmouth Composition Center, responsible for helping international students. His experience as a secondary school English teacher who had worked many hours with recent immigrants was invaluable during the long process of consultation and editing.

In gathering the essays initially, we encouraged participants to work from broad guidelines, reflecting on how the formative aspects of their home culture and values (with reference to such influences as family and schooling) had affected their transition to a foreign college, examining the pleasures and problems encountered along the way. Writers were asked to think about classroom experiences at Dartmouth in the context of intellectual stimulation offered by the college as a learning environment; and about their interactions with mentors, other international students, and American students, exploring the friendships that crossed the lines of race, class and sex. We asked how their engagement in college life affected issues of identity (personal and national), and whether participants anticipated returning to their mother country after graduation.

While the editors worked on a weekly basis with writers there was an effort to keep assumptions about where the individual stories might go in view, but out of the way of the participants. Because the emphasis was on process—facilitating contributors to undertake that most complex of all writerly tasks, the location of voice (a task further complicated for those who were working in a second or third language)—no editorial interventions were made during the generative stage. Although the parameters were necessarily established by the editors, we encouraged writers to develop their own themes and make analytical sense of their experience in ways that gave them back significant meaning for their own lives. All we requested was that their thinking, feeling and writing be as honest as they could possibly muster. There was no assumption on either part that the story was "there," waiting to come out ready formed, as if from the head of Zeus; rather, there was the shared belief the story had to be "found"—built little by little as patterns emerged and themes asserted themselves.

It was the writers themselves who decided when their first draft was complete, at which time the discretionary work of revision began in earnest. Some writers went through three drafts, while others did as many as eight re-writes. It was a labor-intensive job that surprised and challenged many contributors and required editorial choices that were at times agonizing—the business of inclusion, preclusion and hovering between these cruelly opposed options turned out to be too complex for criteria that might work for less personally charged anthologies. Indeed, the relationships formed between editors and participants felt deeply privileged, which added to the always demanding task of selection.

The thirteen narratives that comprise this book represent Asia, Europe, Africa and the Caribbean. How, indeed, did we choose? Sometimes it wasn't our choice at all, for instance in the case of a brilliant Southeast Asian student who withdrew his completed essay because he was cautioned by his friends that some of his sympathetic views towards gays and Jews might hinder him in a future political career. And then there was the more ambiguous gesture of a South

American writer who withdrew his essay after five revisions, perhaps because he was at the limits of his self-understanding. It is possible that for others who withdrew the opportunity for writing and self-reflection through the independent study was always more important than the possibility of a later publication. Once the "therapeutic" purpose had been served within the confines of the academic term requirements, there was no further incentive for revision. The nimbus of these "lost" essays informs those that are visible here in something the same way that the bands of colored light available to the eye at any given time point to others that exist in a larger relationship to the visual world.

Informing the revision process at all times was the belief that student writers can best build confidence in their approaches to personal prose incrementally, finding the detail that resonates with their own memories and perceptions. Because of the nature of these essays and the purpose of the book, the variation in tone, facility with the English language, degree of self-analysis and style of expression which were deliberately cultivated did not get flattened into one editorial mold. Manuscripts ranged in original length from 30 to 120 pages. Some writers took two academic terms, while others reached a publishable stage in ten weeks. We consider that the process of generation and revision was deeply collaborative and reflects the editors' teaching emphasis on reflective learning.

Indeed, the editors firmly believe in the educational value of personal memoir, both for the writer and the reader. In the ten years that Garrod has worked with college students writing personal memoirs—in three editions of *Adolescent Portraits*, and in *First Person, First Peoples*, and three other collections in progress—he has found students overwhelmingly open to the invitation to make sense of childhood and adolescent experiences that up to then have been inchoate, unintegrated, and insufficiently reflected upon. Seldom at college does academic coursework surrender authority to the student or confirm for the student the validity of his/her most personal experiences and analyses. Generating personal narrative is not only a process that is essentially writerly—requiring precision, nuance, and a suppleness of syntax—but also one that offers both a therapeutic and a hermeneutic opportunity. For some students the text that is developed can act as a template in later stages of development, when increased sophistication will allow the material to be fruitfully recast.

It is incumbent on the supervising teacher, then, to be sensitive to the therapeutic, cathartic, interpretive and compositional dimensions of the task. In our own editorial roles, we have felt deeply privileged in aiding the student writers to deeper levels of self-understanding and into gaining purchase on the world through reflection and articulation. Most importantly, at the end there is an artifact, the essay—often compelling, brave, vivid—to show for the labors, one that could enlighten and embolden student readers for generations to come.

The thirteen essays are grouped thematically: in the first section, "Opening Worlds," writers explore the various influences of their pasts in relation to the sense of displacement experienced at Dartmouth. This section reveals the extraordinary resources, intellectual as well as material, available to the international student and their initial perception of a burgeoning world of unlimited possibility. "Challenging Expectations"—the middle section—deals with the emotional and intellectual accommodations that had to be made in order to fit into this opened world, and uncovers some of the assumptions carried from the provenant reality into the new one. It is in this section that we learn how exposure to academic courses, readings and fresh ideas prompted a writer to update his or her interpretation of "home." In the final section, "Re-Viewing Identity," the ordinarily tumultuous process of adolescent identity construction is amplified by the cross-cultural educational experience. As Marianne Hirsch points out in her Forward, an international student may bring "an already culturally hybrid bi- or multi-lingual identity" into the encounter with American ideologies, values and language. How is the resulting "self" experienced when it might be seen, as Lai Heng Foong so poignantly observes, to belong both nowhere and everywhere?

Taken together these essays offer the reader a rare opportunity to understand from the inside the experiences of recent outsiders. We are invited not only to appreciate the courage, resilience and insight of their changing perspectives but also to re-examine the United States as these young writers see it—with a freshness and precision that is sometimes unnerving.

After five years of work on this project we are indebted to the editorial skills, energy and enduring support of a great many friends and assistants. Special thanks for moral and administrative help are due to Judith Mackenzie and Guilan Wang, former and current Directors of International Students at Dartmouth College, respectively. Several friends—Karen Maloney, Dody Riggs, Gail Taylor, and Kari McCadam—generously offered close readings and helpful editorial suggestions at different stages of the manuscript's preparation, right up to the night before manuscript submission. We are also deeply grateful to past and present Dartmouth students—Cabell King, Abigail Klingbeil, Will Taylor, Keith Zorn, Megan Cummings, and Julia Webb—for their assistance in preparing the manuscript; we owe a special debt to Matthew K. Nelson and Kelly Hsieh for their meticulous checking of the manuscript immediately prior to publication. John and Karen Sanders are also owed many thanks for their gracious gift of home and heart on Jay's numerous trips to Hanover.

We particularly want to grant special recognition to *all* students who worked with such industry, openness and courage to bring their stories by stages from the realm of the strictly private into public view. Those who do not show up here gave no less generously of themselves, and we are in their debt. Finally we salute the perseverance, insight and honesty of all those whose essays make this book.

Introduction

The exile therefore exists in a median state, neither completely at one with the new setting nor fully disencumbered of the old, beset with half-involvements and half-detachments, nostalgic and sentimental on one level, an adept mimic or a secret outcast on another.

Edward Said
Representations of the Intellectual

Neither myself nor my narrative can have . . . a single strand. I stand at the crossing point of too many social and cultural forces; and in any case, I am forever on my way. My identity has to be perceived as multiple, even as I strive towards some coherent notion of what is human and decent and just.

Maxine Greene
Releasing the Imagination

The word "translation" comes etymologically from the Latin for "bearing across." Having been borne across the world, we are translated men. It is normally supposed that something always gets lost in translation; I cling, obstinately, to the belief that something can also be gained.

Salman Rushdie
Imaginary Homelands

I will probably always find myself in the chinks between cultures and subcultures. . . . It gives you an Archimedean leverage from which to see the world.

Eva Hoffman
Lost in Translation

This is a book by and about young women and men who traveled thousands of miles from their homes to attend college in a foreign land. They are Bulgarian, Chinese, Nigerian, Bosnian; they are student assembly presidents, war veterans, feminist scholars; they hold up mirrors to our culture that are alternately warmly thankful and coldly damning. Intertwined throughout this fundamentally complex mixture, however, is a common thread of difference, of spaces occupied in their college lives that are an amalgam of cultures, memories, contradicting values. Using their own voices, these students write about discontinuities as they straddle cultures—about presents lived in environments extraordinarily different from pasts.

In a very real sense, these writers have crossed customs, not so importantly in their presentation of passports but in their integration, or rejection, of distinctly American attitudes and traditions as they simultaneously discard, adapt, or insistently maintain the attitudes and traditions of the countries that have been their homes. They must constantly make decisions about how former lives and values may be reconciled, if at all, with American ideas and practices. If, as Mirsky and Kaushinsky (1989) suggest, immigration is a "deep internal process in which a meaningful interaction—one which brings about significant change in both parties—occurs between immigrant and society" (731), then these students offer important insights into what it means to be on the margins working in, to occupy a middle ground that is truly neither here nor there, to be, at an elite American college, an immigrant. Through their stories, we may better understand how international students at college follow, in Marianne Hirsch's phrase, "the developmental trajectory of the hybrid, multicultural self."

And this trajectory is one being followed by an ever-increasing number of students at American colleges and universities. Indeed, "American education institutions are to the modern world what Alexandria in Egypt was to the ancient world during the beginning of the third century" (Udadigbo 1997: 1). For the seventh consecutive year, foreign enrollments have shown modest growth, leading to an all-time record in 1996–1997 of 457,984 students enrolled at U.S. colleges and universities (Desruisseaux 1997: A47). Although this figure seems impressive, foreign students in the United States actually account for only 3.2 percent of all postsecondary enrollment, as compared with Britain and Australia, where they now represent 12 percent and 10 percent, respectively (Desruisseaux 1997: A47). These percentages may be affected worldwide in the near future, as a result of the severe economic turmoil in Asia (especially the hard-hit countries of Indonesia, Malaysia, South Korea, and Thailand, all of which rank in the top ten as countries of foreign students origin), which may influence the number of foreign students sent abroad (Desruisseaux 1997: A47).

Visitors to the United States come, overwhelmingly, from Asian countries, with Japan, China, the Republic of Korea, and India sending the largest numbers. Statistics in "Open Doors, 1996–97" show that Asia, in fact, accounts for 56.9 percent of all foreign students, 46,292 of whom came from Japan in 1996–1997. Europe comes in second at 14.9 percent. Interestingly, of the top ten countries of origin, Canada is the only non-Asian representative (Desruisseaux 1997: A47). More men than women (59% as compared to 41%) enroll in American institutions, 48 percent to study as undergraduates and 42 percent to pursue graduate degrees. Foreign students studying in the United States are surprisingly self-funded, with 67.2 percent relying on personal and family resources to fund their education. U.S. colleges and universities contribute 16.9 percent to the funding pool, while home governments and universities furbish only 5.5 percent of necessary monies.

Business (21%) and engineering (16%) are clearly the favorite areas of study, with physical and life sciences, mathematics and computer science, and the social sciences each drawing 8 percent of students. The states that enrolled the largest number of foreign students are California, New York, Texas, and Massachusetts, and Boston University, with 4,657 students in 1996–1997, has the single largest enrollment among all U.S. educational institutions.

If we look at the fields of study foreign graduate students select, we see they are more likely to pursue degrees in science and engineering than are U.S. graduate students. "In the academic year 1993–94, 37 percent of all foreign master's degree recipients earned a degree in science or engineering, compared to 16% of U.S. recipients" (Young and Bae 1997: 1). Upon examining foreign graduate students' postdoctoral plans, we find that, of those who earned doctorates at U.S. colleges and universities, students from China and India are more likely to stay in the United States (92 and 89%, respectively) than students from Korea (49%), Taiwan, and Canada (40% each) (Young and Bae 1997: 1).

The contributors to this particular volume are students at a small, yet highly competitive college in New Hampshire—an extremely homogeneous state that enrolls the eleventh smallest number of international students (1,869 in 1996–1997). At Dartmouth College, where undergraduate enrollment is 4,300 and the graduate student population is 1,200, international students in 1996–1997 filled 232 undergraduate slots and 196 graduate slots. These numbers have practically doubled in the past ten years, showing positive trends in foreign student enrollment.

With such vast numbers of students from other countries continuing their education in this country, it is difficult to make generalizations about "the international student experience." The literature on international student issues is as far-ranging in research goals as it is varied in the populations studied. Also, as with all college students, the international student's experience of university life depends on that student's own unique set of family, religious, racial, geographic, linguistic, and political circumstances: The experience at Dartmouth College will be extraordinarily different for a white woman from South Africa and a black man from Nigeria, a man of mixed African and Chinese descent from the West Indies, and a Chinese-Malaysian woman from Kuala Lumpur. Compounding the difficulty of isolating patterns and variables is the simple fact that college students—even international students in their early twenties—are still experiencing the transitions of late adolescence. However, while broad-based generalizations are tricky at best, the editors have found compelling patterns of experience and reaction in our contributors' experience that resist dismissal. They also find that these patterns reinforce some central findings of research on international students in general.

As intuition suggests, the uprooting involved with studying in a foreign country goes far beyond the typical separation faced by American college students. Simply put, "International students are more likely to experience more problems than students in general and have access to fewer resources to help them" (Pedersen 1991: 24). At precisely the moment when most that is familiar has been left behind, very little that is familiar surrounds the international student. Often these students struggle to maintain possession of Erikson's (1950) "sense of identity [that] provides the ability to experience one's self as something that has continuity and sameness, and to act accordingly" (37). Removed from the cultural environments that have molded their identities, international students often find themselves disquietingly unsure of how exactly their conception of self relates to the new environments that surround them. As a result, "Foreign students are more vulnerable to psychological disturbance" (Klineberg and Hall 1979: 369).

This psychological disturbance, and the success with which individuals negotiate the challenges it presents, comes in a variety of forms. To measure the different stresses that confront the international student, Sandhu and Asrabi (1994) developed an acculturative stress scale—a scale that assesses the relative importance of different challenges in international students' lives. The most significant cause of stress was a sense of perceived discrimination/alienation; the second major factor was homesickness; and perceived hate, fear, and stress due to change and guilt all played significant but less important roles in students' lives. In their own groundbreaking work on international student experience, Klineberg and Hall (1979) found major causes of stress to be ethnic prejudice and discrimination; loneliness and homesickness; and, less importantly, negative evaluation of the actual university experience and the teaching encountered. Crucial variables that determine the level of stress experienced seem to be the duration of time in the United States—university stay of longer than a year has a much higher rate of depression—and the level of academic preparation the student had before arriving in the host country (Furnham and Trezise 1983).

In their processing of what it means to exist in Said's "median state," caught between the assumptions and expectations of different cultures, international students often experience a gradual separation from the home country as well as from internal representations of identity that are connected to the home country. Mirsky and Kaushinsky (1989) have conceptualized this separation process in terms of Margaret Mahler's (Mahler, Pine, and Bergman 1975) separation-individuation model of infant development. Seeing immigration as a late adolescent representation of Mahler's stage theory, Mirsky and Kaushinsky describe a pattern of development that they have observed in their work with immigrant students in Israel. First, the international student may experience initial elation, thrilled by the freedom and autonomy that the new environment offers. This is soon followed by a practicing stage, where students immerse themselves in becoming oriented and applying their skills in a new environment. Concurrently, however, many international students also experience what Mahler termed "low-keyedness," where the awareness of loss and of their own internal changes takes center stage; Hoffman (1989) writes of this transition in *Lost in Translation:* "After the immigrant's dendrites stop standing on end from the vividness of first impressions, comes this other, more elusive strangeness—the strangeness of glimpsing internal landscapes that are arranged in different formations as well" (265).

The internal emptiness that can result from this new awareness may bring a prolonged realization stage, where the loss of homeland connections is acutely felt, and the sense of alienation can be at its strongest of the immigration process. Students at this stage often frequently feel anger toward the host country or host university, and also often search for symbolic connection with objects and people that represent the home country. In Mirsky and Kaushinsky's final stage, naturalization, students' success in ultimately negotiating the challenges of immigration depends on their ability to reconcile their past identity and connection with the developing sense of self. "Mature, post-ambivalent interpersonal relationships and intimacy develop at this point, and search for the individual lifestyle begins" (Mirsky and Kaushinsky, 1989: 738). Whether choosing to remain in the host country or return to their homeland, these students will leave college as dramatically different human beings—men and women who have been molded by, and have in turn molded, the university environments that they inhabited.

And it is precisely the affecting/affected quality of many international students' experiences that prompted the collection of narratives for this book. The thirteen essays assembled here reflect the vastly different college experiences that would be expected from vastly different people; at the same time, however, they cohere because of the writers' common experience of change, of evolution in how they see their college, the United States, their homeland, and ultimately themselves. Although they are all students at a highly selective liberal arts college, the issues they address are relevant to all foreign students in the United States. They speak in voices distinctly their own, yet their stories bear out the observations of the researchers cited earlier. In so doing, they suggest commonalities of experience that offer compelling insight not only into what it means to be an international student at an elite American college, but also into what it means to be human in the midst of startlingly rapid change, what it means to feel that "our identity is at once plural and partial . . . that we straddle two cultures (or) at other times, that we fall between two stools" (Rushdie 1991: 15).

Whether straddling or falling in between, our contributors write at times poignantly, at times humorously, at times incisively of being between cultures. Every contributor to this book writes of specific moments at which the dissonance of cultures was most profoundly felt—a dissonance that often spurs new insight simultaneously into both cultures involved. For some, the dissonance is humorous, a relatively light reminder of difference. Devyani Sharma becomes hopelessly bemused when trying to decide which international address to give as her "home address" on registration forms; Yu Chen's upbringing in communist China does not prepare her for quarter-requiring laundry machines in her dorm basement; Stephen Kobourov actually has headaches his first week as the air is "too clean" after the smoky haze of Sofia, Bulgaria.

For others, the awareness is searingly painful, a specific moment in which their distance from all things familiar becomes disequilibratingly difficult to bear. Ian Sue Wing gasps to breathe as his lungs struggle with the subfreezing air on his way to an 8:00 a.m. class in February, while his thoughts are two thousand miles away in dusty streets at the Caribbean festival that he knows will be lingering still from the night before; Maria Popova realizes that much of the social warmth she has experienced is actually very superficial, a "silky thin chain of 'Hi's' and 'Bye's'" that ultimately do not reflect personal connection; "Devneesh" sits in a hammock by a frozen river, contemplating suicide as he struggles to reconcile his "old" identity with the expectations of his "new" society.

This struggle of identity is for many students an unintended by-product of their journey to the academic world of Dartmouth—unintended precisely because their goals and desires for their time here are in many cases external to personal or emotional development. Every international student we worked with (both those included in the book and those who are not) observed that intellectual growth and academic achievement form the foundational *raison d'être* of their coming to America. Whereas most Dartmouth students anticipate development that is on academic, social, athletic, artistic levels, international students at the college are strikingly focused on their lives within the classroom and libraries; not incidentally, three out of eight recent valedictorians are international students. Seeing their time here as an opportunity for access to a remarkably rich array of intellectual resources, our contributors cite the educational advantages of Dartmouth's liberal arts program as their original draw to the United States.

They also see this "array of resources" to be as varied as it is rich. Many of our writers marvel at the access to over a million books, what Stephen terms "an awesome repository of knowledge that no one lifetime can assimilate," and "James" likens to a "river of knowledge" that can be almost paralyzingly inviting. Others speak warmly of the attentiveness of professors, and the personal investment that many faculty members seem to have in the intellectual and personal growth of their students. As an extreme example, Yu Chen actually worked with a Dartmouth professor while studying at Beijing University—an interaction so illuminating of possibility that she came to this college in search of similar interactions that would transcend the limitations with which she had become increasingly frustrated in Beijing. Many writers can highlight an individual class or area of study that was solely responsible for epiphanies of development: Like Yu Chen who finds in her women's studies classes the strength and confidence to "sing the unsung songs" of her female ancestors, Georgina Gemmill uses her work in women's studies to look "through a new lens" at gender roles in her native South Africa; Ian finds connection with his ancestry through the Chinese classes he could take in addition to his engineering major; Devyani, amazed by the flexibility of her study at Dartmouth, discovers in her literature and psychoanalysis course the abiding passion for linguistics that has informed her career path; Aassia Haroon finally finds community in her creative writing classmates—a community of writers committed to using language to effect both personal and societal change.

Such epiphanies only intensify the amazement of our contributors at what they perceive to be the general intellectual apathy of their American peers. Many of the American students take for granted a wealth of resources that stuns Maria and Stephen after being raised in communist Bulgaria with the kind of perpetual denial that cultivates burning curiosity and desire for knowledge. Although "Misun Kim" is generally impressed by the intelligence of her classmates, she is consistently depressed by their lack of intellectualism. The American classmates often do well in their courses, but there is in many cases a stark dichotomy of seriousness with their international counterparts, a gap in willingness to explore complex topics in depth. Skimming glibly and competently over the surface of their studies, some of the host country students frustrate their "guests" with what appears to be the superficiality of their academic interests, their acceptance of a level of learning that ensures educated cocktail party conversation but little real mental engagement.

This surface-level learning also too often applies to the level of curiosity that American students show in the backgrounds of their international peers. A general lack of geographic understanding and knowledge of international affairs amazes students raised in environments that are by necessity far more attuned to the political and social climates of neighboring countries. Having barely survived a firing line in the midst of a Bosnian war, Almin Hodzic is stunned by his American friends' complete ignorance of eastern European conflict. In a lighter, but equally frustrating vein, Ian vividly remembers a young woman at a fraternity party gyrating on a desk while asking him if Trinidad was in Asia. For Maria, it was more subtle, in the form of feigned interest in her background, but no genuine desire to see her as any more than a "quota."

Even more disturbing for some of our writers is the difficulty many of their American peers have with understanding multiethnicity and multinational heritages, and the resultant stereotyping that must constantly be endured. "Devneesh" lives with a bigoted first-year student who refers to him as "Karma Man," and who expects him to smell of curry when they first meet. While not persecuted in the same fashion, Lai Heng Foong sees herself as a "culturally transcendent" product of her international education spanning four continents, and is deeply resistant to the expectation that she can offer simple answers to the question, "So, where are you from?" For Ian, Dartmouth is the first time in his life where his race was an issue; coming from Trinidad where his skin color did not matter, he finds himself pigeonholed as "black," with no account at all taken of the complexities of his personal and racial history. These contributors all regret that fewer of their classmates understand, in Edward Said's (1993) words, that "no one today is purely one thing. Labels like Indian, or woman, or Muslim, or American are not more than starting points, which if followed into actual experience for only a moment are quickly left behind" (336).

It is partially these labels too rarely being left behind that initially causes such social difficulties for many of our writers. While Stephen finds the friendliness of people on the street in Hanover, New Hampshire, to be a thrilling surprise after his childhood in a society where "ill-hidden hatred radiates from crowds like a deadly cold wind," the vast majority of the students we have worked with in the past five years speak to the superficiality of interaction that characterizes their social lives on campus. As has been shown in many different studies (Klineberg and Hall 1979; Furnham and Trezise 1983; Mirsky and Kaushinsky 1989; Sandhu and Asrabi 1994), host nation students have far less at stake emotionally in interactions with international students. They are consequently complacent enough in the familiar comfort of their surroundings not to need the risk of interaction across cultural barriers. What this means for so many international students we have worked with is a perceived insincerity and only polite warmth from American students in social situations. What Americans have internalized as a social trope, more often mere affirmation of recognition than precursors to deeper conversation, many international students see as a lack of genuine interpersonal connection. Combined with Maria's observed silky thin chain is Devyani's descriptions of the "pseudo-indications of contact" represented by "Howyadoing" and "What'sup?" As Sandhu and Asrabi (1994) note, "The end result of superficial pleasantries is a sense of alienation that is far more severe among foreign students than others."

The contributors to this book also often have difficulty relating to both the concerns and social roles of their American colleagues. Coming from cultures that have established rituals for recognizing gender, some of our writers are confused by such rituals of masculinity as binge drinking in fraternities and the kind of social posing represented by a roommate placing sexually explicit posters on the wall or using derogatory phrasing to refer to women on campus. Other writers cannot understand the pettiness of some of their acquaintances' concerns, particularly given the struggles that all of our writers have overcome before arriving at Dartmouth. Almin will never clearly understand the frame of mind of a student in class whose largest ethical dilemma was self-reported as "whether to let my roommate copy my CDs or not"; such "dilemmas" ring somehow less than life-consuming when seen through the eyes of a man whose extended family was decimated by a war that uses religion to justify death.

Finally, and not incidentally, language barriers can frustrate the most well-intentioned social attempts. While so gifted with language, as their essays here attest, many of our contributors find the subtle nuances of conversation and humor escaping them. Yu Chen struggles to form relationships, continually stymied by the language barriers she finds. An accomplished polyglot, Devyani becomes intensely frustrated by her difficulty grasping the fine shades of humor in colloquial language—a frustration that is disequilibrating for a student who relies on her abilities of self-expression. For anyone attempting to thrive in a different language, the gaps between what is known and what is expressible can be debilitating; only after much time does one realize Eva Hoffman's (1989) wisdom that a gap in languages can also "become a chink, a window through which [one] can observe the diversity of the world" (274).

This is not to say that none of our writers found meaningful contact with American peers; to the contrary, many developed lasting relationships that became crucial to their sense of self. Frode Eilertsen finds in an American roommate the closest bond he has found to the friendships developed in war; "Devneesh" finds in a Texan Jew the acceptance he needs to nurture a different side of his personality—a side that allows him to leave Dartmouth a more emotionally sure person; "Misun Kim" writes that her friendship with J.H.—a Korean American—was "the main support that kept her from falling through the cracks of academic indifference and social disappointment" at Dartmouth. Unfortunately, however, these are more the exception than the rule in our work with foreign students, and it is far more often the case that international students befriend other international students, often forming best friendships that are with students from continents other than their own, but that can organically grow out of the fertile ground of shared feelings of alienation and questioned identity.

And it is the area of questioned identity that ultimately contains the greatest potential for growth in the international students who have written for this book. Those international graduates who have the strongest sense of identity and purpose when they leave Dartmouth are invariably those men and women who have had to confront whole ranges of expectations, cultural assumptions, and countless conflicting influences on their sense of self. Not only are there the preconceived assumptions and stereotypical expectations from Americans, but also entire sets of expectations from their families and home countries. Having come from the collective "we" of South Korea—the country of her family that expects her to go to medical school—"Misun Kim" is not willing to go against the roots of her cultural identity by pursuing the American "I" and indulging her love of philosophy. Aassia also writes of identity pressures from "home," in her case a Pakistani society, where personal fulfillment was considered sinful and a woman's smile was seen as "the beginning of anarchy." Eva Hoffman's (1989) observation on language certainly applies: "Like everybody, I am the sum of my languages—the language of my family and childhood, and education and friendship, and love, and the larger, changing world—though perhaps I tend to be more aware than most of the fractures between them, and of the building blocks" (273).

It is of course these building blocks that reside in the "gap"— between cultures, languages, belief systems, external expectations— that offer the most enriching growth potential for international students. Certainly our writers have at times felt themselves falling into Rushdie's gap between stools, caught in a "double bind, . . . between old values of native culture which they cherish and new values of the host culture which they must adopt or adapt to in order to succeed" (Sandhu and Asrabi 1994: 446). At these points, the individual must try to answer the fundamental questions that Rushdie (1991) poses: "What are the consequences, both spiritual and practical, of refusing to make any concessions to [foreign] ideas and practices? What are the consequences of embracing those ideas and practices and turning away from ones that came here with us?" (18). For most of our students, then, the essential process of identity development is the negotiation of their middle ground, their space in between, their building blocks combined from an incredibly diverse range of materials.

Happily, every contributor to this book has come through this negotiation with some degree of success, now turning their attention to life beyond Dartmouth. For some, that which has been learned here— lessons of patience, assertiveness, academic schools of thought, adaptation strategies, resistance strategies—will be applied in their country of origin, with Georgina hoping to return to improve the roles of both white and black women in South Africa, Aassia finding creative inspiration for her writing career in the uncertainty and danger of Pakistan. Others will embrace the cultural freedom and opportunities of the United States, at least for now, testing the waters of naturalization: Stephen married to an American, "Misun Kim" in medical school. Yet others, both those even now at Darmouth and those who have moved on long since, still consider the building blocks they have to work with:

Frode literally loses sleep, "contemplating the question of where to go from here," and Devyani has no final destination, knowing only that she will "flee the consistency and stability of America."

Out of the crucible of cultural adaptation, these thirteen writers are emerging with a more finely honed and tempered conception of self. Their stories of adaptation are told in voices that compel with their honesty, self-revelation, and insight into both American collegiate culture and the cultures from which these students came. Through reading these stories, we better understand narrative's simultaneously synthesizing and generating nature, better understand what Eva Hoffman (1989) knows to be true about memoir: "It's only after I have taken in disparate pieces of cultural matter, after I've accepted its seductions and its snares, that I can make my way through the medium of language to distill my meanings . . . to hit home" (276). These student writers have taken in disparate cultural pieces, and they have distilled their meanings. In doing so, they have certainly hit home.

REFERENCES

Desruisseaux, P. (1997). 49% increase in number of foreign scholars at U.S. universities. *Chronicle of Higher Education* (December 12): A47.

Erikson, E. (1950). *Childhood and Society.* Middlesex, England: Penguin Books.

Furnham, A., and Trezise, L. (1983). The mental health of foreign students. *Social Science Media* 17 (6): 365–370.

Garrod, A., and Larimore, C. (Eds.). (1997). *First Person, First Peoples: Native American College Graduates Tell Their Life Stories.* Ithaca: Cornell University Press.

Greene, M. (1995). *Releasing the Imagination: Essays on Education, the Arts, and Social Change.* San Francisco: Jossey-Bass.

Hoffman, E. (1989). *Lost in Translation.* New York: Dutton.

Klineberg, O., and Hall, W. (1979). *At a Foreign University: An International Study of Adaptation and Coping.* New York: Holt, Rinehart & Winston.

Mahler, M., Pine, F., and Bergman, A. (1975). *The Psychological Birth of the Human Infant.* New York: Basic Books.

Mirsky, J., and Kaushinsky, F. (1989). Migration and growth: Separation-individuation processes in immigrant students in Israel. *Adolescence* 29 (25): 735–740.

Oei, T., and Notowidjojo, F. (1990). Depression and loneliness in overseas students. *International Journal of Social Psychiatry* 36 (2): 121–130.

Pedersen, P. B. (1991). Counseling international students. *Counseling Psychologist* 19 (1): 10–58.

Rushdie, S. (1991). *Imaginary Homelands.* London: Granta Books.

Said, E. (1993). *Culture and Imperialism.* New York: Knopf.

Said, E. (1996). *Representations of the Intellectual.* New York: Vintage Books.

Sandhu, D., and Asrabi, B. (1994). Development of an acculturative stress scale for international students: Preliminary findings. *Psychological Reports* 75: 435–448.

Udadigbo, F. (1997). Recruitment dynamic of foreign students into the United States postsecondary institutions: The implications for education and international development, Paper presented at the Annual Conference of the Community Colleges for International Development, (February 2–4).

U.S. Department of Education. (1995). *Digest of Education Statistics 1995.* Washington D.C.: U.S. Government Printing Office.

Young, B., and Bae, Y. (1997). Degrees earned by foreign graduate students: Fields of study and plans after graduation. *Integrated Postsecondary Education Study Data System* (November).

CROSSING CUSTOMS

Opening Worlds

The Presence of the Past

Stephen Kobourov

Bulgaria

My grandmother has a favorite saying: "Don't dig up the past. Dwell on the past and you'll lose an eye." But then the saying goes on: "Forget the past and you'll lose both eyes." Since I came to study in the United States, two urges have been struggling inside me. The first is the urge to cast off the past, to defy it, erase it completely, like a nightmare that was real and terrifying, but which by morning has all but vanished from conscious memory. I could make a clean break, start a new life as different and distant from my past as one's waking hours are from the sleeping hours. Indeed, what is the sense of waking from the nightmare if only to spend the rest of the day cowering before its images? Why leave Bulgaria if only to go through life recounting, rethinking, revisiting my difficult and often miserable experiences there? The second urge is the all too human desire to unload what I have been forced to keep hidden inside me, to speak of my unspeakable past, to allow to flow freely in my life the effects of the painful and dehumanizing circumstances of growing up in my native country.

I don't remember when I first realized I was not born in a normal country. I must have been quite young when I came to realize that the people I saw every day, the things they said, and the lives they lived were not normal. When I was still in high school I read *Animal Farm*. I read it over and over, and couldn't help thinking how much my world in Bulgaria resembled the one that George Orwell had envisioned. The pigs ruled, the horses toiled, the sheep obeyed, and the rest of the animal kingdom kept on shouting empty slogans. Orwell's best-known novel, *1984,* describes even more precisely what communism really meant. This book depicts communism's most destructive characteristic: not the system's unlimited power, but its constant control over everyone's thoughts and actions—a control that destroyed whole nations in less than half a century.

Coming to the United States at the age of twenty-one, I could not help but compare the lives of Americans and Bulgarians, their different societies, their different values and attitudes. In Bulgaria people grew up and aged much faster, both physically and spiritually, as ordinary lives were confounded by countless forces completely unimaginable to people here. Children growing up in Bulgaria were deprived of almost everything that American children are entitled to. We were forced to learn early to survive in a world that devours the weak and destroys the strong; we had already lived a lifetime before reaching adolescence. In elementary school we were taught to admire a Russian kid named Sasha Morozov, who turned his own parents in to be killed by the communists because they allegedly "conspired against the Great Revolution." He was a model to learn from, a hero to emulate. Truths today were lies tomorrow and truths again the day after. We had writers but no literature, artists but no art, musicians but no music, statesmen but no state. And, above all, we had enemies. Every member of our society was branded either a communist, or an enemy, and was dealt with accordingly.

Our lives were predestined by this concept, primitive and contrived as it was. A small agricultural country, Bulgaria had never developed a rigid class system and had never been plagued by the class conflict that the communist theories blindly predicted. Nonetheless, in accord with this ideology, supposedly the vanguard of the people's interests, the communists fabricated social divisions that had not existed before and terrorized our nation under the pretense of some universal class struggle for human liberation. In this "best" of social orders, normal human relations were quickly destroyed by constant fear and suspicion, and life lost all meaning as the specter of communism settled in yet another godforsaken country.

For our communist leaders, the larger than life, omnipotent, and ever-present enemy warranted every injustice and every atrocity. As people throughout the history of mankind have felt the need for a deity, so the communists needed an enemy, without which the party, the regime, and all of its macabre trappings would have seemed nothing more than paranoid insanity. The regime blamed the enemy for every hardship of life, for all the government's tragicomic blunders, for the gargantuan economic disasters perpetuated by its incompetent leaders. That the enemy was everywhere around us sabotaging our bright socialist future justified the terror, the concentration camps, the summary trials and executions, the KGB and its Bulgarian equivalent, the State Security Service.

Since they were responsible for everything bad in life, our enemies were to be hated, and the corrosion of hatred dominated our lives. We hated Western capitalism, imperialism, and expansionism; we hated our past national heroes, kings, and czars. There wasn't a moment when we were not inhibited by apprehension and hatred, which emanated from everywhere and were absorbed by everyone. We were born and grew up in a gray fog of suspicions and lies, robbed of the happy and carefree naiveté that is the luxury of youth. Fear and animosity were passed on like a plague from person to person, relationship to relationship, infecting our schools, offices, homes, our private lives, our very consciousness. We found ourselves unable to trust friends and family we had known and loved for years. Genuine friendship became a distant concept as everyone was a uniformly impersonal comrade. We got accustomed to the way that nothing actually was as it seemed, or as it was supposed to be. We lived in a world in which our internal selves bore no resemblance to the faceless masks we wore in public. We confided in no one, looked for hope nowhere, found solace in nothing.

I will always see life in Bulgaria grotesquely distorted through the prism of my own and my family's experiences in a homeland where we were considered enemies. In the communist nomenclature, my family fell into the bourgeois category under the "enemies" label. Both of my parents had university degrees: My father was a doctor and my mother a biochemist. To be an intellectual in Bulgaria was considered one of the most certain signs that you were opposed to the regime. Highly educated people were treated with suspicion and ill-concealed hatred by our rulers, most of whom lacked even a secondary school degree. For example, T. Zhivkov, the secretary-general of the communist party and president of Bulgaria for more than twenty-five years, never graduated from high school. Because we were living in a state where everyone was supposed to be equal, there wasn't much difference in the salary of an unskilled laborer and that of a scientist. Regardless of their qualifications and professional skills, enemies were paid only enough money to survive.

My parents were quiet, patient people who never complained about their hardships. Although unhappy about raising children under the difficult conditions in Bulgaria, they remained hopeful that things would change for the better. They found escapes from the nightmare of our existence: My father had a little piece of land at the foot of the mountains not far from Sofia, and my mother had her books. My father's farm meant everything to him. He developed his land into an orchard, and even managed to build a small house. By the time I was born, the farm had become a tiny oasis in the desert of pollution and destruction that was so typical of Bulgaria. It was my father's obsession: He read dozens of books on fruit growing and cared for the trees as much as he cared for his patients. He spent every free minute there, and when I grew old enough I went with him to help. Our weekend retreats from the city and from real life into this peaceful, quiet world were among the few things that kept our family together. They were an escape from the atmosphere in our home, an apartment in the city center, where the telephone was tapped, where neighbors spied on each other, where the air was hard to breath from the pollution outside. Our retreats also gave my mother more quiet time to read. Books gave her the freedom and happiness she otherwise lacked, let her visit other worlds that she would never see. She even studied foreign languages so she could read more books.

Everyone developed a defense mechanism, a kind of obsession without which it would have been impossible to survive. My father had his farm; my mother, her books; my grandmother never missed a new play or an art exhibition; and my brother constantly played the piano. My brother's tragic story always comes to mind when I want to explain how living in Bulgaria affected me and people dear to me. He is a typical example of how talented people in Bulgaria were destroyed. George was a brilliant musician. He had the rare gift of being able to play a new piece of music perfectly, after only a couple of hearings. He worked hard to make the best of his talent, and at age fourteen was one of the most promising young pianists in Bulgaria. Only one high school specialized in music, and its students were accepted only after numerous qualifying exams. Out of hundreds of applicants from all over the country, my brother placed second. Several weeks later, however, my parents were notified that George was denied admission. The communist regime never missed an opportunity to remind enemies such as my parents that their sins were not forgiven and that these sins passed from one generation to the next.

My brother was deprived of his hard-earned chance to become a professional musician. Although he continued to play, his hope and zest were fading by the time he was drafted into the army. Military service was and still is the horror of every young man in Bulgaria. In the army, little time was spent on physical education and military training; service consisted mostly of working on construction projects without pay, and of endless brainwashing in the form of classes in dialectic materialism and the history of the Soviet communist party. My brother's squadron spent some of the coldest winters on record working in the open, often without gloves. After the two years of obligatory service he came out a different man. His hands were crippled from the exposure to cold, and he could hardly play the piano. He had lost his ambitions, his will was crushed, and his life was all but destroyed.

Only my grandmother could find reassuring words for George. "A dead lion is no better than a living donkey," she would remind him and all of us. During her eighty years, she had seen good and bad times in Bulgaria. She had received an excellent education, graduating from the Italian College, one of the most prestigious in Bulgaria at the time. There she studied Latin, Italian, religion, music, and all the other disciplines that were considered important. She had visited many European countries, and could compare the old times to the present. Rather than send George and me to kindergarten or day care my parents had my grandmother look after us. She raised us on parables from the Bible, folk stories, and fairy tales. She was exceptionally proud, but knew how to appreciate the little sources of happiness left to her and how to ignore the hardships and troubles. She preserved traditions, kept the household going, and settled all problems that arose in the family.

My grandmother never got used to the lies that flowed from the TV, radio, and newspapers, but she reserved her most comprehensive hatred for the telephone, which she saw as an instrument for spying on and controlling our lives. Often when conversations would die out in unspoken thoughts, she would go to the telephone, pick up the receiver and deliver the monologue that always made us laugh: "We know you are there, and you know that we know it, right? So we won't say what we think, because you know what we think anyway, right? Why don't you go and give yourselves a break, have a cup of coffee, while we're talking about other things, eh?" But, fortunately, the tapped telephone

lines, the jammed radio broadcasts, the Secret Service arrests all ceased
with the initiation of *perestroika* in the late 1980s. I was also given a
chance that my parents did not have: I was allowed to leave the
country, a right that Bulgarians had been denied for the past fifty years.
By the time I graduated from high school, the communist system was
falling apart. The sole inheritance of the old regime was chaos in every
institution: schools, universities, hospitals. Although Sofia University
had been one of the foremost centers of higher education in the
Balkans, the only resemblance it now bore to a normal institution of
learning was its name. As a student there, I saw only another example
of the pervasive destructiveness of the communist regime. The damage
inflicted during fifty years of gross mismanagement would be hard to
repair.

I felt a liberal arts education would be best for me because of my
interests in various disciplines, but liberal arts schools were nonexistent
at home. I soon realized that it would be difficult to pursue my interests
in computer science and applied mathematics in Bulgaria, and decided
to try and complete my education abroad. Sofia University had about
10,000 students, 500 of whom were majoring in computer science.
Computers were very expensive, so most students had to rely on a
handful of obsolete machines in the university computer center.
Because so many students shared so few computers, we never had
adequate time to accomplish anything. I did my best to learn what I was
taught, but you don't learn computer programming by reading books
alone. Our education was characterized by a high student/faculty ratio,
lack of tutorials and personal contact with the professors, and
monologue-style lectures. Only the exceptionally talented and studious
managed to keep up, but after graduation even they rarely found
employment appropriate for their qualifications because the economy
was so lacking in opportunities.

In contrast, U.S. colleges, especially the good ones, offer all that a
student could want. For example, a good college in the United States,
such as Dartmouth, offers limitless opportunities. Professors are
engaged with their material *and* interested in their students' welfare.
Everyone has computers connected to the Internet, and the library has
thousands of books and journals. Even after two years at Dartmouth,
I'm still amazed that I take courses with a handful of students who call
the professor by his given name. I am still amazed that I can play pool,
go to lunch, or go to parties with my professors. Most Bulgarians

cannot imagine or understand such an environment, whereas many Americans take it for granted and underestimate its power. Nevertheless, people find it hard to believe that educational opportunity could be the main reason for someone to come to the United States, especially from a country like Bulgaria, dismal in so many different ways.

I didn't seriously consider applying to colleges abroad until my first year at Sofia University, when I realized how inadequate it was. Then I wrote to more than two hundred universities, and applied to each one that did not require any financial support from my family. This campaign required tremendous effort, made more difficult because I could not afford the application fees or provide official transcripts from my high school and the university. I wrote hundreds of letters explaining my situation. What started as a mere experiment to see how I could do on the admissions tests grew to a full-scale application campaign that consumed most of a year.

Even though I was accepted almost everywhere I applied, there was little chance of going to the United States, as most of the colleges asked for more than one thousand dollars. I received many letters congratulating me for being accepted and for having earned large scholarships, but to me they meant no more than the few refusals that I received. Dartmouth was the only college to offer me a financial aid package that left less than a thousand dollars for my family to pay. However, even this amount was too much when added to the travel expenses, as it was much more than my family's yearly income. Fortunately, an international foundation awarded me a grant that helped cover the remaining expenses.

Except for a week's visit to Russia, I had never been out of Bulgaria. But I had heard stories—hundreds of stories of people who had been abroad. Also, I knew a lot about the United States from reading and the movies, and I did not expect any big surprises. When I set forth on my first trip far away from home, I was convinced that only good times lay ahead. My first stop was Zurich, Switzerland, where I had to change planes and stay overnight, and my first surprise came there. When I reached the passport control post, everyone in front of me showed their passport and went through; but when I showed my passport, I was told to wait. I had to stand for hours with a bunch of other people holding conspicuous-looking red passports while countless others passed by. We all felt somewhat guilty and embarrassed; we

looked at our feet and didn't talk much, waiting for the guards to pay
attention to us. At last our passports were collected and we were given
temporary passes that stated, in huge red letters, "The holder of this
pass is allowed to stay in the country for no more than 24 hours." A list
of restrictions followed. I had never felt any particular affection for my
passport, but being forced to part with it left me feeling vulnerable.
This experience spoiled the first day of my international journey.

Because of my welcome in Zurich, I was at least somewhat
prepared for the treatment I received upon arrival in Boston. I have
always wondered how immigration officials succeed in making
everyone feel like a criminal. After talking to the stone-faced officer
who was dressed in a uniform that was painfully reminiscent of officers
at home, I felt as if I were Judas himself trying to pass through the gates
of Heaven. The officer made me feel that he would never admit
someone like me if he had a choice, and he looked genuinely upset
when I finally was allowed to cross the red line. From Boston I took
another plane to Hanover, and by the time I reached Dartmouth it was
late at night. I had been traveling for a long time.

I had expected my first weeks in the United States to be hectic and
busy, but I was in fact utterly exhausted by the time classes started. I
had lost more than ten pounds living on cigarettes and sodas, since I
had only twenty dollars upon arrival. It was only after a few weeks that
impressions started to sink in: the fresh air, which caused a month's
worth of headache to adjust to; the young people in the hallways who
said "hi" to me every time we met; the professors I talked to, who
seemed sincerely concerned about my course selections; the old ivy-
covered, red-brick buildings; the pristine campus; the great variety of
fresh food. I had expected the big shopping malls, the quantity and
quality of the products available. What I had not expected was the
attitude of the people. The way people deal with each other in the
United States, or at least in Hanover, New Hampshire, took getting
used to. Whether you are with an administrator or a faculty member,
whether you are in a shop, in the bank, or on the street, everyone seems
happy to talk to you and willing to help. This attitude contrasts starkly
with that of people in Bulgaria, who seem to take pleasure in colliding
with you on the streets, who do not smile, and who are unwilling to be
of any assistance.

In Bulgaria's zeal to mimic the Soviet Union in government,
economy, and social order, our people also assumed the behavior of the

Soviet citizens. My week in Moscow had been a worthwhile educational experience. Just being there was terribly depressing; walking through the streets drained all my strength. I felt I was in a vacuum created by the masses of faceless people trying to blend into the crowds, the gray shabby clothes, the big furry hats that everyone hid in, the blank expressions on faces that seemed to scream, "Don't get any closer!" Returning to Bulgaria, I saw our little crowds as copies of the bigger ones in the Soviet Union, and I realized that life was the same all over eastern Europe. Why are the people in these countries like this, I asked myself. How could half a century turn people into mere shadows of themselves? Perhaps my idea of prewar Bulgaria is idyllic, but I do know we were a nation famous for hospitality and kindness, a place where strangers said "good day" whenever they met. Now it is different. Hostility, distrust, and ill-hidden hatred radiate from crowds like a deadly cold wind. Whenever I go out in Hanover, with its atmosphere of indestructible gaiety, I'm reminded of the sad contrast with the streets of Sofia.

When I arrived at Dartmouth I was twenty-one, the age at which most students here graduate. Nevertheless, I soon made friends. I helped the student next door with his Russian course; I helped several other students with their math homework. I began to receive so many requests for help that I hardly had time for my own assignments! But I didn't mind; it made me feel less out of place. Even so, when my new friends tried to include me in their social life, I had difficulty getting involved. I found that we shared few interests: frat parties, American football, shopping, and watching TV simply did not appeal to me.

I have often wondered whether I would have fit in better if I had come to the United States when I was seventeen, instead of twenty-one. Would things that seem foolish to me now have seemed so then? Would things of no importance to me now have mattered then? Would I have been closer to my peers, shared their interests, and become more involved in the social life of the college? To some extent being younger might have made a difference, but I think that most things would have been the same. My past experiences will always create a gap between me and my peers outside of Bulgaria. American teenagers spend their lives in what seems like blissful ignorance of the surrounding world and its culture. They do not seem to learn much in high school, and they are not used to studying for hours every day. Few read daily or consider reading a highly positive experience. The hours they devote to

TV and sports cannot possibly provide them with the level of knowledge that every eastern European acquires by the same age. For example, most Bulgarians at my age have some knowledge of art, music, theater, and literature, without having taken any classes and without having any special interest in those areas, whereas most American students I have met seem to lack this basic knowledge unless they have taken a course in art history or drama or music. Their knowledge of music is limited to the most popular rock groups at the moment; their appreciation of art is expressed by having a reproduction of Matisse ("beautiful squares, aren't they?") lost among posters of Star Trek, pop stars, and cute little puppies. Many have never been to a theater, and the most-talked-of authors on campus are the likes of Stephen King, Tom Clancy, and John Grisham.

I do not want to suggest that Americans are completely ignorant, but I have met few who seem to care about the greater world. Perhaps when you're content with what you have, the world you live in, and your life, you do not need to search for more. Maybe one important motivation for the desire for knowledge is its denial. Whenever a book was banned in Bulgaria, nothing could stop me from trying to read it, but if it had been available in the library, perhaps I would not have thought of reading it. The same applies to the proscribed films and the jammed radio broadcasts. The forbidden fruit is the sweetest, and maybe all intelligent and cultured Bulgarians actually owe a lot to the censors. Strange as it may seem, I'm thankful to the communist regime for making knowledge so desirable. Had I been born in the United States, I would have been completely different, possibly without the ideas and interests I have now.

For most Bulgarians, reading was almost a mania, although (maybe because) we were denied the best books. All you could buy in the bookstores were hundreds of volumes about communist heroes or the politically correct books about the big revolution and the building of socialism. In their efforts to become "more Catholic than the Pope," the Bulgarian censors even banned books that were legally published in Russia. It was not until the 1970s that the first translations of Western authors began to appear on the shelves. These were books by writers critical of capitalist societies, like Dickens and Steinbeck, or those the regime found otherwise acceptable. Such books disappeared hours after they arrived at the stores, and we worshiped them.

A family's library was its pride. We constantly exchanged books with friends, thus managing to read what we could not buy. Then there were the smuggled books. People studied foreign languages to be able to read books that would never be published in Bulgaria, and people ran great risks to smuggle them from abroad. And finally there were the *samizdat,* illegal, home-produced books, that circulated secretly from friend to friend, and whose publishers ran even greater risks than the smugglers. It is no wonder that publishing was the most flourishing business after the collapse of the old regime. All the books that people had wanted to read were suddenly available, and everyone wanted to have them. Since no one had enough money to buy them all, we borrowed from friends. Friends made sure that each bought different books so we could read more. Books of hundreds of pages were read in a single day, then passed on immediately to the next person. This hunger for books made me perplexed to find that many Americans regard reading as a waste of time. I was stunned when I read, in a preparation guide for the SAT, advice on how to manage to read three whole books in a single year. This number appeared ridiculously low and seemed nonsensical until I came to the United States, where I realized that this advice could actually be useful to some. I couldn't believe that people read so little, especially in a country where nearly every book ever published is available.

Besides the desire for knowledge and culture in my country, there was little that was positive or uplifting. People were frustrated, disappointed, and disillusioned, and the only "treatments" available were tobacco, alcohol, and drugs. The drug abuse problem that the United States faces today has always been routine in Bulgaria; the only difference is that no one cared about it there. Even when we could not find meat, milk, or bread, alcohol and cigarettes were always in stock, and their prices were disproportionately low. For the price of a pound of beef you could buy a carton of cigarettes or a couple of bottles of hard liquor, and although the alcohol and cigarettes were of poor quality, these relatively low prices encouraged people to drink and smoke—which they did in great quantities. Bulgaria is covered from end to end with a thick carpet of cigarette butts and broken bottles. Everyone drinks and smokes—fathers, mothers, teachers, friends—and by age thirteen or fourteen most people already smoke and drink regularly. These habits were among the few vices we were permitted, and we engaged in them with all our hearts.

The attitude toward drinking and smoking in the United States is quite different from that in Bulgaria. In the States, the popularity of these habits is mainly a function of fashion. Right now it is not fashionable to smoke cigarettes, but it is fashionable to smoke cigars. And it is still, as always, fashionable to drink in college. In Bulgaria, fashion has little meaning, as people cannot afford to keep up with the latest trends. Instead of being part of a fad, drinking and smoking are part of everyday life. People smoke on the streets, at home, at friends' homes. People drink constantly, with no need to justify it: No convention dictates that you drink only at parties or on Friday nights. The only difference at parties is that people drink even more than usual. The quantities of alcohol and cigarettes usually consumed at such parties would make even the brothers at a U.S. fraternity house blush with shame. However, unlike Americans, Bulgarians rarely lose control, no matter how much liquor they consume. Those who do get too drunk are usually less experienced, and still learning that you do not throw up something for which you've spent your last penny.

In Bulgaria, I rarely asked myself why our lives had been overtaken by cigarettes, alcohol, and drugs. Only after I came to the United States did I see the meaninglessness of my life and how close I came to the point of no return. Like most of my friends, by the age of twenty I already had problems caused by smoking and drinking. But I did not even think of changing my habits until I left Bulgaria. Coming to the United States undoubtedly brought about other significant changes in my life, good and bad. Back home the feeling of hopelessness discourages even the most talented from trying to find meaning in their lives. The greatest virtue one can possess in Bulgaria is patience. People patiently stand in lines for hours. They patiently wait for something nice to happen. They patiently drink themselves to sleep, hoping that tomorrow will be different. In the United States patience is almost a character flaw. Here you are in control of your own future and you make tomorrow different.

Thankfully, Bulgaria is on the road to recovery now. New generations will grow up without having experienced the horrors of the past, but I hope they will be able to salvage a valuable lesson from their country's history. Although Bulgaria was a People's Republic in name and the ruling party called itself communist, in reality our state was not a republic, our country didn't belong to the people, and there was no communism. Our totalitarian regime was much closer to that of Hitler's than to the order envisioned by Marx and Engels. Communism and socialism have become dirty words, not because of what they originally stood for, but because they became synonymous with the dictatorial regimes behind the Iron Curtain. When the Soviet Union was still intact, Western countries like Canada, Sweden, and France were much closer to socialist states than any country with the word "socialist" in its name. From the very first days of the Russian Revolution, the admirable ideals of freedom and equality were replaced by Lenin's Red Terror and the dictatorship of the proletariat.

Even though the Bulgaria I grew up in was not the best place in the world, I do not regret anything or envy anyone who was born and raised elsewhere. Living in Bulgaria taught me to cherish the freedoms we were denied and appreciate the opportunities we didn't have. Somewhere along the way, I succeeded in reconciling my past and my present, instead of forsaking one for the other. I now have a much broader perspective, as I need not accept or reject either Bulgaria or America, but can embrace only the positive from both. Regardless of where I choose to spend my life, it will not be because of the past or the present, but because of the future I can make for myself there.

An Escape to Return

Aassia Haroon
Pakistan

I always feel a little claustrophobic when I am in Pakistan. It has something to do with the air, perhaps. It is oppressive. It bears down upon you, heavy and variously filled with the smells of gasoline, exhaust fumes, fuming rubber-seats left too long in the sun, and the sudden contrary whiff of expensive perfume imported from London, Paris, or Dubai. The atmosphere tires and irritates the mind, so that after a few hours in that air, you want to descend into the bliss of afternoon sleep. There is nothing relaxing about the daytime world outside, nothing that an air-conditioned chamber and a good book might not better provide. Ours is a different relationship to the outside world than the one Hanover encourages, with its inviting green, autumn hues, and its canoes and rivers to dive into. The only water I ever dived into in Pakistan was the dirty, salty sea. I dreamt often of escape when I lived in that molten, apathetic land. Such escape came to pass only rarely.

There was the time we drove far outside the city, the thumping beat of hip-hop resounding from the CD players in our cars. We drove to a farm near the mountainous, tribal province of Balochistan, and I remember my excitement as we approached the end of the highway and turned onto a dust road. I had never before been in a Pakistan that looked like this. I had been to farms in the past, but only in minivans with multitudinous relatives and pots of curry. This was different; this was like feeling a trapped thing inside me, fluttering. This was a physical longing to get out of the car and be porous, so I could absorb the silence and brevity of the landscape and take it back to the raging city with me.

It was a day of reflection for me. I went for a walk, to the edge of the fence that enclosed us, separating us from the networks of lonely dust roads and stone and sand hillocks that pointed toward the Balochi Mountains. The landscape was not colorful, but it was the absence of color I loved. In a city that dresses itself up in fine silks and travels from party to party, this landscape made no pretensions to beauty. There was a cool wind blowing, a wind I now physically crave. It reminds me of a relationship to Karachi, the city in which I have lived for the past nine years, which is, for once, a relationship to place. Pakistanis are a people who live indoors. I was never free to walk the streets at home, never free to know the land except in air-conditioned cars that move from air-conditioned house to air-conditioned house. It was from such a house that I had come to this place.

I have never felt so beautiful, and so free, as I did then. The little cart that carried me to the edges of the fields, when I expressed a desire to travel outside the farm gates, could not have known what emotion it was carrying. We rattled along a dirt path among rows of shrubbery, the gatekeeper walking beside us. It was as if we suddenly broke free of foliage and stopped at the edge of absolute silence. After having airplanes descending overhead every five minutes in Hong Kong where I was born, after driving through the screeching anarchy of the bus depot at Saddar every morning to get to school in Karachi, I treasured this. There was no noise—no cars, no people as far as I could see.

When I stand in Hanover and look at New Hampshire's famed Green and White mountains, I feel I am an alien. The Balochi Mountains were quiet and sand-brown: more mine, somehow. I want to walk among them someday, if only to shatter the dream that there I can find some sort of acceptance, for I know that acceptance is elusive in Pakistan. In remembering that day, I suppose I am expressing my search for a perfect solitude of soul, a place where I can be both creative and serene. Yet I recognize more and more that because of the pattern of my life, my true creativity is born not from serenity but from disequilibrium, from maelstroms of emotion. Although my mind seeks peace in that image of the silent mountains, I know that it is a transient, illusory moment. Such is the irony: The feelings I had then remind me of everything that my life in Pakistan is not.

The metaphor of my life there is escape. I was told when I was young that God could see inside my mind and would be angry if my thoughts were "bad." I could not help but worry at my deviance, my inability to think as I supposed other girls did, girls who seemed to conform mentally and yet be happy. When my relatives would tease me and my female cousins about our future marriages, I would seethe with anger. My cousins would only giggle and agree that the time for their weddings was not far away. We were age thirteen. I supposed I was the only girl who nurtured hatred against those adults who prevented women from leaving the home, the only girl who loved reading and writing. But on all these counts, I was wrong.

I have realized, by watching people's eyes, that escape is something every girl and woman in Pakistan yearns for. Even those who do not admit it: I can see the longing in their guarded glances toward me, thinking I have managed it by coming to America. I understand their shadowed study, their darting pupils, because I remember watching others who had left before me with the same envy, the same disbelief. "Why couldn't I leave?" I always used to think. Why wasn't that me, with the fresh-faced just-returned-from-abroad look? And now, when I am the incarnation of that image, I find I disappoint the meaning of the word "escape" because my version of it is illusory. Although I am at school in America, I cannot break free.

I am in a curious position; in this distant place from which I write, I find that I want to return to Pakistan. I feel the beginnings of a genuine love: the love of a writer for her subject, of an artist for her landscape. Pakistan can be a shockingly alive place, awakening one from the general apathy of existence. I miss its surprises and paradoxes. One night, a series of bombs exploded in our neighborhood. We knew nothing about the bombing, except that an Irani man had lived there but was away the night they shelled his sorry house. When we drove by to inspect the damage the next afternoon, we saw a naked grenade on the sidewalk, and I thought: "This will tempt an urchin child and I cannot remove it. I am helpless." Although explosions are not a common occurrence where I live, I know that when I return to Pakistan, it will not be long before I want desperately to leave again, while also overcome by a perverse fascination to look destruction in the face. Yes, Pakistan is like looking at a bomb and knowing you can stay and watch it detonate, or leave while it explodes at your back.

When I began my time at Dartmouth, I did so after making a promise to my father, who very reluctantly but lovingly gave me the permission, and the financial capability, to study in this country. I promised him that after four years I would return home. Perhaps the knowledge of that promise also colors my desire to return, since I might as well look forward to the inevitable. But it is more than that: It is a recognition that to leave would have no meaning anyway, unless I had made my peace with home. If and how that process of reconciling myself to Karachi occurs remains to be seen. I do feel the beginnings of it in my writing, which for me is a process of creative therapy.

When I am in Karachi, I feel hidden, I feel as if I am a snatched-moment: I feel that I am, in my entirety, nothing more than a stolen dream. Perhaps this is because we all hide ourselves there, at least as far as I have seen. Most women in Pakistan, even the most daring, are mistresses of the art of deception. It is dangerous to admit to real emotion, because in doing so you provide your enemies with ammunition. I was taught never to speak honestly to older people, because my simple words might be used to taint my reputation. For instance, if I expressed a genuine fondness for a male relative (quite without romantic overtones), it might be twisted into a story of depraved lust. And a woman's reputation is everything to her family—valued far above goodness, or the ability to seek wisdom or speak truth. No one dares admit to any emotion outside the realm of polite, certain reality, so that our lives become constructions, simulacra—copies without real originals. Things are whispered, that is for certain, but no one speaks out loud because our lives are lived in undertones, and activity is primarily subliminal. Because of the glare of Karachi sunlight, which is very harsh, our eyes squint. They begin to water, drop by slow, painful drop—forced to emit water, something genuine, only by the sun.

When I was young, the places that I hid from the sun were tiled, pastel, cool—I hid in bathrooms and cried. I have spoken to other women about this, and yes, we all have locked our bedroom doors, and then moved even farther from our parents, our lounges, and living rooms into the cool bathrooms, with the taps running to hide the sorry fact that we are wasting precious tears in an arid country. Real emotion is reserved for the world of closed doors, because it is felt so deeply that it is embarrassing to watch, and harsh. Small things are magnified in our lives until they consume us.

It is hard to make those outside of my life understand how tiny were the incidents that evoked deep emotion. Here, they would be considered insignificant. When I am home, at the moment when a desired pleasure is unfulfilled, or is broken by others who wish to deny me, I react intensely, enormously. I have a difficult relationship with pleasure there, which affects the way I feel pain. I crave pleasure because of its elusiveness and its unpredictability. We live our lives at the precipice of it. When we snatch a moment of it, we hold our breaths and live that moment gaspingly, for there is no rational order or continuity to the universe of happiness. When no pleasure can be taken without knowing that its course, its ability to give you bounty, is completely outside your control, you feel a great anger at life. And so at society.

I began to grasp at pleasure tenaciously, even in very little things, because the act of seeking personal fulfillment was considered sinful. If a girl or woman asks for something, she is automatically denied it. For instance, when I was thirteen, I once wanted to go to a friend's birthday party. I begged and pleaded, but I was told I could not because there were "men" attending (meaning only the prepubescent boys who played soccer in the school yard). I swallowed my misery and asked to go a female friend's house instead. I was then yelled at for wanting "to always leave my home" and sent to my room in punishment. The reasons for this were not rational but rather whimsical, and had to do with power and subordination. I rebelled, through my writing and my reading, against a society that dictated I should only find pleasure in that which pleased the fat old men around me—or what I came to call "society." And so I began to take pleasure in any way I could, since when I asked others for something, I had to beg humiliatingly; often it was still refused me. That was when I began to live a double life and reconstructed myself as an image without an original, a platonic horror—an "ideal" girl who really only pretended to be ideal.

I remember my mother once telling me, when I was reading *King Lear* for my literature exams, that she identified with Cordelia, who opens, however tragically, her aging father's eyes. She explained to me how a woman is surrounded by hypocrisy in Pakistan, by "that glib and oily art, to speak and purpose not" that Cordelia so despises, and has to spend her life delivering slippery words to others. All of our lives, she told me, we are servants. We live to make an abstract "society" happy. We seek approval through the perfect flavor of a cup of tea and the consistency of the gravy in a curry. Pakistan is a country that has not yet learned to take pleasure in the individual accomplishment.

I have heard some in Pakistan remark that women should not be happy for too long. Something dangerous is thought to lurk within a woman's smile, perhaps the beginnings of anarchy. Young girls are scolded when they are at the threshold of adolescence for their wanton movements. They might be asked to shield their breasts, thus painfully heightening the shame of the changes that are happening to their bodies. They might be scolded for speaking to members of the opposite sex, for an obvious crush on an older boy or a man. Thus, life is checked through denial and the subsequent beginnings of a self-awareness that is centered on suppression of emotion toward men. Many fathers withdraw from their children. Women might not hug or kiss their fathers after the age of twelve, unless it is a quick peck on the forehead, and some wear scarves in their father's presence.

I spent the first twelve years of my life trying desperately to satisfy the image I had built of the paternalistic homeland based on vague utterances by my parents. I was so good. It may seem an innocuous phrase, but do not underestimate the importance of "goodness" for a Pakistani girl. The ultimate goal of a girl is to imbue herself with *sharam-o-hiya*. *Sharam* is a word that means "shame." *Hiya*, perhaps, is "purity" (I cannot translate for you directly because I understand only the feeling behind that phrase). Pakistan, in my infant and then adolescent eyes, was filled with this elusive elixir. From my distant perch upon my bunk bed in Hong Kong, where I was born, I imagined a land of accepting people, a land of pure light. In Hong Kong, then, I had what I suppose was a sense of nationhood. Perhaps I lost it when my uncle once told me I had to wear a scarf to show my *sharam*. I was twelve. All I know is that I lost it after I moved to Pakistan, and I rebelled against the image of the country I had been taught to love.

I remember when I first moved to Pakistan, I could not live without a magazine called *Jackie*. *Jackie* is a British magazine, created especially for little girls who imagine that they have grown up and know what it means to be a woman. It is similar to *Teen* but perhaps not quite as hip as *Seventeen* or *Cosmopolitan*. Obtaining the weekly magazine from a newsstand in Clifton, a suburb at some distance from where I then lived, was my foremost desire. I would travel there and anticipate the perfect moment when I could lay my hands on it and begin to read. I remember that I arrived at the stall one afternoon, only to find it shut, and I began to cry. I wouldn't talk to my bewildered family, I was so angry. I went home and I played my favorite album, *The River*, by Bruce Springsteen, lying on my orange carpet. I loved the sound of his voice. It was rough, it was filled with pain and resentment against the vagaries of existence. It was not happy. I don't often tell anyone this, largely because it's the sort of thing that is easier to construct in writing than to speak, but Springsteen and *Jackie* got me through the torment of moving to that country. I was crying not only for my magazine; I cried for the cumulative effects of my transition from life in Hong Kong—which was solitary and happy—to Karachi life, which choked and confined me. Here, I could not leave my home unless my mother came with me in the car. My music and my magazines were the only facets of my identity that belonged exclusively to me in a new country that was trying, desperately, to mold me.

I have a habit of gesticulating rapidly when I speak. As I become more and more excited about an idea I am examining or an incident I am recounting, my movements become more expansive. My hands fly. When I first moved to Karachi I was told to abandon this "attention-getting" style. I remember my hands being held down and the abrupt command, "Now speak!" I could not. I felt a voice deep down attempting to rise in my throat, but it needed my hands, which struggled against those confining fingers for release. I remember another Pakistani woman telling me that she was scolded for her laugh, which tinkles and is beautiful. She was told to calm herself if the tinkle ever burst forth, and as she was telling me, I could see her eyes become hard with her buried anger.

I admit I feel a deep residual resentment and frustration at the thought that my childhood was sacrificed at the altar of Pakistani society. I was an experiment for my poor bewildered parents, who were themselves returning to the mother country after years away. An experiment, thank goodness, that they have now abandoned and that we often look back on amusedly. They wanted their children to fit the image of what an ideal Pakistani child should be. I was the guinea pig, since I was the eldest child. I was eleven and a half years old when we moved to Karachi, and I suffered tremendously. I will never again cry as much as I did in those first three years in Pakistan. My parents saw in me the possibility of an "ideal" young Pakistani girl. Yet I thought I had been their ideal in Hong Kong. Now, I was not allowed to wear jeans, or other Western clothes. I could not talk about boys or mixed parties. I had to appear demure and chaste. I had to cover myself "decently." I had to read the Quran. I had to serve tea to members of my extended family. I hated it; I hated the country with a passion because I saw that it hated what I represented. Pakistan hated me.

Yet in spite of this, I still want to return to Pakistan; it is the most honest and deeply felt thing that I can do. Since I was very young, I have worshiped creativity. Creativity cannot, in my opinion, be constructed. It arises out of life and is challenged into action by specific experiences, which become the momentum for the creative outpouring. It does not lie, because it cannot. This is the paradox of my life: My creativity is awakened by Pakistan and the emotional and intellectual challenges I encounter there. It is not awakened by the problems I see here, although they fascinate me intellectually. My creativity has to be both emotional and mental for it to be successful. I am tied to Pakistan because it evokes the synthesis. Although a part of me longs for oblivion or escape from my country's problems, I know I will lose that by which I define myself—my writing—if I sever my ties with it.

Although I still smile when I see my stack of *Jackie* magazines, and still get an irrational lump in my throat when I listen to *The River*, I do not need them anymore. As I grew older and began to build a life in Pakistan, I replaced those adolescent crutches. The new instrument of my separation was my pen. I sorted out my inadequacies on the pages of my school notebooks, which I now laugh at when I read them. I constructed grand theories of the Pakistani psyche, of religious issues, of anything that I saw as troublesome or imprisoning to me. I went through a period of admiring Kemal Atatürk, the Turkish leader who once had all the self-appointed clergy (the *mullahs*) drowned in the ocean. And I kept on reading. I edited my school magazine and scribbled letters constantly. I defined myself by my ability to evoke emotion or thought in my readers. I worshiped intellectual and emotional honesty because I saw myself as dishonest—ostensibly a part of the system that I secretly loathed.

In trying to understand why I was so tormented by Karachi while growing up, and why I constantly sought to expose its failings, I realize that my self-identity was tied up in refuting a model Pakistani identity. I could not have lived with myself had I not hated Pakistan—even while I came to secretly love it. Such relationships, with a person or a place, are unhealthy I suppose. But I have thrived on the challenges that a place like Karachi provides my mind and my identity. I feel I am constructed in opposition: That being in opposition has molded my behavior more than any other thing in my life.

I sought to write about only the truth, even if it shocked me. The act of uncovering what I perceived as "truth" needed constant challenges by the surrounding lies and falsehood. I remember an image I created when I was fifteen: It was of a pile of beautiful silks—purple, orange, magenta, green. Underneath the pile, I remember writing, bred cockroaches. That was my metaphor for Pakistani society. I was tormented by what I saw as the hypocrisies of the average Pakistani, both as citizens and as religious beings. The ills of society became catalysts for my creativity. I wrote morally, even though I despised dogma, because I thought there was so much wrong with Karachi—the way women were treated, the amount of emphasis that was placed on public prayer and sacrifice, the love of money and power. I am sure that these ills are present in all societies, but they seemed particularly acute to me there.

My foremost desire between the ages of twelve and nineteen was to study in the United States, to leave Karachi. I tried everything to get permission—arguments, tears, blackmail, copious prayers. Nothing seemed to work. But then one day, as I was sitting in my brother's bedroom having a discussion with my father on the merits of the Islamic banking system, he announced that I could study abroad if I wished. I remember how I ran screaming to my mother and I recall the silly smile on his face, knowing what he had given me. I could break free, I could break free.

It was an illusion that was shattered when I came to the United States. By the time I came to Dartmouth, I had already rejected two lands, Hong Kong and Pakistan. Perhaps feeling skeptical about the third was inevitable. I felt quite old already. What I did not realize when I was jumping with joy in my brother's bedroom was how much my struggles had fatigued me. An apathetic feeling persisted throughout my first year at Dartmouth, except in academic pursuits. In fact, this apathy still haunts me. I feel as if the depth of emotion of my adolescence in Pakistan has numbed me to almost all my experiences here. They do not compare—I do not let them. I am tired of feeling deeply. I have the luxury here of being what I have always appeared to be in Karachi, even when it was untrue: disconnected. I think my distance from many students I encounter here is because of my fuzziness, my indistinctness. I hear the usual lines—"Oh my God, you're so exotic!" Or "You're weird, you're so intense," which is what my roommate would say to me fondly. All the words I hear from others construct me at a distance: a safe, observing distance. Those few people that have broken it are mostly other South Asians, although that is less true the more time I spend at Dartmouth.

Amel is from Egypt and has lived near Boston since the age of seven. We are housemates this summer, and I remember sitting up one night at the kitchen table and discussing what we felt Dartmouth had given us. We discussed how our time away from our homes, which are very similar in their outlooks because we are both from Muslim families, has helped us. She explained how she now better understands the peculiar constructs of her life, ones that she had taken for granted and assumed applied to everybody. Dartmouth has also allowed me to understand myself better. It is my respite, my reflection. It allows me to see myself as someone who has an identity separate from the one I am given at home. I analyzed my self at home too, constantly—but it was analysis wholly connected to rebellion or hurt. I lived in constant opposition. Dartmouth is relatively calm, which is a luxury. It is the only time which I can honestly say exists for just *myself*. I sometimes wonder whether I will ever again be as self-centered as I am here. For the peace, external and internal, that Hanover allows me, I value Dartmouth greatly.

However, in spite of this gift of calm, I find I am desperate to get away from American malls and cutoffs and fake smiles (although many a fake smile has been flashed my way in Pakistan). I want to see another world, a world that moves me much more deeply and confuses me much more than life here—but ultimately, a world that is much more real to me. I am remembering when my family used to drive to Burns Road on Friday morning, through the old section of Karachi, to eat *aaloo poori*, the "little things." The shop was perched slightly above the road and was lit by naked light bulbs and gas lamps. Huge metal *matkas*, or containers, held the churned yogurt to make *lassi*, which is an icy drink, delicious in that heat. The shadows seemed accentuated by the way I perceived dark and light after my A-level art class. A man churning yogurt in a *matka* cast a deep charcoal shadow beneath the metal, falling to the street below. Us sitting inside the roughly built shop at dirty tables and my mother talking about the difference between our cushioned lives and this. Yes, I crave that shop because I am sick of pretending Pakistan does not exist. After two years of hiding from my home in this little town, I have begun to crave a return to reality.

When I think of Karachi, I think of atmosphere. The shop stood on a back road, which smelled of oil and breakfast and the Friday prayer at the mosque. It smelled of fumes from errant exhaust pipes and my father's cigarettes. As much as I resent Karachi for my relative confinement there, I love to observe that city. When I think of Karachi, sitting here in Hanover, I often want to cry because of the way my city moves me. Perhaps I know that there are so many reasons why I should cry that I cannot possibly voice them all and still retain my hidden love. If I speak, I am scared I will be engulfed by bitterness and the sarcasm of analysis and forget that it was Karachi and the things that happened to me there that give me a voice and words with which to write. There is nowhere in the world where I feel more pain, and I suppose that is why I have temporarily come away. But there is nowhere where I am challenged more, where apathy is more a cover for revelation, and where the mind dreams up new landscapes, fearful and beautiful, to escape the sorrowful gaiety outside. There is nowhere that I am more creative because creative wisdom, I feel, is born from pain.

I am a masochist as I court pain; it helps me write. However, the two are not connected linearly. The relationship is circular. I felt pain first, in moving to Pakistan at an awkward age; it imposed itself on me unwillingly. I turned to my writing to escape it, and then I sought out the pain and confusion again when I knew it helped me write, create. The Shiites, a sect of Islam, use knives and implements to slash their chests in an effort to mimic the pain religious leaders suffered many centuries ago. They bleed in memory of Ali, a cousin of the Prophet Mohammed who was killed. I have only now begun to understand their impulse, which had eluded me. Their psyche is constructed around the memory of suffering and pain, so that God can truly be reached only through the knife-catalyst. Perhaps that is what I mimic when I write. I draw on the confusions and the challenges of Pakistan, which sear me in the process, for my creative instinct.

And so, I feel a peculiar prickle when I recognize my ties to Pakistan and how they have molded me. Inevitably, I wonder: "What are the things that my time at Dartmouth has given me?" Many things spring to mind, many images. I think of the time I danced down the hall with my two freshman-year roommates and sang *You Are My Sunshine* to our undergraduate advisor. I think of the house I live in this summer, along with five friends. I think of late night coffees and conversation. And most of all, I think of my relative peace.

While I sometimes see the residue of the tension of Pakistan flash in my life here, on the whole it has disappeared. Distance has been a productive exercise for me—at first, the mindless distance of freshman year, and now, the thoughtful, analytic distance of long-term resolution. I know my contradictions will not be solved easily. In fact, I wonder if they ever will. I do value Dartmouth for allowing me to seek peace, even if it is an elusive peace. With this relative calm descending, however, I cannot shake the feeling that I am an observer. When I say this, I do not mean that I am objective and utterly detached. My position is more that of a court jester, a fool who is so much a part of the fabric of the life that surrounds, who exists as a commentary. I see my past and the characters that inhabit it with a sharp and often cutting vision. In my writing, that bitterness can sometimes surface. However, like a fool, I am self-conscious of the tragedy of my own place in the vision. I see others clearly, I suppose, but as I laugh, I also see myself fade and shrink and disappear into a Shakespearean storm.

Perhaps this feeling of shrinking is accentuated by how I am perceived by others at this college. I feel I am an anomaly. As an international student, I am seen as inhabiting a space separate from other students—a space that is entirely individual, because of the absence of family and community, and yet collectively representative of the curiosities of culture, history, and geography. In some ways, I am the incarnation of Pakistan for those I encounter here. Their perception of me, as a dual shadow (for, of course, the burden of my identity also makes me an outline to them, unreal), has influenced me. I never feel as if I quite "get" life here. Just as I am an outline to most of those I meet, they remain unshaded outlines to me.

As my most pressing issues derive from Pakistan, I usually feel alienated here. I do not find much honesty here among most students, because this is a very image-conscious school. Most people—although not all—seem to live in fear of real emotion because they do not want to be different from others; or, alternatively, they want to be the same in a constructed differentness of lifestyle. My obvious differences combined with my "normal" appearance become my downfall, because people either resent me for my self-containedness or dislike me for my love of ideas, thinking that I perceive myself as "above it all" and others as unworthy. They see me as having no identifiable place, other than perhaps the role of "international student." Quite a perceptive irony. I have reconciled myself somewhat to the idea that most people I meet will misjudge me, at least at first. It is another haunting pattern I have come to recognize.

When I speak to friends at Dartmouth about their perceptions of me, I find that they all comment on my smile. "You always smile— look at you, always happy." I know, however, that many of them find my smile disconcerting because they know what can hide behind it. I smile because I cannot help projecting a uniform exterior, no matter what I am feeling. This also retards my ability to communicate honestly, although I struggle to make sure that my conversations have meaning. So many people have told me that I appear trouble-free, spaced-out, and unaware of the burden of self. That they can reach a conclusion so polar to my own perception of myself interests me. I suppose I am a dichotomy. Like a fool, I am an example of the difference between appearance and reality. However, this dual perception causes me to feel split sometimes, not quite in touch with my "self," whatever that is. I feel as if I am diffuse: Like perfume and gasoline and rubber tires all floating in the same air, I consist of too many parts to understand them all separately.

I suppose that such problems were true of my time in Pakistan as well, where most students perceived me much as I have just described. Perhaps this sense of disconnectedness is a universal problem, and is only accentuated by those who have had to travel across culture and geography. This idea reminds me of a grand theory I constructed as I was falling asleep last night. I thought: "Being international is merely an accentuation of the loneliness of nationhood—it is the natural loneliness we all feel drawn out more sharply." For that fuzzy and sleepy moment, when I understood my similarity to others, rather than my differences, I felt warm and connected to everyone around me.

I often let myself forget that my feelings of detachment are not peculiar to Hanover. When I lived in Karachi, I did not feel I was quite a Pakistani. There, too, I felt I was a shadowy outsider observing some elusive "real" Pakistani life and representing something distant, perhaps something of Hong Kong. I feel I am neither here nor there. I am caught, perhaps quite luckily, in a place where I have damaged my ties with what it means to be "Pakistani" (if I ever was that) and yet I have not replaced this with a profound love for a new concept of place or of identity. I am thus in a place where I alternate between loneliness and brokenness—and ecstasy at my freedom.

This sense of brokenness and isolation is something I always thought was peculiar to me. I imagined myself as uniquely pained by these issues, not out of a sense of egoism, but more out of a sense of my own "difference" from people in Karachi and in Hanover. However, I have learned to challenge myself on this, because of an independent study in creative writing I am participating in. What I do in English class is the most exciting part of college for me, because it uses my distance from home both to help me understand myself and my experiences in a constructive way and to realize that I might not be as different as I first thought.

This course is the first time I have seriously read non-Western, mostly South Asian, authors, and it is helping me articulate my issues and understand that some of my perceived detachment is not peculiarly mine. "But we were coming to a parting, Pakistan and I. I felt supped full of history, hungry for flavors less stringent on my palate, less demanding of my loyalty," writes Sara Suleri in her book *Meatless Days*. I have found that some of the problems that move me are common to intellectual and emotional life among expatriate South Asians, among English-language speakers who image themselves in a tongue that cannot adequately express the burdens of their heritage. Most writers are tied, in their anger, their bitterness, and their fascination, to what it means to be both distant from and yet connected to "home." It is interesting to me that they also perceive themselves as curiously detached, curiously alone. They are self-conscious—maybe self-conscious to the point of emotional paralysis. It seems that they hurt for their countries, largely because they can never blindly accept their nationhood. As a writer, one takes on a peculiar burden. In writing about a place like Pakistan, I open myself up to suffering and empathy, criticism and resentment, as other writers do in relation to their own homes.

As a hopeful writer, there are two forces battling within me: on the one hand, I want to express these various thoughts about what it means to have been me, to thus connect; on the other, I am defensive about writing on the subject in this country because I do not want to be put in a box labeled "South Asian Womanhood" and judged according to the resulting Western paradigms. Because I grew up in Hong Kong and moved back to Pakistan when I was eleven and a half years old, I think in English and judge Pakistan by what the language suggests to me. It is the voice of my emotions and my dreams, what I converse in with my family. When I write, I write to people who think and dream like me. So I cannot express myself to most of what is considered my country, because Urdu, the national language, is more hazy to me: a pidgin language sometimes fun to speak along with English. I also cannot write comfortably to people in the United States about Pakistan, because I feel the burden of representing my country, the burden of their condescension. I have no right to represent the country, I think, since I am not even a very good example of what it means to be Pakistani.

While I have been at Dartmouth, the most frequent question asked of me has been: "Will you go back?" There are many who do not even bother to ask; they simply assume I will never return. At Denny's Restaurant once, with a group of friends, I mentioned that I would return home. Someone literally dropped her cup in shock and looked at me and said, "No! You're joking, you aren't really going back? What about grad school?" I smiled and reiterated that I was going home. There was a long and awkward silence before we resumed drinking our coffee. At another point, a professor I worked closely with announced to me: "You should do a Ph.D. in philosophy—you have to. It would be a waste of your mind not to." There was nothing I could say in either case because a part of me agreed with them. However, the more I write, the more I realize that going home, in spite of its burdens, might be the best thing for me.

I am returning to an old vision of Pakistan—one that is perhaps not so rosy, but that is accepting. I am calmer now that I have been away. I have ceased to define myself wholly in opposition to that country, although the impulse hasn't left me entirely. My life has moved me in strange and contrary directions, both chronologically and spiritually. It has been lived in flux—Hong Kong, Pakistan, America—but when it stabilizes, I seek out the flux again. Thus, as I savor this Hanover peace, I also see it as ultimately doomed. There are savage tribesmen in Balochistan who roam the mountains I wanted to escape to. No, I will not walk in sand-brown and silence, unless I go never to return. So where, I wonder, does that leave me?

Since I have begun writing seriously again, I have made more of an effort to meet people because I am constantly analyzing myself and those around me and I feel the need to talk about the analysis, to be challenged. A friend told me that my attitude toward Dartmouth has changed since my reimmersion in writing. Being an international student is not comfortable unless you are comfortable with your self-perception. You cannot let yourself be perceived through the eyes of others, which is what I let happen in my first year or so. Because I was distanced from most other students, I distanced myself from myself and remade myself in their eyes, forgetting how deeply I had avoided that denial of self.

I struggled very deeply for an individual identity in Pakistan, largely because I thought people were trying to stifle me; here, I am apathetic about asserting my "individuality" and my sense of self. There I used to start dancing in the school yard when music played in my head; when students would look at me, I would smile at them and dance a little more. Here, however, it is not often that I spontaneously break into a two-step to assert my space. Is it because I no longer feel I need to, or because I have forgotten how important it is to try? I sometimes feel I am lazy now because of the lack of challenge to myself in this society. I feel the United States cannot impinge on my Pakistani experiences enough to challenge me. I crave that kind of a challenge, and when I get it I feel alive. When I used to write in my journal in Karachi, my images were of things shattering, things like dogma and norms. I do not want to lose the conviction that drove my reflections and actions in Pakistan.

Yes, the greatest danger for me here as a writer is to let myself be apathetic. I need to think constantly, to be alert, happy. I have found very little discourse here, no intellectual or emotional excitement, no dialogue, except in connection with dating and drinking—things that do not personally obsess me. Discourse is something I greatly miss about my life at home. I often wonder why it seems that people here talk less, although they do talk more superficially. Most conversations I have are profoundly unsatisfying to me. I feel unchallenged by them and excited when a conversation is "real." Then I realize how sad that is, when most of my conversations in Pakistan were all too real. Perhaps it is because we feel life so deeply there, being denied access to so much of it. So many women and men I knew in Pakistan thought they had been wronged by society, and they talked about it. They expressed, at least among friends, that sense of frustration. They analyzed and categorized and ranted and cried. Maybe constant conversation exists only in the realm of the powerless and the distraught. We were our own psychologists, I now recognize, and I miss that sharp, cutting understanding that we often reached.

As I attempt to pin down the comparison between my life at Dartmouth and Karachi, I have a sneaking realization that I am romanticizing Pakistan from this distance. Do not discredit what I have written, because it is all true. But I have shown what I wanted: the moments when I was alive and saw things in sharp relief. Life was not always like that, although there were many epiphanies. When we read *A Passage to India* in literature class in my senior year of school, I remember that my friends and I latched on to a line E. M. Forster uses to describe the bewildered and alienated British woman, Miss Quested. He said that she had lived most of her life at "half-pressure," thereby giving those moments of fullness that she later experienced more importance in contrast to the general dullness. We too felt that we lived at this reduced pressure, where "most of life [was] so dull that there was nothing to be said about it." When I return to Pakistan, I crave the fullness that it can hold, but I also dread its emptiness, which knells like the sound of a hollow metal bell.

I do not know if I have become addicted to a life of emotional imbalance after the initial imposition that I experienced upon moving to Pakistan, or if the maelstroms I have described are an intrinsic part of my personality. I often wonder if there is an essential self that is released by experience, or whether to be international (which really only means to be displaced), is a constructed thing. I often feel constructed, not quite real, but then, I also feel this to be true of others I meet who have always lived in one country. I find that through my writing, I am seeking justification for the place we live in, although I wonder at the relevance of the word "we." I may merely be imagining a community that does not exist and is fragmented spiritually.

I find it interesting that I use the word "community" in a positive sense. Growing up, it was a word I abhorred because it signified a loss of individuality. Like the word "society," it brought with it images of the worst that Pakistan could be. In school, I avoided being a part of a certain "group." At Dartmouth, too, I have chosen to stay independent of a Greek affiliation, for a combination of reasons. I do not function well as part of a whole. A group identity tends to make me possessive of my sense of self. Yet I am finding that I am less scared of group activities now. Perhaps it is because I have come into contact with more people who share my interests now that I have begun writing. Perhaps I am less scared of interpersonal communication now that I create my own social barriers, rather than having them imposed on me. Whatever the reasons are, I am seeking that which I shied away from: a sense of belonging or community. I cannot return to blind nationhood to find it; I cannot seek it in an American identity. I wonder if I can find it in a community of writers (which is in itself a paradox, as writing is such a lonely thing), but that remains to be seen.

Writing combines my love of history and my desire to erase my memory. It is at once a future, and a recapturing of feelings and incidents from my past. It is an act of communication, with others and myself. It is also a major part of my self-identity. Thus, when I attempt to envisage the years ahead, although I cannot see very far into my future because of the Hanover mist, which is thick and hazy, I see many sheaves of small black type, concise and sharp, with ink scribbles in the margins. I also see fear: the snatching of the pen, the laughter of a country that might not care about my writing. Although most of the time I feel disconnected and essentially split, I fleetingly banish that dichotomy when I write.

Perhaps the best advice anyone ever gave me about my writing was that endings are artificial, constructions that do not adequately reflect real life. I have had the tendency to take endings as absolute, to imagine that at the close of every incident and every piece of writing, my understanding is complete. I must remember, though, that each closure brings with it change and makes me different from the moment before I wrought it. While in the process of creation, it is easy sometimes to forget how temporarily art reflects real life. It is momentary, holding within it the knowledge of the past and the intuition of the future: illuminating, but never definitive.

Drinking at the River of Knowledge

"James"

Nigeria

"Who am I? Where do I come from? Where am I going?" If we all find occasion on which to ask ourselves these fundamental questions, then I have found in Dartmouth College an endless supply of such occasions. When I came here, I loathed this place; now I could even be described as being fond of it. This change in attitude toward a college that initially was such a disappointment to me is a complex one. I have written this essay to better understand it, and to better understand my own journey.

The origins of my path to Dartmouth can be found in the well-to-do Yoruba family into which I was born. My father was a doctor, his father a judge, and my maternal grandfather a wealthy property developer. After qualifying as a general practitioner in Nigeria, my father sought further medical training abroad, and it was during this training that I happened to be born in Britain. This British citizenship would later prove to be a great advantage in fulfilling my ambitions—ambitions that have come to define my identity.

My family lived in Britain for the first few years of my life, returning to Nigeria at the close of the 1970s. This was an era of great optimism in oil-rich Nigeria, which was prospering dramatically due to the rise of world petroleum prices. Things went well for the first few years after our return, both of my parents having obtained well-paying jobs. We enjoyed a luxurious standard of living, having a large house in an upscale part of Lagos and retaining the services of a maid, a cook, and even a chauffeur. This charmed life was not to last, however:

Within three years of our return, world oil prices returned to more modest levels, and Nigerians fell on quite hard times. My parents did not escape these difficulties, and we had to adopt a far more modest lifestyle than we were accustomed to. We let go of all but one servant and moved to an apartment in a middle-class section of Lagos.

As a child, I was not adversely affected by these changes. I had no more annual trips abroad and had to change to a closer school, but this new school was a good one. Its facilities were top-rate, and I thrived there. By the time I was eight years old, I was at the top of my class.

By age nine I had developed an addiction to reading, and was willing to read nearly anything that came into my hands. From the usual child's fare of comics and illustrated science books, I soon worked my way through my mother's novels and my father's books on philosophy and medicine. I was like a reading machine; I even managed to read through the abridged Oxford English Dictionary, from cover to cover. I did all this before I was ten years old. Looking back now, I cannot overstate the importance of this reading background in my life; my passion for reading has been what sustained me through the various transitions that have marked my life.

In those days I was not aware that my interest in reading was atypical for a child. From an early age, I had been inclined to solitary preoccupations, and had little interaction with children of my own age, including my brother, since the two of us had few interests in common. I also detested the presence of adults, deeply resenting their attempts to exercise authority over me. Being so isolated in my own world, I never realized that my interests were out of the ordinary.

In my final year of primary school, I began to realize that there was a gap between myself and most of my peers in terms of intellectual pursuits and abilities. In that year, with the goal of gaining admission into secondary school, I took several nationwide entrance examinations, managing to come first or second in the country on all but one, and this in a nation of one hundred million people.

As a result, I had my pick of schools, and settled on a government school in Lagos, which was one of the most prestigious in the nation. I enrolled as a boarder, primarily to establish that I could be independent of my family, and the experience proved to be a shocking one. The living conditions were spartan, and our lives were highly regimented. There were times for everything—eating, sleeping, reading. I had been accustomed to reading till late at night and waking up late, but now I had to be in bed at 10:00 p.m. and up at 5:00 a.m.. The upperclassmen also did their bit to make life difficult, demanding that first-year students defer to them and run all kinds of errands. We called any student in a class above ours "Sir," and we were forbidden to fraternize with students not in our own class. First-year students also had to clean the dormitories and do the upperclassmen's laundry. I found these menial duties and the obligatory deference particularly demeaning. At home, I had been accustomed either to speaking with my elders as if with peers, or, if this were not possible, to avoiding them—options I no longer had as a boarder.

My academic adjustment proved scarcely any better. I had never been exposed to the idea of systematic study, and had done well in school without any organized effort. Now, I was expected to take notes, pay attention, and read boring textbooks. I found this impossible, spending most lecture periods doodling, talking, or sleeping. My academic performance suffered as a result. Some of this can be traced to class absences. Although attendance at all scheduled events was usually compulsory, in practice there was some flexibility in class attendance, which I took advantage of. I spent most of my mornings browsing in the school library, which I consider my one source of good fortune in those years. I learned far more from the books I read in the library than I actually learned in class. I feel that it was in the library that I got my real education in those years, and I consider the various libraries I have known in London and at Dartmouth to be the best teachers I have had.

During secondary school, I was away for nine months of the year, and when I was home things were none too pleasant. Despite the fact that my tastes and intellectual leanings are similar to my father's, I have not modeled myself after him; to be honest, I feel no great affection for him. As for my mother, her extroversion has always differed from my introspection, and our relationship has suffered from what I considered to be her bias toward my brother. Indeed, I got the impression that my mother cared about me only when I did well at examinations, taking visible pride in my successes. The only times I got better treatment than my brother in high school were on report card days, where I surpassed my brother's achievements. Academic performance counted for a great deal in my family, far more than did interpersonal relations.

I felt embattled in those years. My school life was terrible, and my home life was no great success either. I came to feel that there was no one I could lean on, and that everyone was a potential adversary. When I was at school I would dream of being at home, not to see my parents again, but to have the chance to sleep and eat well once more. Conversely, when I was at home and felt ignored or criticized by my family, I would find myself actually asking if school wasn't a better place to be, for at least I had friends there.

As it turned out, school was *not* a better place. When I advanced to fifth form (equivalent to eleventh grade in the United States), I had expected to find better conditions. Instead, there were actually more ridiculous expectations, and an intensification of the humiliations, beatings, and deprivations that we had to endure from the student prefects in the dorm. Prefects were exempt from most of the absurd regulations we had to endure, and they were determined to get as much out of their leverage over us as they could. For nonprefects, it meant sleeping in wet, filthy clothing almost every night on the floor outside the door of some prefect's room after being soaked in a mud pool. It meant being woken in the middle of the night and subjected to countless lashings. It meant being made to do press-ups for hours on end without a break. The punishments and humiliations came at random, which was by design. The prefects realized that the most effective terror is that which cannot be anticipated. They kept us all permanently on edge.

After a single term of this madness, I was fed up. No amount of "character building" was worth all the suffering that I was going through. I told my parents that I could take no more, and that I had to leave boarding school. It took some doing, but, seeing how determined I was, my parents managed to get me out of there and enroll me in a nearby day school.

My transition to day school highlights how different the pressures of day- and boarding-school cultures in Nigeria are. Until I became a day student, I had been quite insulated from the pressures of normal adolescent social life. In fact, my interaction with young women of my age had been virtually nonexistent. Consequently, as I began to be reintegrated into the outside world, I often found myself awkward around my peers, particularly around young women.

This awkwardness was not alleviated by the fact that my brother quickly picked up friends in the right circles and had become one of the "in" crowd. Soon many young women were calling our house; no one else would pick up the phone, since any call was usually for my brother. I of course envied his success, and I dedicated myself to mastering the "social game."

My planned climb up the social ladder was a highly considered process for me, and I approached the whole affair with the same calculation that my peers employed. People rationed their time and energies based on whom they might bump into, which parties they should or should not go to, which bits of gossip to plant in which tattletale's ear, and so on. When I first started to engage in socializing, I felt very excited; I started to see a whole new world, and the people I met seemed impossibly advanced in comparison to myself. The guys displayed a level of confidence and "coolness" in their interactions with women that I wished I could exude myself. As a result, I became an assiduous partygoer and glad-hander, trying to make every introduction count as much as possible. I became such an inveterate partygoer that everything else at school became secondary to finding out where the next big party would be. Everything depended on having the right image; I did not feel I could act otherwise.

Writing this now, I am amazed by the priorities I had at that point in my life. I seem then to have been more like a politician than anything else, the kind of politician who wants the love and adoration of the crowd, but dreads dealing with people on an individual basis. When I watched Oliver Stone's *Nixon* I felt I could empathize with the Richard Nixon portrayed therein; when I saw the Nixon who was introspective and yet capable of flashing a phony smile at will, I saw myself. When I saw the Nixon obsessed with being respected by the public, who saw himself as an outsider who could survive only by sheer dedication and hard work, it felt like it was my story being portrayed on the screen.

My schoolwork, needless to say, suffered greatly in this period, and with it my home life began to worsen. My tensions with my mother increased due to my mediocre academic performance, and I was made to sign on with after-school tutors in several different subjects. I had ceased to do more than the barest minimum required of me, so that I could preserve my energies for the socializing, which I considered vastly more important. I stopped attending lectures altogether, preferring to spend lecture periods exchanging gossip.

When I did go to class, I usually sat where I would draw the least attention from the teacher. I took no notes, and hardly ever did homework. I dreaded my mother visiting school, since I knew the long litany of complaints about my laziness she would receive from my teachers. My problem was not an inability to understand what was going on, since I still displayed the occasional flash of brilliance whenever I found myself able to concentrate; I simply couldn't bring myself to care about school. This whole period in my life now has an almost unreal feel for me, as if I had become a different person altogether from my true self.

With this separation came emotional trouble, and by my middle years of high school I had become bad tempered and irritable toward my family, was suffering from chronic anxiety and occasional panic attacks, and was a ruthless social climber and a mediocre student. There was little continuity between who I was in those years and who I had been at age ten or eleven. By the time I was fifteen, I was no longer capable of the concentration required to read a long book at one sitting, and socializing prevented the deep thought that I had developed such a liking for. To those I lived with, I must have been intolerable; to be honest, I was not too fond of who I'd become myself.

I began to realize that the road I was on could only lead to a life of regret at wasted opportunities. What social recognition I had gained from my peers had not made me feel noticeably happier or more contented. In fact, the reverse was true—the harder I tried to scramble up the social ladder, the more I feared falling back down it. Ironically, it was a ladder in the library that finally changed my life direction for the better.

Despite my preoccupation with social climbing, I had never completely abandoned my love of reading, and would sometimes wander into the school library and browse through titles I picked at random from the shelves. One day, high upon a shelf I came upon a 1960 Time-Life educational book about physics. While I once had deeply loved the sciences, four years of tedious rote learning had made them seem simply sleep-inducing. In fact, it was only out of sheer boredom that I even bothered to pick up this dusty old volume.

I will be forever grateful that I did. As I read through the pages on modern physics, black holes, the seemingly paradoxical predictions of quantum mechanics, and the counterintuitive notions of relativity theory, I remember feeling shocked. Physics could actually be interesting! I also remember the feeling that I was lucky to be alive at a time when such exciting things had been discovered. If such marvelous things were known in the 1960s, I thought, what wonders were being discovered in my time?

This one book, and my enjoyment of its intellectual wonders, finally renewed my active involvement in the process of learning. I realized that, much as I desired the love of the crowd, I loved learning even more. I felt a need to really understand the physics I was reading about, and realized that to do so I would require a great deal of mathematical knowledge. In the process of studying the high-powered mathematics needed to comprehend modern developments in physics, I came to see the beauty of mathematics itself. What we had been studying in class was a poor substitute for real mathematics. Real mathematics was a thing of incomparably greater elegance and power, and at age sixteen, seduced by the Queen of the Sciences, I decided to become a mathematician, a decision I have not doubted even to this day.

Soon enough, the time rolled around for my Senior Secondary School Certificate (School Cert) examinations. This was the examination that determined a student's fate, and as a result it loomed over every ambitious high school student's head like some visage of Fortune in a Durer woodcut. Needless to say, my lack of attention in high school left me terrified at the tests' approach. With less than six weeks left before the examinations that would decide my fate, my fear of failure finally provided the willpower I would need to study. Desperate, and not trusting my own powers of concentration, I emptied out a room in the house, leaving inside only a chair and a desk with my textbooks on it. I then asked my mother to lock me in that room from the outside and to let me out only to eat, use the bathroom, or sleep at the end of the day.

I began to study frantically. I had wasted virtually all of my senior secondary school years on socializing and extracurricular reading, and now had to learn in six weeks what I was supposed to have learned in three years. All too soon it was time for the dreaded examinations. Yet somehow, after all, I achieved a "Distinction," which meant that I had performed excellently in virtually all of my papers. Through panicked effort and the benefit of my outside reading, I managed to escape the consequences of three wasted years.

With my School Cert exams out of the way, my parents began to search for ways to send me off to study for A levels in England, which serve informally as university entrance exams. The idea was that I should go to England for two years of private tutoring before proceeding to a university there. I was excited about the thought of going to England to study, as it meant for me the opportunity not only to gain access to books, museums, and art galleries, and to see new places and ways of life, but also to escape my family and peers, with all their pressures and demands, and to start anew.

My parents intended that I stay with my uncle and his wife in a quiet, suburban part of London. This arrangement worked for a while, though conflicts about personal space became unmanageable. Eventually, it became clear to all parties that we would all be better off if I lived in a more central part of London on my own. Now that I had won for myself almost complete autonomy, I had to determine what to do with my newfound freedom.

Most important, I was able to further develop my identity as a student. The more accustomed to studying I became, the less unpleasant a task it seemed. In fact, when I had been working for a while on a complex problem, solution would bring with it a great feeling of intellectual satisfaction.

However important my renewed academic commitment was, no man subsists on knowledge alone. My books were not my only concern during my two-year sojourn, and I still had quite a bit of free time on my hands. As I had left Lagos partly to leave behind my days as a socialite, I was now faced with the problem of what to do with my leisure hours. I decided to try and live free of pressure from "friends" to act in certain ways or to engage in activities I had no real interest in. I wanted the freedom to act as smart and sophisticated or as stupid as I pleased, the freedom to visit the Tate Gallery instead of a trendy nightclub, and the freedom to spend my money on books about number theory instead of on rap music and the latest fashions.

Yet, despite my resolve, I sometimes felt isolated. Having chosen to cut myself off from all the people I had known before, and lacking avenues to make new acquaintances, it did not take long for a feeling of emptiness to set in. I often used to leave the television on simply so I could hear a human voice. Whenever my feelings of isolation became more intense, I would buy a bus or subway pass so I could make round-the-clock use of the city's public transport system. I would visit the entertainment district or tourist attractions, as I found it easier to do my leisure reading with others around me. I also would visit London's many museums and art galleries, and the great bookstores such as Foyle's and Blackwell's that line Charing Cross Road.

At the same time, I did not always run from my isolation. One positive thing that solitude provided was plenty of time to think. I had never before had the opportunity to think in a concentrated fashion about a single thing for days on end and without interruption, and now I did. I thought about many issues, but mostly about who I was and what I wanted out of life.

One thing I learned was that I did *not* want ever again to spend my days trying to climb some social hierarchy. I found that I could fill my days with satisfactions that did not depend on comparing myself with others. It may have been lonely at times, but I grew to love my life in London—going to museums and art galleries, taking walks in Green Park or Regents' Park, traveling around the city admiring its architectural landmarks and soaking up its history and culture. I even began to develop a feeling of identity as a British citizen that I never really had before. It was a case of creeping acculturation, a gradual forgetting of my old frame of mind. It became apparent to me that nothing could be more pleasant than the life of the bachelor who has enough money and leisure time to indulge his aesthetic tastes.

Why then, if my stay in England was so enjoyable, do I now find myself residing in the United States? Plainly put, however well educated a nonwhite person is in England, entrance into the upper classes is essentially closed off to him. One might make one's way into a middle-level job of some sort, but the truly important positions in society (whether in business, politics, art, literature, or architecture) would always be shut off. It is difficult enough in England if one has a Liverpool or Cockney accent; what chance is there for a member of a numerically unimportant minority?

It is also true that, despite Britain's illustrious history as the center of the greatest empire the modern world has seen, it simply is no longer at center stage. While I do not see my mission in life as climbing to the top, I want to be where the greatest excitement is, and Britain is not that place.

Thus the United States began to attract me; with its immigrant heritage, its ethos of self-advancement and social mobility, and its sheer size, wealth, and diversity, I came to believe that there was nowhere else in the world I would rather be. Few nations in the world define themselves by such fine ideas as liberty and opportunity, or hold in high esteem such a statement as "Give me your tired, your poor. . .," even if the American reality has often fallen short of this lofty idealism.

It took time for the idea of studying in the United States to gain prominence in my thoughts. I had always been told that little money was available for international students studying in the United States, and that competition for the limited funds available was fierce. After being in England for eight months, though, I decided to try to obtain a copy of the SAT practice test. I did well enough that the idea of trying to get into an American college was not as impractical as I had earlier felt it to be.

By the autumn of 1993, I felt sufficiently motivated to ask various U.S. colleges for application forms. I also practiced seriously for the SAT examinations, making a score of 1,590 four times in a row on practice tests. I knew that if I failed to get into the colleges I applied to, it would not be due to my academic record. There seemed to be good grounds for optimism, especially as my varied background might be attractive to admissions offices.

In the end, I applied to six or seven universities, with Harvard my first choice, Princeton my second, and Dartmouth my third. There were reasons for this order. The first was the name recognition. Harvard and Princeton simply possess a far higher profile than Dartmouth. The second reason was Dartmouth's (unwarranted, I now believe) reputation for being a hotbed of right-wing activity. The final, most prophetic, reason was the impression that I had from the various college guidebooks about the intellectual climate at Dartmouth. I read such statements as "Dartmouth is the least intellectual of the Ivies" and "Dartmouth students view their class work as a chore to be gotten out of the way." I did not see how my own renewed passion for learning would fit into the climate described in these books.

In the end, however, attend I did, as my first two choices declined to choose me in return. I was of course at first disappointed and bitter, but decided I had best try to develop some enthusiasm for Dartmouth. After all, I had wanted to study in America, and now I had my chance! From the moment I received my admission letter, my thoughts about the future focused entirely on the United States. I felt as if my life was to be one epic adventure: I had left Nigeria for Britain, and now I was on my way to America! I felt like a character in one of those once highly popular novels about the poor but ambitious immigrant who rises to the top by dint of talent and hard work.

After that, my time in England passed very pleasantly, though this period ultimately made my transition to Dartmouth difficult. With my future no longer riding on my A-level results, I had been able to relax a bit and decided to spend the rest of the summer visiting family friends who lived in Cambridge. With its rich history and marvelous architectural heritage, Cambridge University was a delight. The students seemed to be alive, curious, and possessed of a maturity that I would find lacking in students at Dartmouth. For many of the students I met at Cambridge, the life of the mind was more than just a hollow phrase.

My visit to Cambridge only made me more impatient to get to Dartmouth, and yet it also set me up for disappointment. I had not forgotten what I had heard about the intellectual climate at Dartmouth, but I still doubted that the place could be as bad as it had been made out to be. Sadly, I was wrong. From the first night of my Dartmouth Outing Club hiking trip (a tradition for all entering freshmen), I had a premonition that things were not going to work out as I had hoped. My fellow freshmen spent the whole day talking about television, marijuana, chewing gum, and other such trivialities. After having spent the last two years in mental high gear, this kind of conversation was difficult, even offensive, to my sensibilities, and I did not wish to participate. Things did not improve for the rest of the trip. Feeling a growing sense of frustration and anger, I decided to pull away from the pack and march out in front, and even ran up Mount Moosilauke and back down. The physical exertion required to stay out in front gave me something to concentrate on other than the people I was with, and thus provided some relief. I did not like my fellow trip members, and they grew to dislike me. My difference, my "otherness," could hardly have been more clearly highlighted.

Overall, as I suggested in the beginning of this narrative, my first year at Dartmouth from this point on was one of the worst of my life. Indeed, my current love of the school seems far, far removed from my initial feelings of antipathy. I found most of the people I met to be excruciatingly boring: Virtually all the students exhibited a lack of direction or purpose to their lives. Few had passions for anything other than fame, wealth, security, or political renown of some sort. The average student I encountered lacked any desire or willingness to explore new avenues of thought just for curiosity's sake, without regard for immediate applications. The general attitude seemed to be "If it won't help my GPA or career goals, I don't want to learn about it." For me, in contrast, there is no greater pleasure than learning new things and seeing unimagined vistas open up, and the anti-intellectual attitude I found among my peers came as a rude shock. I frequently tried to involve others in conversation about the things I was interested in, but with little success. I found I could engage in pleasant enough discussions as long as I kept my passions to myself. It was only when the ugly specter of intellectualism raised its head in the form of, say, a discussion of the influence of the Bauhaus movement on modern architecture, that problems started to arise.

I remember taking as a freshman a senior honors course in mathematical logic, where I learned about reason and its limits, including the concept that even our belief in the consistency of mathematics is an act of faith. This idea was startling and disturbing to me, as it seemed to indicate that having certain knowledge to any meaningful degree was impossible, and that the most we could hope for were fair guesses. When I realized the implications of this notion, I felt the urge to seize everyone I met by the shoulders and shout, "Do you know what this means for us all?" Yet other students regarded said notion with utter indifference. I find it hard to believe now that I actually expected my fellow students to be interested in what I had to tell them about an issue so seemingly remote from their daily concerns.

And in actuality, this was only one of the many exciting things I had been learning at Dartmouth. Dartmouth seemed, with its wonderful libraries and professors, a mighty river of knowledge. It could not possibly be that, presented with such an opportunity, so few students would be drinking from the river. And yet it seems to me now that most students who come to Dartmouth do indeed make very little use of what this place has to offer. They attend lectures, write papers, and take exams, and some do these things very well indeed, but they are not the sort of people who burn with excitement about what they do.

A college student's mission, as I saw it then and still do, is to learn as broadly and as deeply as possible about the kinds of things a college is particularly conducive to teaching. College is a place one goes to expand one's mind and to learn to think clearly, in a concentrated fashion. It should not be a place merely for learning how to "get along" and how to socialize. Yet my fellow students spent any time not utilized in doing their class work in idle banter, playing juvenile pranks, or discussing such profound topics as how many glasses of beer they'd managed to down without passing out the previous evening. My attitude may seem arrogant, but I really did not care for the company of people so obsessed with trivialities. My lack of interest in those around me left me at times feeling deeply isolated, enough so that I considered transferring. On the other hand, I dreaded the thought of having to settle in all over again somewhere else, and I could not be sure that things would be better anywhere else, so I stayed put.

During this depressing period, I remembered the lessons of my book on physics back in Lagos. I decided that my only hope was to immerse myself in what the school offered, instead of lamenting over what it did not. I had known, even before coming to Dartmouth, that I wanted to study mathematics and physics, and my experiences with the courses I had taken in those subjects at Dartmouth confirmed that decision. It became ever clearer to me that my goal should be to work toward obtaining a Ph.D. in mathematics, and that this goal could provide the focus I lacked.

Regardless of my peers' own apathy toward their studies, I, at least, could throw myself into my academics with passion. During my sophomore year I became even more engrossed in mathematics. By reading on my own, and by taking several graduate courses, I began to get a feel for what the frontiers of knowledge were in my favorite mathematical interest, the theory of numbers. I began to realize what the unsolved problems were, who the cutting-edge researchers were and where they were doing their work, the history of various fields within mathematics, and much else. In short, I began, as some mathematicians like to put it, to acquire mathematical *culture*. I already had ideas as to which topics I would someday like to do my Ph.D. work on. The feeling that I was making rapid progress gave me a great deal of satisfaction, and I began to feel that my ideas could actually make a difference: The day might actually come when I would discover something that no man before me ever had. I do not know of many feelings that rival this one.

While I was engrossed in the study of mathematics, I did not neglect all other subjects. Instead, I spread myself rather thin, and found that I was constantly struggling to fit all my interests into too little time. MIT students like to say that being at their school is like drinking from a fire hydrant, that they have to absorb far too much in too short a time span. I feel that this is a pretty good description of how I have often felt about the situations I put myself in. I have read books on topics as varied as modern architecture, Oriental and Roman history, cosmology, genetics, virology, astronomy, neoclassical and monetarist economics, and Arabic calligraphy; by no means have I confined myself to the study of mathematics. For this, I also give much credit to the flexibility that Dartmouth's administration and faculty have shown in letting me take advanced courses in my field of interest. Although I would never have predicted it in my freshman year, I think I have been getting an excellent education at Dartmouth. I know far more now than I did when I first came to Dartmouth, and I have no complaints about the academic resources available here.

I also discovered during my sophomore year just how beautiful my physical surroundings were. It is amazing what one can fail to notice, and during my freshman year I completely missed the beauty of the college's surroundings. I think the change in my attitude only began with my discovery of the great Japanese haiku poet Basho. What makes Basho's work truly great, in my opinion, is his ability to make one see the beauty in even commonplace things. Inspired by this new way of seeing, I began to realize that Dartmouth, and the surrounding New Hampshire woods, offered a visual bounty. I think there are few things more pleasant than looking out of one's window at dawn, to see the low-lying fog enveloping the nearby hills, or to stroll on a foggy night across the green and watch the streetlights glow like fireflies. Everywhere I turn there is something to appreciate, whether it is the plain, understated beauty of Dartmouth Hall on a moonlit night, or the stately pines that jut into the sky behind the new dorms and Wilder Hall; aesthetic enrichment can be found outside the libraries' walls as well.

With the opportunities that Dartmouth provides me to indulge my eclectic interests, the great resources available here for me to learn from, and, by no means unimportant, the sheer physical beauty of the campus and the surrounding countryside, I don't think it is hard to see why I have come to love Dartmouth. The way I have come to feel about Dartmouth is akin to the way a person feels toward someone he or she is attracted to. At the outset there is a great deal of projection, and the affection one feels is often due more to a desire to believe that person has certain qualities than to any real understanding of his or her essence. Then comes a period of disillusionment, when one wonders what one saw in the other person: This is where most relationships fail. For those who surmount this obstacle, there is the final stage, which I call the stage of reconciliation. It is at this stage that one reconciles how one would like the other to be with the reality of what that person truly is. One comes to like the true essence of the other, not what one hopes this essence to be.

So it has been with me and Dartmouth. Dartmouth is no Cambridge University, no college of dreaming spires. This college is not a place where young men discuss lyrical poetry while drifting down the Cam River, nor is it an institution where young Isaac Newtons and Maynard Keynes storm across the campus, thinking thoughts that will someday shake the world. On the other hand, it has offered me in its faculty and its two-million-volume library the resources to pursue my passions, and for that much I am quite grateful.

As I have come to terms with Dartmouth, other things have gained in importance in my thoughts. I am now a junior, and am planning on applying to two graduate schools—one in the United States and one in England—that are the leading institutions in my particular field. Beyond graduate school, however, I am unsure what I shall do. In fact, despite my avowed love of mathematics, I would probably choose to devote my life to literature, painting, music, photography, and architecture, were it possible for me to ignore financial realities. This may seem strange coming from a person who is planning to pursue a Ph.D. in mathematics, but in fact I am now equally passionate about the arts. I have chosen to continue studying mathematics because the mathematics Ph.D. offers relatively safe career prospects, an important consideration, as I will someday have to take financial care of my parents.

At the same time, I would be lying if I said that I am entirely comfortable with the compromise I have come to. I feel that there are so many things I could do, and I believe, or perhaps wish, that somehow it should be possible for me to do them all. I do not need to be told that it will be a tall order to carry out all the things I would like to do, but I really believe my scheme can somehow be made to work. Unlike many people, I do not see myself as being in a race to rise to the pinnacle of financial success, and I do not reject the idea of just floating around, taking life as a series of learning experiences without any final destination. Whatever the future holds, I am pleased with how things have turned out so far.

Living by Leaving Behind

Devyani Sharma
India

Dartmouth College, Hanover, New Hampshire, was the last place I would have expected to go to college. While all the students in my final year of high school sharpened their no. 2 pencils to fill in endless rows of small ovals on the American achievement tests, I didn't give it a second thought. This international school in Geneva was my eighth school, and having had experiences in Indian, British, American, and international schools, I thought I knew where I belonged. My most numerous encounters of unabashed ignorance had been in an American school in Boston and among the American students in my other schools. When I came from Bonn to Boston, for example, I was asked whether Hitler was still the prime minister of Germany; much later, when we were being posted out of Geneva, I found that my American lab partner did not know that my prospective hometown, Berlin, existed. My efforts to explain were met with a blank and friendly smile. Such moments, combined perhaps with an old-fashioned and irrational Indian awe of England and a minor obsession with a British singer, persuaded me to limit my college experience to Europe at least.

Changing countries every couple of years has had a somewhat kaleidoscopic effect on me. I glimpsed countless faces, colors, sounds—immersed in each small world but never really being aware of it. For many years I assumed that I was living a very normal life, since most of the children in the schools I attended were from similar backgrounds. I did not pay attention to where I was the way my parents did. My actual introduction to my own strangeness occurred when my father was first posted back to India. We had been in America for a brief and happy year, and to my thirteen-year-old mind I was about to return to a country filled with people like me. I thought all Indians would be like me. Upon arrival, I discovered that the real India was not simply a larger and longer version of my intermittent vacations. My only other extended experience of India had been at a boarding school when I was seven years old, a dim memory littered with occasional details that still retain the heightened clarity of a child's view. Now a teenager, I found that I could not participate in the Hindi-English banter between classmates; I did not recognize the names that bred political or cinematic gossip; and above all I was not accustomed to the level and pressure of study.

The response of a population to the introduction of an alien element into its environment reveals the entire breadth of its prejudices, fears, and even desires. There I stood, "freaky" (my alleged nickname, as I later discovered) and demanding categorization. It was quite similar to the situation I sometimes find myself in at college in the United States, although then I had to contend with the brutality of adolescence—mine and theirs. I was inept in most classroom situations: I wouldn't stand up when teachers spoke to me; I failed to address them as "ma'am" and "sir"; I spoke to members of the other sex (seen variously as either insane or lascivious); I was peculiar in appearance; I knew no Hindi slang; the list goes on. Factions formed. Many of my classmates viewed me with extreme suspicion and not much seriousness, having decided I was "from America." To the hip crowd, this last stopover, which had almost nothing to do with where I was "coming from" myself, induced a little awe, a little envy, and probably considerable disappointment that I was so unglamorous for all my foreign (Western only, of course) travel. I made no friends among this group, and received only grudging invitations to parties. But I stayed in India for three years at that very formative age, from thirteen to sixteen. The reason I feel thoroughly Indian is partly because our life-style as I grew up always remained so, but also to some extent because I was in India during these years.

The dual power of language to be disruptive or creative first became noticeable to me during those years. Language seemed to be an even greater hindrance than my lack of participation in practices such as music, dance, or various community activities. Not only my poor Hindi but also my "different" English caused strange barriers. Extensive arguments over the pronunciation of "Agatha" or "mass" or

"Beethoven" provoked bewilderment on both sides; I had never encountered their use of English, and they were bemused by mine. Although I struggled to achieve a functional level of fluency in Hindi within two years of my arrival, I was never able to speak as my classmates did. Linguistic tools such as jokes, irony, innuendo or slang are acquired only in the final stages of fluency and are so crucial to social interaction, particularly at the age when what you say matters much less than how you say it.

During this time, when I was at school in Delhi, I decided what I wanted to study in college. Except for my school experience in Delhi, I always did equally well in everything in school. This often left me with the impression that I was not, in fact, particularly good at anything. But I have always liked to draw. In Delhi, it seemed that there were two distinct attitudes to the education of children: quantity versus quality of knowledge. A few of my friends thought art was "cool," some thought it was a commendable decorative skill for a wife to possess, others could not conceive of the notion of studying it as a serious pursuit. In retrospect, I imagine it was this last group of people that made the decision for me. Acquaintances or family members who would say, "Oh, Babli's son is an aerospace engineer. . . and her daughter paints pictures" gave me my final incentive. So I began at an art college in London.

My college experience so far has been the reverse of most students. I started out immediately studying a very specialized subject and living alone in an apartment in London, a rare situation for first-year students in America to find themselves in. Only gradually did I begin to consider the breadth of subjects that could interest me, along with a slow realization that hostel or dorm life was something I was missing out on. That year I spent most of my time with one particular Yugoslavian friend who, straight out of school, had also flung herself enthusiastically into the London art college scene. We had both done the International Baccalaureate Diploma in our schools; this was in fact one of the first conversation triggers. There is a curious bond that links IB victims. A few words, numbers, and a knowing nod of the head on either side establish a sort of understanding between the most unlikely acquaintances. And so we both understood that first seductive taste of the expanse of possible knowledge that the IB introduces. It is a remarkable course of study; I often realized that within the slightly oppressive environment of Geneva's international school, my only source of happiness was the novelty of such fascinating learning. And yet, perhaps the other moments of disillusion and hopelessness were equally important in how my ideas later formed.

Only through talking with this friend in college did I sense how much I had sacrificed in choosing art college. We spent whole nights exchanging dim memories—which sometimes focused into glorious detail—of historical eras, social revolutions, and literary wonders that had just recently so enamored us. Invariably, the dialogues would find their sleepy end in the mutual worry that art college was making us "stupid." She has shown perhaps greater dedication than me, by completing a full degree from art college, but still often considers combining it with more academic study. Only now can I begin to understand that we had been expressing a much more complex dilemma.

While art college may be limiting, it is not in itself "stupid-making." On the contrary, it is more demanding of a mature and abstract intellect than many other post-high school pursuits. This is precisely the problem I had with it, for although I was bringing a heavy load of academic and cultural baggage with me, I had no understanding of myself yet. To my mind, it was enough to want to draw all the time. But visual communication is often more conceptual than technical, and I simply had no deep, organized well from which to fish out the necessary references or information to make relevant art. After all, it is often called "applied art," indicating that it must apply to other parts of human experience.

My room in London, almost like a small flat, had one wall lined with books. Obsessed with my rapidly declining IQ, I would make sure I was reading at least two of the books at any given time. In this way, I retained a consistent layperson's flirtation with subjects outside the sphere of art. I would often find myself heavily influenced by novels (and later, when a TV was temporarily within my reach, also films and documentaries) that dealt with the violent exclusion of an individual from society. Perhaps I identified a little with them, but I believe my interest was usually a much more objective curiosity about the human condition. Two nonfictional authors with whom I was particularly taken up were Desmond Morris, now somewhat suspect, and Lewis Thomas; their writing was a kind of pop anthropology that made common concepts of the field accessible to me. Through them I found the world of human studies, the possibility of placing our entire species before a giant mirror.

London was a first in many ways: I was living alone, I was no longer in school, and I was in an entirely English-speaking environment. Of course I did not make the most of its theater and concerts—as always, intending more than achieving—but I at once immersed myself in the only language in which I have always felt comfortable. Somehow the subtleties of my English, the accent, intonations, or diction, feel more pronounced here in America than they were there. London was too heterogeneous, at least in its college atmosphere, for me to be aware of my particularities for very long. After a year's course, I chose to do a degree in graphics in Berlin. Apart from a few of my art tutors in London, who knew the reputation of German graphic design, most of my friends were baffled that I would choose a Teutonic lifestyle over the delights of London's culture. Somewhere along the line, I was obliged to decide which I valued more: a rigorous, impressive training in my field or a sense of comfort and belonging. Berlin could offer me the former, but not the latter. After resisting leaving London by all conceivable, illogical means, I started a degree course in visual communication at the Berlin University of Fine Arts.

My German had been resurrected intermittently over the previous five or six years, so it was in a state of ill-grammared fluency. This is possibly the worst language level with which to enter a foreign land, because you give a misleading impression of fluency. In spite of my stumbling adjective endings, I believe the professors and students imagined that I was more or less expressing all I wanted to. Quite to the contrary, I would articulate only the barest shadow of my actual thought in order to simply communicate it—and I eventually became so stymied that I ceased to even think any further than I had to, knowing it would never reach the point of expression. I spent every evening alone in my room reliving the day's anguished moments of maladroit verbal exchange. A single mispronunciation or failed experimentation with slang would make me forever self-conscious with the people involved, even if they never noticed. Toward the end of my first year, when I knew I was coming to the United States, I had actually made a few friends. Their surprise at my reasons for moving is probably proof enough that my linguistic ineptitude existed to a large extent only in my mind. Had I stayed on, I may have gradually become indifferent to the fact that I was living in a foreign language. But it was impossible to continue in an environment where I had to think out remarks and jokes hours before trying them out, only to be met with sudden silence and polite, uncomprehending smiles. I often consider this when I see students struggle with English here: We so easily forget that they are really saying next to nothing about themselves, that we know nothing about who they are.

Struggling through the stoicism of the German character and language had its benefits. For one, I realized that, for the most part, I myself was not like that. I found I missed that crazy mixture of nationalities which, of its own accord, allowed people to transcend their accent and appearance, for as soon as everyone is "exotic," no one really is. Even my art foundation course in London was expressly planned for foreign students. In retrospect, it is very clear to me that when I have been in a homogenous environment, mainly my school in India and the Berlin university, what people expected me to be was derived much more from my background than from my own character. I felt so uncomfortable in the culture, and particularly the language, that my negative conception of U.S. colleges began to change.

My general directions of curiosity, as I finally began considering applying to American colleges in all seriousness, seemed to focus around subjects that had been inaccessible to me in school. In the final months of the IB, we were required to take a course called Theory of Knowledge, which offered the faintest hints of philosophy, psychology, anthropology, and so on, as if to say, "And this is what we forgot to teach you about. . . ." Somewhere in my unconscious, the knowledge then settled that I could officially "study" people. During the two years of art college this little temptation danced in my mind until I finally capitulated. By this time, I imagine, my parents were resigned to having a pathologically indecisive child on their hands.

My parents have been the source of many fortunate dilemmas and mistakes, through their sheer permissiveness. Even when I was fifteen years old in India, I was excluded from the parent-bashing conversations of my friends, many of whom suffered under traditionally despotic Indian parents. My mother almost never limited my activities, except maybe when we both knew I was being idiotic. My father once (perhaps only once) went to a PTA meeting, and was told he should look for my teacher not in the eighth but in the tenth grade. So his problems were of a far greater magnitude than knowing where I was at a given time of day. Humane parents like these were somewhat alienating. Later, as my friends were herded into the few respectable paths of study—engineering, commerce, medicine—I was happily taking German and painting classes. When I chose to pursue humanities after the vicious tenth-grade board exams, some of the students used to say, "But you shouldn't give up; I'm sure your grades will be good enough to get into the Eco or Bio section," as though I had fallen miserably into the hopeless field of humanities by sheer default.

I often think of how different my outlook would have been had I not always had the support of my parents. The only constant for the four of us, when moving from home to home, is each other. People laugh at my liberal use of the word "home"; for example, I currently use the word for four different places, and that excludes all ex-homes. Ironically, my most "home" home is where my parents are posted in Kazakhstan—a place I have not even seen yet. Every term at registration here in Dartmouth, I am asked in a perfunctory manner for my home address and telephone number. A few minutes later, the impatient official will look up to see me thrown into profound confusion by this request.

Over the past year or two of separation, my father has begun to come to terms with the notion that I am, in fact, a thinking adult. We began to have occasional conversations, or rather interrogations by me, about subjects that I was only starting to think about. He studied and taught English literature for twelve years before becoming a diplomat and, like most of his own family, is afflicted with a voracious appetite for comparative religions and cosmogonies, along with other innumerable pet academic pursuits. As the IB unfolded the vast worlds of English, history, philosophies, and knowledge to me, I ran first to him, knowing he was the infinite well from which I had to somehow coax similar discoveries and huge links and parallels in knowledge. I am sure he is unaware of this, but my most inspiring moments of learning were rarely in school, sometimes in books, but most often while talking with him.

My father's input into my way of reading and thinking inadvertently defined much more: my political views, academic scavenging, and probably how I view myself in relation to everything I experience. After an initial phase of impulsive, reactive atheism that most teenagers go through, imagining themselves to be rebels of society, I developed a curiosity for my father's interest in questions of the spirit and the mind. I decided there must be something to it if it could so sustain his unflagging interest. I picked up tidbits of Hindu as well as Western theology and cosmology; I read and asked him about cosmogonies, theories of existence, hypnotic regression, "other" lives, and related topics. I was foraging. In the process, bewildering parallels began to emerge across both the breadth and depth of time, so to speak. I was awed by how Hindu parables of creation, of matter being energy, of illusion and scale, echoed in the most contemporary astronomy. I was thrilled to read about moments of mutual acknowledgment, such as when Robert Oppenheimer, upon watching the first controlled atomic detonation, recalled Krishna's words from the *Bhagavad Gita:* "I am become death. The shatterer of worlds." And I was puzzled by conscious segregation such as Stephen Hawking's disregard for ancient Asian mythological cosmologies.

I think I keep wanting to scrutinize human existence within this immense, immeasurable universal state. But rather than through philosophy, or even cosmology—apart from within an anthropological framework—I like to discover clues of what we are through seemingly minor tangible symbols, occurrences, and patterns such as language. I often feel that I can gauge a person's political inclination from how they view spirituality. My politics, and also my notion of myself, stem from a kind of spirituality that has helped me control recurring moments of panic, isolation, and bewilderment, and that therefore means a lot to me.

I became vegetarian about five years ago, on June 18 of my sixteenth year. On that day, my cousin, a "soul-sister" if I ever had one, left Delhi for a boarding school in southern India, leaving me alone after two years of almost compulsive togetherness. I had been vaguely looking for an appropriate date to fully renounce the consumption of violently procured guileless flesh, so to speak, and this date seemed suitably unrelated and yet momentous. In any case, this is a topic I have remained fairly militant about for years now. One of the few aspects of life that seems not to vary much between Europe and the United States is people's attitudes to animal activism. I do not include this with environmentalism, for there are some differences. I encounter the same disproportionately large number of people who cannot conceive that someone could take the issue of animal exploitation seriously, and then the rare individual who has given some thought to the question and is not quite as shocked by my suggestions.

I find everywhere that most people do not question my motives for making a vegetarian, and also anti-fur and anti-leather, choice because they assume it is religious. By some happy union of the Holy Cow legend and my nationality in their minds, I invariably lose any chance of talking about theories of human violence and hypocrisy. There are some issues that I find are treated with a curious, archaic kind of ridicule, often issues that are very important to me such as animal liberation (a *bad* word!), sexuality, or even anarchy. To my mind, these are subjects that were central to the kinds of impediments or anger I felt while growing up. In Europe, I found extremists more genuinely extreme and critics more genuinely critical. The American mentality tends to consist of rather prepackaged opinions.

As far as anarchist thinking (by this, of course, I mean more than the usual offhand definition of anarchy as something misanthropic and terrorist) goes, I think there is more open consideration given to it in Europe and India because both regions have had more immediate contact with socialist and other noncapitalist efforts. America, to my mind, will always have a lingering aftertaste of its McCarthyite past when encountering almost any suggested lifestyle other than capitalist. Anarchy, since it cannot find much expression within straightforward politics, seems to become allied instead with "softer" approaches, such as the hippie or environmental movements.

Dartmouth is the first place where I have been conscious of my politics, as opposed to my hypothetical ramblings. The strength of conservative thinking at this college is evident to me through the fact that I have become very aware of how apparently leftist or progressive my views are. In art college I suppose it was taken for granted that you were, to some degree, a nihilist and were deeply indifferent to ambiguous sexual orientation. The Dartmouth Film Society recently showed a film by Derek Jarman, a well-known gay filmmaker in London who has AIDS. This film, *Edward II*, dealt concurrently with themes of homosexuality in the story of Edward II as well as the current gay rights movement. Despite some weaknesses, his style is so loaded with witty symbols, ambiguity, shock, beauty, and ugliness that it cannot fail in its effort to confront. But I could barely follow the film for all the laughter, hoots, loud remarks, and louder departures from the hall. In this community, I always see this incredible vulnerability, for want of a better term, to be so easily shocked and bigoted that any rational discussion of compelling current issues, whether one agrees or not, is lost. This is what frustrates and yet fascinates me. It is probably this violently conservative predominance that has made me want to be consciously political.

Wherever I have lived, I have rarely belonged to a homogenous clique. One exception was perhaps in India, where I eventually had quite a fixed circle of friends, mostly from the same background. In fact, as we got to know each other it would very often happen that some family friendship could be traced. I was bewildered by these recurring connections because I began to feel how I really belonged to an insular circle of society, for all our similar parents with similar backgrounds had sent their similar children to the same school without even knowing it. An interesting footnote to this pattern is my Yugoslavian friend in my London college. As we talked about our lives, we found that we understood each other uncannily well, almost finishing each other's sentences. Our grandfathers had been generals; our parents were diplomats; politics was an intrinsic part of evening talk in the cities we came from; both our cultures had traditions of tacky Western imitation in fashion and music that we abhorred and adored simultaneously. There is considerably more that brings people together than meets the eye! And people from very different parts of the world may find that they have, in fact, very similar backgrounds that led them to the same kind of educational institution.

As a rule, in international schools and otherwise, I used to avoid being inextricably involved with the Indian subcontinent cliques that invariably formed. I think people did and still do see this as some kind of snobbery. If anything, it was quite the reverse, for it began as shyness and awkwardness—I did not listen to Indian music; I did not learn any form of Indian dance or music; and I sometimes seemed more out of place among them than when I simply mingled in the school or the city. I am too much of a cultural concoction to feel either condescension or awe for a particular group; some part of me will rebel because I belong, in bits and pieces, to all of them.

Awareness of individual identities seems to develop only during those early adolescent years in school, largely as a result of observing students and ethnic cliques different from oneself. When I was ten and attending a British school in Bonn, West Germany, I observed a classic exchange of insults between a very small girl from Nigeria called Sa'adatu (however accurate my imitation of the pronunciation of her name sounded to me, it sent her into paroxysms of laughter) and an

American called Debbie, whom I envied for some forgotten reason. One day, after PE, Debbie called Sa'a a "chocolate cookie," in return for which Sa'a single-handedly labeled Debbie and all her formidable gang "cheese crackers." At that age, this only remained in my mind as a curiously culinary exchange. I spent some time trying to think up a snack to match me, too.

Now that I have overcome (or so I like to hope) many of my subsequent adolescent horrors of being a strange, wrong, uniquely hideous, and eternally alone creature, I like to amuse myself by watching my interactions with people here. It is understandable that Americans, with their very cleanly delineated Map of the World, would have a hard time categorizing me, but it is much more fun meeting Indian Americans, whom I have never encountered in such large numbers. They often have an intensely Indian upbringing that either compromises or loses against the surrounding American culture. It is the same exaggerated preservation of customs, and often language, that we notice whenever we move to a new posting. I find that since I do not actively pursue very Indian activities, they imagine that I have similarly "lost" to some other culture; I sometimes become Swiss or German because of my school and "current" home as listed in the freshman book.

These are merely observations; they do not influence my choice of friends particularly strongly. By far my closest friend at Dartmouth is someone who looks more Indian than me but says "Louisiana" when asked where he is from. He has much more mind-boggling encounters than I, because he is basically American but will never be considered so by many of the people with whom he comes into contact. His name will always be mutilated beyond recognition, and he will be interrogated about Indian food and habits at least once every week for the rest of his life. As a result of this stereotyping, combined with painfully conservative parents, his view of India is about as skeptical as mine of the United States.

I suppose that on the whole I gravitate toward people who think like me. But this can mean anything and eventually means nothing. As much as anyone may try, it is impossible to identify a predominant character or inclination that defines who each of us chooses as friends. I cannot say that I befriend either exclusively international students or Indians or Americans, or that people I find myself drawn to have a particular set of interests or opinions. I am more aware of why I am *not* friendly with certain people; I feel as though, by a process of elimination, I make friends by default. On this campus, in particular, I have encountered people with views diametrically opposed to mine and sadly closed to discussion. Perhaps other foreign students have also had the experience of not being schooled in the uniquely American codes of social conduct, such as the pathological need to say "Howyadoing" or "Whatsup" incessantly to each other, with little or no interest in the response. These are very misleading pseudo-indications of contact to people who are more sparing but personal with their greetings.

Other habits of the natives can be similarly problematic. Take, for example, "good weather" rituals. As soon as summer approaches, the collective mood soars and people begin to indulge in any number of patterned, time-worn practices. People's moods are so weather-defined; I am in a guaranteed minority if I say I like the rain, or that I have sometimes felt saddest while watching sunbathers, frisbee-tossers, barbecuers, joggers, baseball players, and every conceivable figure of health and joy parade past me on a sunny day. Of course I enjoy warmth occasionally, but I am more moved by the beauty of a dusty, draining heat, and the celebration of a hot, numbing rain. Summer behavior in the West can be as exotic and alien to me as these sensations are to Americans.

Sometimes I sit alone in this college and feel very fully what the word "alien" means. At times like this, one doesn't rationally reflect on what the source of loneliness is. The person becomes an invalid, unable to move or speak, let alone think constructively or communicate. Perhaps it is cultural alienation, but I have always fallen into similar inexplicable abysses of blackness wherever I am. It is a strange combination of frailties, of insurmountable sadness, of infinite distances between your soul and the people, places, and patterns around you. For that moment you want neither to "talk about it"—the American cure for all ills—nor to receive verbalized sympathy from another. The only interaction that may filter through the arbitrary shields that build around your tight, concentric, monotonous thoughts is noticing that another individual has a true understanding of this state.

At Dartmouth in particular, but also in most situations where "foreigners" are immersed in a homogenous alien environment, it is sometimes only this that induces the clustering of foreigners. However little I may have in common with another international student, I can depend on the unspoken understanding that we have both come to terms with being isolated. Being together cannot alter that—it merely reduces the uniqueness of your own situation—but this is infinitely reassuring. It is easy to see this simply in the body language between two international students. Waving, stopping to exchange a word, the openness of gesture and posture all seem subtly enhanced, or perhaps just slightly more genuine. I feel we acknowledge that each of us has a complex culture that is temporarily severed from us and that is almost invariably disregarded or misunderstood in this environment. By "culture" I mean not only the arts and customs of our countries, but rather the words, gestures, humor, currents of thought—traits that can vary so greatly even within a country.

My most recent and maybe most real experience of recognizing that another person understood what "alone" means was here at Dartmouth. I found it not in a person, but in a book. (This amuses me; it is such a predictable outcome of life at this college—very little deep personal exchange and quite extensive immersion in printed matter.) On some fortuitous whim, I took a course in my second term here called Literature and Psychoanalysis. It covered a wild array of writings, since it was concerned with reading novels as psychoanalytic case studies, and then reading case studies as fiction. Among the readings were theoretical works by Freud, Jacques Lacan, and Julia Kristeva's *Black Sun*. This book was my first reading of a serious and disturbingly accurate perception of what she calls "melancholia," in which she talks of the psychomotor inactivity, the breakdown of symbolic language, the effects of loss, and the fluctuation between euphoria or froth (*aphros*) and melancholia or black bile (*melaina kole*), a balance that is so prevalent while growing up, but that no one seems to talk about. Kristeva talks of the "unnameable Thing" that exists in place of a real loss but that causes the same depressive effect as an object-loss. So much in her assessments of mood, and of language and signs, emerges in other reading I have done, as well as in my own experience. These writers in particular, since they are directly concerned with human and linguistic experience, have made me conscious that certain kinds of emotions and even traumas are not aberrations, but are an integral part of human experience.

Since then, when I read or when I react, I feel at least a slight understanding; I begin to feel that each work I read is a part of every other. Freud, despite his dubious assessment of female sexuality, opened the layers of the mind and all of its possible networks to me—

an endless game. Our discussions of other writings on female sexuality, such as Luce Irigaray's lesbian separatism, supplemented my emerging interest in these topics. On the other hand, I found Lacan and the world of language and existence. At last, here was more about language as a living entity, a transmitted, precarious thing in which all the clues to an individual might lie. Earlier this term I heard Umberto Eco speak on the (European) search for the perfect language—a very different, mythological approach to language. Everything seemed to connect or rebound; it was for this kind of universality that I originally came here.

It is apt that a liberal arts education is characteristic of America, for I feel the same casual, uninhibited sense of openness with the college system as with the country. The country is a potpourri—geographically, demographically, politically—and the same spirit is inherent in a liberal arts education. There is a certain academic irreverence, or at least impertinence, in attempting to approach and comprehend so many disciplines at once. India, in her British way, is quite canonical about specialized fields of study, and also about maintaining a great distance between "teacher" and "taught." Europe is also relatively conservative about academic hierarchy, but the United States fully encourages a self-assertive, dilettante approach. At the cost of some dispensable educational traditions, colleges here tend to allow any form of knowledge-gathering, and I sometimes think that many American students, being brought up within this attitude for the most part, do not realize how much freer and more flexible this system is in comparison to most.

While studying here, my notions of what "America" and "the world" mean have been confronted by the very different meanings that American students themselves ascribe to them. At lunch once, I had two such encounters simultaneously. In the newspaper I was reading, a photograph of a local Waco, Texas, resident was captioned with her assessment of the then-current Branch Davidian Cult confrontation, to the effect that "this kind of thing happens overseas, anywhere but in America." To my mind, this was a complete inversion of how I would view the incident. I would have to think long and hard to name another country in which a violent Christian cult community annihilates itself in the flames of an invasion by a hypermilitarized force called the Bureau of Alcohol, Tobacco, and Firearms. As I looked up from the paper, a fragment of conversation drifted across to me from the next table: ". . . all over the world! I mean, like, in *Alaska!*" Alaska, as an extremity of the United States, was the furthest conceivable place. Many American students have a slightly warped sense of scale, like Western map projections that show the northern hemisphere as twice the size of the southern. This insular worldview is what is most troublesome, for it is not a tangible bias; it quietly permeates into all aspects of exchange. People here will never fail to be surprised by a foreigner's knowledge of "their" language or their cultural idiosyncrasies, like *Monday Night Football*.

Language is an especially well-guarded domain of the West. I once mentioned to someone that I had lived in London for a year in 1991, and he asked if that was where I had learned my English. I was a little disappointed that my English had come across as just a two-year-old acquisition. Many people I meet here are surprised that I speak in English with my parents and Indian friends. One evening I was talking with some people about the bizarre use of the word "like" in English, particularly American slang, when inserted between every few words for no grammatical purpose. I mentioned what an incredibly widespread habit it is, because among friends in India we also often insert it randomly. After fifteen minutes the conversation was becoming increasingly incomprehensible to me, until I realized that they thought I meant that we used the *Hindi* equivalent of "like" and talked only in Hindi. It is certainly regrettable that I grew up being so Anglocentric. Naturally, many young people in India do talk mostly in Indian languages, but most children have a working knowledge of three languages—Hindi, English, and their local/state language—without really being aware of it. We often speak in a mixture of languages. There is little comprehension here of the complexity of ex-empire/commonwealth countries. Against my better judgment, I often find myself pleading with people, ". . . we *do* speak English at home, we *do* wear jeans, we *do* have pavements, traffic lights, microprocessor industries, soap operas. . . ." How does one respond when someone says, "Your English is very good"? I just say, "So is yours."

Eurocentrism was an equally great impediment before I came here (perhaps even greater, for they have substantially more to be centric about). In Germany I was sometimes mistaken for being Spanish, and interest would often drop considerably when I revealed my true origin. The Germans like India as an esoteric, academic pursuit, but they turn to Spain for passion. On the other hand, when I was walking home in East Berlin I was once verbally abused by three corpulent skinheads sitting outside a café who, thinking I was an Arab, babbled pseudo-Arabic nonsense at me. Few people here understand or acknowledge the extent of prejudice in Germany, from violence and slurs to concentrated avoidance—even in a college situation—of people with a different appearance. I appreciate the general lack of such pigeon-holing at U.S. campuses. Despite the stereotypes of India, I don't feel that people are surprised to see a foreigner, and they are not always as overtly convinced that they are superior. With their unique blend of immigrant populations, no American could hope to guess correctly the background of a foreigner (though they never stop trying). Although I may defend my country, I do not feel obliged to represent it, nor do I believe I ever could. One of the unconscious errors of many American students, which can become irksome sometimes, is their constant association of the individual with their country: "Oh, do they do it that way back home?" "How come you both can't talk to each other in 'Indian'?" "I didn't realize Indian women thought like that!" and so on.

On this campus, I have personally felt that my identity as a woman is challenged as often as my identity as a foreigner. One gets used to being a little different and misunderstood as an outsider anywhere, but I am not yet accustomed to the peculiar role-playing options for women here. Personal relations are very heterosexually defined, in that the woman's character develops not on her own terms but according to how she relates to men—compete or concede. In particular, the curious practice of masculine competition at this college is quite new to me. Because of the highly male-dominated history of the college, where women were imported on weekends as decorative, corporeal distractions, perhaps women have felt it necessary to compete more on masculine terms than to forge a more genuine female identity. Feminist self-assertion seems more convincing to me when it emphasizes the strength of women through our difference from men, rather than synthetic imitation. The androgyny of "jock" women forever sprinting around campus in sports clothing or heavily masculine attire is interesting, but I cannot really identify with the espoused "masculized" behavior that accompanies it.

On the other hand, there is a tendency to play a conservative female role that then comes to be expected by males. At least on this campus, there is little room for any transgression of such social codes by a member of either sex. Again because of my two years in the student art scenes in major cities, I was exposed to all degrees of activism, and so I am not surprised by much feminist or gay/lesbian/bisexual activism here. If anything has surprised me, it is the prevalence of insecure, conservative behavior in the form of fraternities and sororities, their somewhat paradoxical counterparts—for isn't the premise of fraternities an artificial clustering of men that legitimizes excessive indulgence in highly masculine rituals? I certainly don't argue that women in Indian cities have a better situation, but I wonder if all the people who have asked me if I wear traditional outfits at home or if I will have an arranged marriage realize that circumstances here are not as different as they imagine. How many American students would ask a male Indian student if he wears traditional dress at home?

I feel very aware that I am privileged to have had such opportunities throughout my life. Even in a city as large as Delhi, women have a hard time getting out if they wish to, and fulfilling goals that may seem unexceptional to a woman here. My friends in India think quite like me, and yet each hope would have to work its way through innumerable kinds of prejudice or apathy, often perishing in the process. The problem is not of exotic and amusing marriage practices among quaint people, as it is sometimes portrayed in the questions I get here; it is huge social and parental pressure against normal, "modern" hopes of women exactly like women here. It is sad to see how the parents of American-born Indians still burden their children with typically Indian limitations on the direction of study or on their social life, anachronistic remnants of practices from the time they left the country. How unfair, with all of the options that this country lays before them, to have to live as though they were in India in the 1950s. I find some expatriate families live by even stricter traditions than people I know in Delhi, perhaps in a last attempt to retain some bond, however negative.

The dynamics and restrictions of the social intercourse of some Indian Americans here are particularly curious, because they attempt to preserve a kind of cultural integrity that I myself have missed sometimes in contact here. Of course, the main aim of conservative Indian parents in forbidding flirtation and romantic involvements, especially with non-Indians, is the view to an eventual arranged marriage and the protraction of an obsolete morality. But however much I abhor such authoritative control of their mature children's impulses, I have occasionally felt a considerable abyss between me and

Europeans or Americans. In both cases, flirtation is an integral part of life from a very young age. As I grew up, I had a fairly tentative approach to it and somehow or other was left out of much of the run-of-the-mill teenage romancing. It seems like a trivial phase in retrospect, but being excluded from these rites of passage can be so demoralizing. I think I went straight from childhood friendships to adult relationships, and now when I encounter the Western kind of casual flirtation, I hesitate. I suppose I have evolved my own adaptation—a little reserved and yet not very judgmental, because neither my different cities nor my parents supplied a standard. This confuses people, especially me, because it is an amalgamation of Indian and Western values. Such pressures are always at play in romantic or sexual interaction between an Indian and an American or European of my age; perhaps I am a little more conscious of it because I feel both inclinations.

I had a "model" discussion on the subject once when I was on a long train ride across Europe. I started talking with a Yugoslav soldier my age who had left Belgrade after fighting for thirteen months and was in a similar state of uprootedness as I was, except that I had planned my next four years in America and he was free to go anywhere, though something of a fugitive. Trains make people talk about love, so we began interrogating each other about our respective pasts and points of view. He was soon winning, because although I had as free an approach as he, I had this fixed notion that I could never have a complete relationship with a foreigner. Until then, I had only expressed this among Indian friends, and we would mostly acknowledge it without really considering why. For once I was now on the firing line, and I found I had no idea how to explain myself. In Europe, and to some extent in America, people are brought up to be individuals; it is much less important what culture they belong to. Children are given far more freedom, and are treated as independent beings who will one day be expected to determine how all aspects of their lives develop. There are few familial or social obligations in their choice of a partner. Even though I have grown up with these notions, I need a person to understand a certain way of being that is very non-European. The difference is always so tangible and yet so inexpressible. However indifferent I remain to a person's background, it is probably some indication that the most substantial romantic involvement I have had has been here, with a person who came to the United States from India as an infant but has a confused enough identity to understand me.

A lot of people of my age seem to be anxious about future intentions and goals, often because of social indoctrination. The big question here is always "What are you looking for in life?" It is this feverish and futile search that keeps the United States—through fads and crazes from New Age spirituality to anorexia—forever on the verge of a collective nervous breakdown. Life is nothing more than a succession of sensory perceptions of the most abstract nature, and its essence lies in this transience, not permanence—in fluidity, not solidity. In Jorge Luis Borges' words: "The truth is that we all live by leaving behind."

All that I have written has been preceded by a highly chaotic past, and anticipates a life of greater confusion. I have hardly ever contemplated settling down, whether geographically or ideologically, for both are highly unlikely and quite undesirable. My great fear is of the stability people exude here, at institutions such as this one. As I encounter people, I begin to unveil a monolithic structure of inscribed views that defends them against incertitude, and against questioning. They are consistent, settled in their views. All my experiences and attitudes, on the other hand, are flavored with a kind of bewilderment, even desperation, that I rarely encounter here. I plan to leave the country after I finish my studies. I adore some of the cities and some of the people here, but my life has not prepared me for the self-contained, insular, paranoid, and somehow clumsy world of America.

Chasing the Dog's Tail

Maria Popova

Bulgaria

In my cozy room in Hanover, thousands of miles and several years apart from the communist regime in my country, I started to read George Orwell's *1984* with the tickling feeling of stepping over a threshold. While reading this book in democratic countries was considered a must, behind the Iron Curtain in Bulgaria, it was a crime even to possess "this evil creation of the decaying capitalism." As I galloped through the pages, I was stunned. I admired the unusual sagacity of the author, who had created a sarcastically exaggerated picture of the communist societies. Newspeak, thought-crime, doublethink, thought-police, Big Brother—as I grew up, these symbols were reality. I could step perfectly in Winston's shoes, and therein lay the paradox. The book was depressing and bleak, but instead of feeling disgust and relief that this nightmare was now over, I felt nostalgia. I remembered that in Bulgaria, I had lacked freedom of expression and choice, and I knew that if the communist system had not collapsed, I would not be here now, writing about myself. But instead of feeling grateful, I was confused. I had been so happy in that absurd and, for the majority of people, painful world that I would have given up my Dartmouth career, with all the great choices it would give me, would have left the freedom, comfort, and safety of my life here for the old Bulgaria that I knew—a world that unfortunately does not exist anymore.

Many would ask me what could possibly have made me happy in that obscure and oppressive society. I could not have answered this question if I had not come to the United States. I do not want to leave the impression that I was happy because of communism. I was happy despite all its dark sides; despite the frustration of my parents, who never achieved what they could have in the West; despite the restrictions on travel; despite the impossibility of even thinking about studying or working abroad freely; despite the lack of nice clothes and tasty food in bright packages; despite a myriad of humiliating restrictions and absurd, but unquestionable, rules.

One might expect that I made plenty of compromises with myself in order to achieve happiness in such a bleak reality, but this was not the case. First, I feel I developed the useful ability to value the minute details of life that sometimes make it utterly joyful. A single banana on a winter day could make me happy, not to mention a new toy or a new jacket. A letter from an unknown penpal from Japan was the biggest event of the week. A new stamp from Mexico was a treasure I would brag about. In a world of regulations, uniformity, and scarcity, everything unusual, colorful, or simply different was a source of happiness.

Second, I was not alone then. There were some side effects of communism that had changed the people's value system for the better. The lack of competition and the people's indifference to their jobs, besides destroying the economy, did something else more positive. People focused all their efforts, affection, and time on their family and friends. At Dartmouth, I have found out that in my personal value system, bonds are much higher than freedom and well-being. I have learned that freedom can sometimes be equal to solitude, and that I prefer to have love and affection than liberty. At some point in *1984*, Orwell makes a rather pessimistic prediction that turned out to be wrong for the majority of the people in the communist society that I knew. Children did not betray their parents; neighbors did not grab the chance to tell on each other to the Secret Police; connections between the people were not destroyed by suspiciousness, hypocrisy, and fear.

There were happy people during the communist era, and I was definitely one of them. That is why it seemed logical to me that coming to a "better" world of unlimited opportunities would make me even happier. High expectations, however, often do not come true. When I came to Dartmouth, all alone for the first time, I found it difficult to feel part of it. Maybe Moses was right in saying that people born in bondage can never learn to be free. But freedom is not the problem in my case. The problem is how to rediscover things I took for granted:

love, affection, connections, communication. Why did I take them for granted?

One of the good sides of life in a socialist country was security. The term "unemployment" did not exist, and the only reason we knew its meaning was that it was often referred to as "one of the scourges of capitalism." There were no homeless people, and those who did not have a home of their own lived in state apartments, paying the ridiculous rent of ten dollars a year. Do not think, however, that life was all a bed of roses. In fact, the more precise word for existence in the communist world was survival. Everybody was guaranteed and at the same time sentenced to survival; to exist was to survive the physical and intellectual dearth. The common hardship and fears incited the solidarity and closeness that prison mates often develop.

But let me narrow the story to my own family. After their matrimonial ceremony, my parents didn't go on a honeymoon trip, not only because my mother's finals started the next day, but also because they did not have the money to go to the Black Sea, a favorite vacation spot for many in eastern Europe. Venice or Paris was out of the question because it was more than clear that they would not have received a visa to exit Bulgaria. They were not even able to live somewhere, just the two of them alone, because there was a twenty-year waiting list to buy a new apartment, private flats could not be lent, and the government gave state housing only to people who had absolutely no place to live. My parents' only option was to live in the family house of my mother's parents and grandparents. It was very uncomfortable, probably a nightmarish scenario for most foreigners— four rooms and a kitchen shared by eleven people from four generations. But for my parents, those years brought a lot of joy.

It was a happy house. I still remember it, although I was only four when they demolished it to build a new bunch of ugly block houses, which soon formed a new project. I can still remember my early infancy, more as a sequence of photos than as a coherent film. Everybody is out in the yard on a warm summer evening. The men— my grandfather, my father, and my uncle—are playing cards or chess. My grandmother, my aunts, and a neighbor are preparing the dinner outside and discussing something that I do not find interesting (maybe it was gossip, or maybe recipes, who knows?). I am running and shouting with my cousin and the neighbors' boy, when I hear my grandmother's voice: "Try to be more quiet because mummy is studying. You do not want her to fail the exam, do you?" Then I see myself sitting in my great-grandmother's lap, listening to stories about my ancestors. She was a good storyteller—I still remember a lot of what she told me. The knowledge of my family history introduced me to a world of the past to which I indirectly belong: a gallery of people that I never met, but who would have loved me because I am their offspring; a number of places where I feel at home, although I've never stayed there more than a couple of nights.

After the house was demolished, the family was separated and my parents got an apartment in one of the new blocks that emerged, bright and equal, as Bulgaria's future was supposed to be. When we moved there, my parents' usual bickering swelled into frequent fights. Maybe they fought because they were getting to know each other's flaws better and better over the years, but I tend to think that the loss of the big family that tied us all together also contributed to this deterioration. Since the move, my family has not been a paragon of mutual understanding and respect. My parents spent a good part of their life quarreling—sometimes over serious problems, many times over unimportant matters. After almost twenty years of family life full of misunderstandings, scandals, and some chunks of bliss, they managed to reach a happy balance—but only after I left the house. What luck.

Nonetheless, I had a happy childhood. I learned to make the most of the rare periods of tranquillity before the storms and enjoyed them as a gift. Then, when my brother was born—I was ten years old at the time—my life changed. I went to live temporarily with my grandparents, saying, "But Mom, Dad, I cannot study when the baby is crying all the time! Do you want me to start getting bad grades?"

I actually never returned completely. I did not want to, because my grandparents made me so happy. Besides their love, which was equal to the love I received from my parents, I received more attention. My grandparents had both retired and spent all their time looking after me. My grandmother always tried to please me, cooking all my favorite dishes and listening to my stories about everything that had happened in school, in minute detail. She was never bored when listening to me, or at least she never showed it. She knew all my school friends, and every time I invited someone to our apartment, she hurried to make a snack. She encouraged me in everything I did, and thus made me confident and not afraid of challenges. She typed the poems I had written and made little books, which my grandfather showed proudly to relatives, neighbors, friends, and even to passengers on the bus. My grandfather is a retired colonel who has traveled a lot, and he always starts a conversation with the sentence, "Let me tell you something that will expand your attainments." During my life with him and my grandmother, I used to discuss politics, international relations, and history with him, sometimes for hours. I spent the summers in a small town with my paternal grandmother, who never got tired of telling me stories about my ancestors. Even though I did not live there, I always felt part of this small community, by virtue of my grandmother's fame. For many years, she had been the town's only midwife, and I always felt proud that everyone knew and respected her. One often recognizes happiness only when seeing it slip through one's hands. I, however, have always been grateful to my grandparents for making my childhood so blissful.

The fact that I have such a profound relationship with my grandparents might suggest that my mother has been somehow out of my life or, perhaps, only in the margin, but in fact, she is the person closest to me. During our eighteen-year relationship we have not had even a single quarrel.

The main reason for my perfect relationship with my mother is our long conversations. They started in the years of my earliest infancy, which are a little misty in my memory. My mom has told me many times that she started treating me like an adult from the time I learned to talk. She has never hidden anything from me just because it is not appropriate for little children, or because I might not understand it. Neither of us experienced the embarrassing atmosphere of the first puberty talk, since it had taken place without us even noticing it. All the major decisions I have made in my life were influenced by my mother: which school to go to, what languages to study, what profession to consider, whether to study abroad or not, and so on. At the same time, she has always seriously considered my opinion in the decisions she has had to make, both personal and professional. To some extent, the fact that I became my mom's best friend since I was two or three years old deprived me of the carefree and blithe spirit of childhood, but I do not regret it. All these shared choices drew us closer than most daughters and mothers. I feel I have been lucky to grow up in a family where three generations of women—my grandmother, her two daughters, and me—lived in perfect accord. It has been a very rewarding experience to have so many people I can trust for anything, to receive understanding, advice, compassion, and help in any situation. My family gave me the precious feeling of being "a loved one."

Being away from my family, consequently, sometimes makes me feel completely alone here at Dartmouth, so alone that I cannot believe it. I sometimes walk along the green thinking, "Does anybody here on this campus care about my feelings? Will anybody notice if I suddenly disappear? Will anybody regret it if I transfer to another college?" It is a pity that the only people I think would are the other Bulgarians at Dartmouth. Why did I come here, then? Why did I exchange my valuable status as a loved one for the status of being just an international student from, where was it? Oh yes, Bulgaria, that is neat! And sometimes it is not even neat. To some people, I am just one of the "bunch of third-world Marxists," who instead of living in their own countries have a whole nice international house on "our" campus. Unfortunately, I am not exaggerating; I have been told these very things. So why am I here? I often encounter this question just when I am rushing headlong toward happiness; sometimes it manages to knock me down. At those times, I turn to new chunks of knowledge I've obtained, and to my memories.

I was the brightest kid in the neighborhood. At two years old, I could calculate anybody's age if given the year of birth, knew all the politicians' names, and could comment on the current international events—all this with the serious face of an adult. Of course, I do not remember those years clearly, but I can easily recollect the praise and the impressed faces of the adults around me.

Psychologists might say that such an attitude toward a small child could have easily spoiled me and turned me into a self-conscious, conceited, and capricious little princess, and they might often be right. However, I avoided becoming a know-it-all kid because my mother always had new peaks for me to climb. She would throw new challenges at me, sometimes half-jokingly, and I would always strive to achieve them. Her suggestions always required a lot of effort and zeal, and made me feel the limits of my abilities.

For example, when I was six, my mom took me to take the entrance exams for the National School for Gifted Children in Sofia. I was perfectly aware what the name of the school meant, and I was determined to do my best, to prove that I had deserved to be praised. I was not self-confident, though, and when my mom found out that I had made a mistake on the exam, I cried desperately all the way home.

Nevertheless, I did get into the school, and I was again the center of attention.

I think that my admission to this school was one of the best things that happened in my life. I liked the school from the day of the exams. The building was unlike any other school I had seen; later, I understood that the "inside" of it was also unique. The school was situated in the foothills of the mountain Vitosha, a few blocks above the center of a rural-looking Sofia suburb called Gorna Bania. We used to play every day in the woods around the school. When I say "we," I mean my class, which consisted of twenty-five children and two teachers. It might sound awfully banal and corny, but now that I have known my classmates for thirteen years (two-thirds of my life) and have spent two-thirds of each school day with them, I feel they are my second family— like brothers and sisters.

Our long acquaintance is not the only reason for our closeness. Just like brothers and sisters, we grew up together, under the influence of our surrogate mothers and fathers—our teachers. Moreover, we lived isolated from the world, in our personal paradise. Almost every other year, we went on tours abroad and had folk dancing concerts. Every summer we went to the seaside, every fall to a ski resort, and studied there for two weeks. Every weekend we visited a historical monument, monastery, art gallery, opera or theater performance, or just went to a nice, secluded place in the mountains to spend the whole day playing. It was the school's policy to build up our attainments and knowledge of the world through concrete contact with it, keeping us together most of the time so that every child could benefit from the others' talents. The method definitely worked, since my class left the school with the sense that everybody was leaving his or her childhood home.

Besides the beautiful relationship with my classmates, I felt close to my teachers. It is not that we behaved as if they were our peers—I would find that disrespectful. We called them by their last names, and addressed them with the polite verb form. But we could also share all our problems with our teachers, ask them for advice without having to make an appointment, or just stop by their office to chat about the future (or maybe the past, whichever we felt like discussing) over a cup of coffee.

Another way in which my school was (and is still) unique is that students have the same teachers over the years. This contributes to the gradual forming of a very strong relationship. My chemistry teacher, from whom I learned both what a substance is and what the basic assumptions of quantum mechanics are, used to say all the time, "I feel like a mother dog who has new puppies every year, raises them until they become independent, and then waits for them to come and visit her. It is sometimes sad that I am always the one that stays, after you go away, but you will come to see your old teacher when you win the Nobel prize, will you not, puppies?"

No matter how much I wanted to put off my graduation day, it arrived--merciless and oblivious of my fear to leave school. I started preparing for it a month earlier, trying to persuade myself that the future in front of me was going to be as exciting as my school years. The ceremony was touching, but I managed to stay dry-eyed through most of it. Toward the end, the principal announced that the first-graders wanted to say good-bye to the graduating class with a folk dance. From the first tones of the introduction, I recognized the music—it was the same dance that we used to dance. Then I realized that they were dressed in the national costumes we used to wear when we were exactly their age. Pictures from my happy childhood started appearing before my eyes until I could not see anything but myself and my classmates in the faces of the children who were dancing. I looked around and saw that all my friends were on the verge of crying, and despite how hard I tried to stop myself, I started sobbing first. When the dance was over, I remember walking to the microphone in a semiconscious daze and sliding the crumbled sheet with my speech into a friend's hand. I will never know what I said. After the ceremony, people came to congratulate me for my successes and wish me good luck in the "real life out there," but I was not listening. That was the most painful day of my life. Someone had just slammed the door of childhood in my face.

That is why I chose Dartmouth—a small school with traditions, rural setting, and a faculty dedicated to teaching. From the few photos and information booklets that I saw, the college looked like a twin of my school. I was sure that time and experience was going to affirm my first impressions. I had forgotten, though, a Bulgarian proverb that warns not to put money on the table before you have seen the check. That is exactly what I did—I took out all my dreams and believed they would come true, before even seeing Dartmouth. When I saw the bill, it turned out that the price for my happiness here was much higher. This is how my "Dartmouth career" started.

It was September 14, 1993. Just an ordinary day of an ordinary fall, but for me it was a critical point in my life: a stepping off into a new land, a new culture, a different life—the beginning of a discovery. The beginning, however, turned out to be trivial, unexciting, and disappointing. The Greyhound bus unexpectedly dropped me off in White River Junction, and the driver said I had to figure out how to get to Hanover myself. I did not panic. I caught a cab that took me straight to the Office of Residential Life. I was surprised that nobody waited for me there to say "Welcome!" and give me the key to my room. The cab left me in front of McLane Dormitory and I was again on my own. I realized that I would not make it to my fourth-floor room with my four suitcases, so when I saw that the lounge was full of people, I walked in and said:

"Hi! My name is Maria. I am from Bulgaria, and I just arrived a few minutes ago. Could someone help me take my luggage to the fourth floor? I am afraid I cannot do it by myself."

They laughed, looked at each other, and did not say anything. Now I panicked.

"Maybe my accent is too strong. I will take care of that soon, so there is nothing to worry about," I thought while dragging the first suitcase up the stairs. I liked my room—clean and green. My roommate had not arrived yet, so I decided to prepare a little surprise for her. I spent the rest of the day decorating my room with pictures from home, and drawing a "MELANIE, WELCOME TO OUR ROOM" poster. As soon as I learned how to use Blitzmail (the campus e-mail system), I also "blitzed" her a welcome message. I spent the following week piling up things I wanted to tell her—an extensive description of my interests, a good number of jokes, my plans for the future, my memories from my happy childhood—and I had a huge list of questions to ask her as well. In my imagination, the whole year would not have been enough to finish the conversation we were going to start from the very first day—had we ever started talking to each other. As it turns out, she did not give me a chance.

Maybe language was part of the problem. Bulgarian is not a popular language, so people at home dedicate a lot of time to learning foreign languages—"windows to the world," as the expression says. Americans, on the contrary, expect others to understand them, because English is spoken almost everywhere. Although I studied English for more than twelve years and had the chance to practice it with native speakers, my language skills are obviously more limited than those of my peers. Not that I do not know enough words to express my thoughts, but subtle things such as intonation, slang, and connotations elude me. I know I sounded awkward when I spoke with Melanie for the first time, but she should have tried to understand that this is not my native tongue. I know "Oh, that's cool!" sounded funny coming from me, but she should not have laughed and said that my accent was hilarious. I decided that there was no need to try again, and I contented myself with the fact that nobody noticed my accent in a paper. Thus, little by little, my roommate and I stopped talking at all because I did not want to be reminded that I sounded funny, and she never shared anything with me. The first strong bond that I had expected to build turned out to be silky thin--just a chain of "hi's" and "bye's," ready to fall apart any minute.

"OK, maybe I just had the tough luck to be roommates with a person who is very different from me, which prevents us from building a close friendship," I told myself, to keep from panicking. I decided to take another approach.

I looked for friends in my classes and I did find them, but they were all from my English class—the "English for International Students Only" class. From my other two classes I did not make a single friend. One girl did blitz me five times a day, but once the midterm was over, she didn't need me to proofread her Spanish papers anymore; I never heard from her again. When we pass, she does not even say hi, and that is definitely not what I call a friend. I was disappointed, but tried to remain optimistic.

I thought, "Maybe I have to meet more people in order to find the right ones. I will start going to parties, like I did in Bulgaria," which I did. But that only discouraged me even further. What I call a party is a night crammed with fun, but not one that is advertised all over campus. To me, a party includes a core group of people who are all close friends, and every one of them brings another friend to introduce to the others. There is a lot of dancing and laughter. There is alcohol, too, but it is definitely not what brings the people to the party. The group may include couples, but they do not need to show how far they can push the limits of decency or lock themselves in a room for three hours. Of course, people might meet for the first time at a party, and discover that they are attracted to each other, but they do not get drunk together and do not introduce themselves in the morning after they have had sex.

I could not find a place in the fraternity parties at Dartmouth: I do not need alcohol to make communication easier, and when I spend half an hour talking with a guy, I definitely do not want him to infer that he can "score" with me.

I decided to talk to my undergraduate advisor and tell her that I was finding it difficult to feel part of the so-called Dartmouth community. She told me that I had to make efforts every day in order to find friends. Her advice sounded like "if you work hard in your classes, you will get an A for your persistence." I did not like the idea as I do not think friendship is a goal or an investment for which you have to strive. It is a gift that you get for just being who you are. Making efforts, as she suggested, implies stretching, and stretching implies insincerity, and I want such insincerity out of my life. Nonetheless, I decided to follow her advice and make an effort to incorporate myself in the community. I know that I always felt my heart racing during community events like carnivals, annual concerts, and formals, so the Homecoming Weekend and the Bonfire seemed to offer an ideal opportunity to make an effort to enter the community. So this is what I did.

I dressed in green like everybody else, ran from cluster to cluster with everybody else, rushed through the spinning door of Baker Library alongside everybody else, even screamed "Harvard sucks" with everybody else. (I didn't like this last "activity"—it seemed to me a negative expression of inferiority, rather than the more positive alternative to say, "Dartmouth is great.")

I looked around me as we were going up Lebanon Street, and I saw that everybody was exultant, almost in ecstasy. But all those faces in the huge mob were somehow alone; I could not sense the common spirit. Maybe because such a negative theme—that Harvard sucks— cannot be unifying, and should not be. Or maybe because it's impossible to feel attached to a community if you are not really attached to any member of it. Anyway, I realized that I was not excited about all this artificial euphoria, that there was no point in staying, so I went to Ben & Jerry's ice cream shop. While I was licking my ice-cream cone, again completely alone (even the saleswoman was out watching, even she felt part of the community), I thought: "Is it my fault that I felt so out of place in the mob? Am I really so inflexible? I always thought the contrary. Will I ever feel that I belong here, or will I continue to live on the margin by myself? Well, not exactly alone, because I already feel part of the international community here. But is that the reason I wanted to come here—to be a minority, to be alone?" I knew the answer only to the last question: I definitely did not come to Dartmouth because I wanted to be alone. I detest solitude when I have not chosen it myself. But, I also knew that I would not change the self I developed over the years just to be part of the majority. I came here to share my culture with the rest of the students, and if they did not want to approach me, then I would live by myself. I am not stubborn, but I already took the first step; now it was their turn.

However, I did not stop attempting to change my life here. I applied for the New Leadership program at Rutgers University, which addressed the role of women in American politics. Even though I did not satisfy the implied and seemingly logical requirement of being an American woman, I was sure that I would be nominated. I knew there would be interest, not necessarily toward me as an individual, but toward the rare species to which I belong—a communist woman, a political attraction. I was indeed selected as one of Dartmouth's five representatives at Rutgers. However, instead of perceiving this as a success, I felt a stab in my self-confidence. The nomination made me confront something I was hiding from: the realization that my presence here was determined by the fact that I add diversity to the campus, rather than by my capabilities. I hate to say it, but the analogy of an extinct exotic animal kept coming to mind.

In the United States, I have noticed that diversity is considered a great asset to every community. Coming from a communist country, where being nonconformist was a sin or even a crime, I can assert that diversity indeed means more freedom and richness. I do not think, however, that diversity should be a goal in itself. It is only a means to encourage equality and mutual understanding of different people—an accomplishment that would make the world a nicer place. But you cannot just put Marie Antoinette together with the beggars and expect that they will become friends; if you do not tell her that if people cannot buy bread, then they cannot even dream about cakes, she will keep saying that their complaints are not fair. Or more relevantly, you cannot expect a student from Somalia to join a campaign to raise funds for the hungry people in Vermont. What is the point in diversity if all people do is say, "Wow, Bulgaria!" when they meet me, and then walk away?

Over the years, I have come to the conclusion that people pretend to value diversity, when in fact they are afraid of it. I realized this when

I went on a foreign study program with twenty other Dartmouth students. In Spain, my peers suddenly saw me not as a mysterious foreign student, but as a well-known Dartmouth person, and the barrier dropped instantaneously. I made a lot of friends on that program because we realized we had a lot in common. Since we were stuck together in an environment equally new for all of us, we had to become close. As the weeks rolled by and we ran out of things to say about Dartmouth, we started sharing high-school memories, political views, and ethical values. To our mutual surprise, we discovered that even though we had grown up in parts of the world as different as Bulgaria and southern California and had different ethnic backgrounds, we had more similarities than differences.

This experience made me change my approach to the people at Dartmouth. Instead of starting out a conversation by saying that I am from Bulgaria, I talk about my major or about a movie. Thus I do not scare people off. Once I get to know them better, and can tell whether they care to hear about Bulgaria, I talk about it, and can do so with pride and love in my voice.

I can also understand now why many people never seemed to be interested in talking to me once they knew I was an international student: They were afraid to ask a stupid question that would offend me. I can also understand why some people were rude or obnoxious: That is the way they were to everybody. Being an international student, like being African American, has made me more vulnerable because I never know whether people treat me as they do for who I am, or for the group I belong to. During another foreign study program, I became very good friends with an African American woman. We stayed with the same host family, and in the beginning, I was afraid to ask her questions that occurred to me, because I thought my ignorance might offend her. Gradually, as we became closer, our questions became more and more sincere, and we learned a lot about each other and about ourselves.

I asked myself whether one has to be isolated in a foreign country in order to venture out of the micro-universe into which we comfortably fit. Dartmouth is perhaps too big and too small at the same time: too big because it is easy to find a few people very much like yourself and thus avoid taking the trouble to get to know someone more enigmatic for you, too small because there are too few people to create various and diverse groups to choose from, so that many people simply choose to get lumped in the cozy majority.

At Dartmouth, we do not have a rich diversity of attitudes. The majority of the people I have met have a common goal—an enlightening and profitable career. Of course, I believe that there are people who study for the sake of gaining pure knowledge, even if it is impractical, or people who just want to have a fun college experience, but they are the minority. In a community that is said to be diverse, the terms "majority" and "minority" should, in fact, be irrelevant.

Diversity of preferences should also exist, as Dartmouth offers so many departments and programs. So why do about two-thirds of each class choose either pre-med, engineering, or government majors? And why does the outdoorsy type predominate so clearly? Why is it that every time I put on something dressy, someone tells me that I look funny? It might sound paradoxical, but in Bulgaria, where egalitarianism was the rule, people were more diverse in their looks, attitudes, and goals. Another paradox is that in Bulgaria, where the state prohibited and discouraged diversity, people were, in fact, diverse. At Dartmouth, the administration makes tremendous efforts to add a different flavor, but success is slow, not due to school policies, but to the slow change in mentality of a big percentage of the students. It is hard to step out and be different because it may mean being ostracized.

Even though I realize that I share myriad experiences and views with many students at Dartmouth, I am constantly reminded that I am different. It may sound like big words, but I think that being at Dartmouth made me realize how a materialistic society shapes one's personality. Growing up in a society where money was of little importance due to its scarcity has had a deep impact on my attitude toward life.

I will never understand why people who have enough money to afford to treat their friends for lunch for a whole week, waste time calculating the percentage of the check that accounts for their meal, so that they can figure out the exact percentage of the tip that they should be responsible for. It will always sound strange and cheap to me that someone would pay their mother to babysit for her own grandchildren. I will never cease to think less of parents who enjoy a lavish retirement, while their children take out thousands of dollars in loans and work three jobs in order to put themselves through graduate school.

In a heated discussion with one of my American friends, I referred to the above-mentioned cases as "examples of super egotism." He claimed that these same cases showed America's belief in the individual's self-sufficiency as the ultimate freedom. I could see where he was coming from, but I could never agree with him. That is why I will always be a Bulgarian, regardless of the time I spend in the United States and the number of American friends I make.

The scale on which I rate the problems that I encounter also distinguishes me from many of my peers. For me, Dartmouth is like a greenhouse, where we are protected from pretty much all the evils of the outside world: crime, poverty, and persecution, to name the biggest ones. For people like me, who have experienced deprivation and lack of freedom, Dartmouth seems like a great place. People like my friend from Chicago, who has witnessed crime and violence, share my opinion. For people on financial aid, the advantages of Dartmouth are a prize they have fought for. However, others who have grown up in a wealthy, safe suburb knowing they will be the third generation of Dartmouth alumni, often perceive all that the college offers as something they are entitled to. For these students, having three papers due in one week may seem like the end of the world; the death of their beloved ferret could be a sufficient blow to cause them to fail their classes. When one has never known real hardship, little problems can seem to be disasters. Moreover, when one has never been confronted by obstacles, one cannot be confident in one's ability to overcome them. What is even worse, one might actually lack the ability to tackle and deal with them.

This fundamental difference in attitude toward problems sometimes alienates me from my peers. Their complaints are not valid according to my scale, and therefore I cannot sympathize with some of my friends. However, I can sometimes help them by sharing my experiences with them, and in such situations, I realize why diversity is an asset, and for once being different is rewarding.

My attitude towards my college has changed over the years. The Dartmouth I saw on homecoming weekend when I started writing this piece is very different from the Dartmouth that surrounds me now. Some acquaintances have become friends. It took me a while to become a happy person again. I had to find another Dartmouth, my own—not the outing club's, not the frats', not my roommate's. I truly believe that happiness is not a gift of fate, but rather an inherent part of the self that some people have the talent or perseverance to discover. For many people, happiness is like a dog's tail—they chase it unsuccessfully for years. For me, before I was able to grip my tail again, I had to learn that in order to be happy, I did not need to re-create my childhood at Dartmouth nor uncover a small Bulgaria in Hanover. I had to look at Dartmouth from the window of my Dartmouth room, rather than from the little crack in the wall of memories. I realized that no matter how much I wanted to make my Dartmouth experience a smoothly flowing continuation of my childhood in Bulgaria, it was impossible. After all, Dartmouth *is* part of another culture, and I choose to join it.

Challenging Expectations

Changing Stencils of the Past

Georgina Gemmill
South Africa

Five of us squeezed into the small Toyota, having little in common; some of us were meeting for the first time and would probably never meet again. What united us was the desire to mark our "X" on the ballot that was to determine the future of a new South Africa. Professor Light, a visiting South African professor, nervously shifted gears, averaging 45 m.p.h as we headed south from Hanover toward Boston. We talked about everything possible—college, the weather, and so on—but no one dared to reveal their true thoughts. No one dared to betray a single sign of how they would vote or what they thought of the dramatic changes that were taking place in South Africa. How I longed to be back home, to be a part of the tension and the excitement of white fears combining with black liberation in an explosion that could only be revolutionary in its effects on South African society. So, I closed my eyes and followed my imagination to the land of my origin, where the heat filled my pores and the dust swirled around me. I pictured the coil of citizenship wrapping itself around and around the polo field as men and women came together, waiting in line to cast their votes. How could I miss this revolutionary moment? How could I miss the moment in which I would acknowledge my fellow black patriots who had stood invisible behind me, serving me, sharing my school with me, but never being one with me and my country? The 26th of April 1994 marked a day on which I, and indeed all South Africans, would come together as one nation to cast aside the old political regime and sow the seeds of a new beginning, a new birth.

It is ironic that the South African elections came at a time when many of my own preconceived ideas were being challenged and changed. At a time of political and social revolution at home, I was involved in a personal revolution of my own. My views and attitudes had been shaped by apartheid and a history of colonialism. I had been raised in a bed of stereotypes regarding race and gender roles, and was unaware of the extent to which I had adhered to the status quo of a strongly patriarchal, authoritarian society. In coming to America, I have gained an increasing awareness and a greater sensitivity to South Africa's politics, gender relations, and environmental concerns, or lack thereof. While my thoughts and actions are often still motivated by the social and parental influences of my childhood, I have, over the years, come to view South Africa and many of my own attitudes through a different stencil—a stencil modified by an American society dedicated to freedom, democracy, and equality. Thus I have experienced a paradigm shift, a personal revolution that will, I believe, prove extremely rewarding to me as I attempt to become reabsorbed into a changing, post-apartheid South Africa.

With the changing of many of my own attitudes over the years, the love for my homeland has remained constant, acting like a magnet that draws me back to the rolling hills of the Natal midlands and the sun-parched scrub of the African bush. I can imagine the dusty roads of another dry winter season. The grass that stretches from our farmhouse down to the dam in front is prickly, stiff, and green-brown. When the rains come, they bring with them a peace whereby everything becomes calm and still. The dust on the road settles, the trees are clean, and the whole land seems to sigh with relief. The drought is momentarily broken and the azaleas are ready to face another stretch before the next rains. Even the puddle in the middle of the sun-parched dam seems a little higher.

In the summer the storms come. Toward the end of a long Sunday lunch, the clouds gather—thick, black, and threatening. We see them approaching over the Drankensberg as we sip our deep red wine and discuss the political storm brewing all around us. A flash of gold announces its arrival as we take cover under the protection of our home. Losia and Ennie are called to help clear the table, to get the cushions, the tennis rackets, and the food inside before the rains come. From the family room we watch the storm raging, sometimes accompanied by hail that batters Dad's trees and ruins Mum's vegetable garden. By nightfall, the sky would once again be ablaze with stars, and the farm has a fresh smell that comes only after a good rain.

But the rain doesn't come often, and when it does, it's short and hard—violent in its omnipotence. As a result, the land is often bare and eroded. The hills through Zululand, Lesotho, and the Transkei are overgrazed, lying exposed to the unforgiving climate. As a result of overcrowding, poor farming methods, land shortages, and traditional customs, many of the African homelands—so designated by the government in the 1960s—lie wasted and barren. The African sun shows no compassion; when rain does come, it evaporates immediately, leaving the land cracked and dehydrated. But out of this harsh climate grows the *bushveld* that is the heart of Africa.

We were never a very religious family. My father saw in religion a sign of weakness—a need to seek comfort and help from some supernatural power when life became too hard to handle oneself. But that is not to say we never had a religion in the sense of an identity or a commitment to something. The *bushveld* was Dad's church, his love for the simple pleasures in life was his religion. In the bush, we would get up with the sun and attempt to track down a lion. If we were lucky, we would find him dozing under a tree, his golden, dusty mane thick and powerful. And the birds—oh, the birds! The most beautiful bird was a woodland kingfisher, fluorescent blue with a white chest, sitting perched on the branch of a tree. It is wonderful just to listen to the bush: the constant chirping and buzzing of nature at work, and the heat and dust that seem to carry a sound of their own. There are no neon lights and no false wrappings. What remains is the expansive landscape lying exposed in all its freedom and honesty to the unforgiving African climate. What remains is home.

When I first thought of leaving this home, I found myself questioning whether I wanted to be alienated from all that was familiar: My family, my friends, my familiar landscape. Did I want to distance myself from my land of origin during a time when my high school friends would be meeting other South Africans and becoming more rooted in South African society? Yet I was tired of the security and restrictions of a familiar society in which I was an unquestioning subject entrenched in its traditions and customs. I wanted the adventure of a completely new world, the challenge of an Ivy League institution, the challenge of being truly alone. In retrospect, I feel that I have become somewhat detached from South Africa in following such goals, that I am a solitary, critical observer viewing both South Africa and America from a distance. But out of this detachment and loneliness has grown an individual who is slowly breaking out of the ideological mold of her parents and her society, who is moving into an unrestricting realm where she is free to question and form her own identity.

Many of these identity-shaping questions were raised during a visit to South Africa with four of my Dartmouth friends during my sophomore year. During this visit, I became acutely aware of distinct cultural differences between South Africa and America, which were evident in their behavior and possibly even more so in my reactions. While my reactions were often based on the influences of my upbringing and my adherence to social customs and manners, they also illuminated a marked difference in maturity and in experience between me and my American peers. The manners that we considered appropriate at home—the mature handling of alcohol, the ability to interact with one's parents and to enjoy and feel comfortable doing so—seemed new and unfamiliar to them.

Such differences in manners and behavior became apparent at our first dinner together. The dining room table was set perfectly, with a white table cloth that contrasted with the red candles that cast a dim light over the room. Thinly sliced smoked salmon appetizers lay on the glass platters at each place, while the deep red wine curled around the luscious shape of the clear round glasses. Andy, thinking this was all he was getting, quickly yelled across the table, "Hey, Sarah, if you're not eating all that, pass it up this way!" I looked at Mum. Andy gobbled up his food while keeping up a stream of conversation, and gulped down his wine. I looked at Dad. I had been taught to sip my wine and never to stretch across the table, let alone to eat the leftovers off someone else's plate. But Dad kept filling their glasses, Mum offered more food, and conversation was stimulating, free-flowing, and friendly. After dinner, Andy accepted Dad's offer of a cognac to end the evening and (not usually being a smoker) asked Mum for a cigarette. I looked at them both.

The evening finally came to a close, and I slipped back to my room to reconsider the events of that evening. I may have overreacted in my anger and disappointment at my friends', specifically Andy's, behavior; however, Andy's actions challenged the social graces that I had been taught represented respect and appreciation. I perceived Andy's disregard for our social customs and traditions as a direct insult to my family and my home. In my experience, the German and South African societies are, and have long been, societies entrenched in discipline, in which traditional manners and customs are respected and followed. As a product of a German mother and a South African father with a strong English heritage, I have developed a respect for tradition and discipline, embodied in my manners and in my acceptance of the status quo. Americans, however, seem to have fought against the social customs of traditional English society. Instead they have promoted individual freedom and escape from such a colonial society.

Based on the American myth, epitomized by Thoreau's belief that a person stripped of his or her false niceties is left in a more purely sincere form, many Americans, like Andy, appear to resist gentlemanly laws of social etiquette. As a result, they appear more open, friendly, and relaxed in communicating with all people. Yet although I felt immediately comfortable and welcome when I arrived in America—warmed by the loud, continuous conversation and the confident, open personalities—I have found over the years that such openness is often superficial, preventing me from reaching down into the depths of a person and his or her true feelings and emotions. Thus, I wonder if one can ever escape the "false niceties" of traditions. For in defying existing norms and customs, are Americans not establishing a whole new set of "traditions," which, in turn, become equally worn, mechanical, and false? Is not the social pressure to be loud, talkative, friendly, and confident often as insincere as the gentlemanly social customs?

I still have a high respect for manners, but I am becoming increasingly aware of the need for social diversity. South Africa's manners (and the importance that we, or I, have placed on manners) make it hard for me to accept those people who are not familiar with such social etiquette, or who choose not to follow it. While I disapprove of Andy's behavior, I may have been more accepting of him had I not held on to my own social customs; I might have appreciated him for his energetic, unique personality instead of criticizing his actions. Before we, as South Africans, can try to accept people across racial, cultural, and gender lines, I believe we need to be more open to change and less rigid in our tendency to judge people according to our traditional ways. My time in America has allowed me to challenge such ways. The questioning and breaking down of social myths, although frightening and often painful, has been absolutely necessary in order for me to be open to the creation of a new South Africa.

My reactions to Andy's behavior, however, stemmed not only from a difference in social customs, but also from his own apparent personal disregard for me and my country. At one point during the visit, Andy jumped over the protective fence of the game park in which we were staying and ran to the water hole and back. Not only was this action extremely dangerous, but it also signified a disregard for my homeland and for Dad's "church." To me, it showed a lack of appreciation for all that my parents had done for my friends. Above all, however, it represented a disrespect for the wild and the undisturbed serenity of the sleeping bush.

Andy's behavior was, I felt, not only disrespectful but immature. His actions, and to some extent those of my other three friends, reminded me of many of my concerns about differences in maturity between me and my college peers. Having grown up in a very open family as an only child, I have been treated as an adult since I was old enough to reason. My experience in a boarding school, and especially my four years in America, have caused me to take on more responsibilities than many of my peers. At Dartmouth, I find that many students who have been protected by familiar Puritan attitudes and the competitive drive to achieve are only now being exposed to the real challenge of maturation and development. As a result, my four friends were unfamiliar with how to handle new situations or how to regulate their alcohol consumption in a mature, civil environment. They were unsure as to how to behave in a different culture and, possibly, how to behave around parents in a mature yet friendly, relaxed environment.

I believe American Puritan attitudes and the rarity of family members sitting down for a meal are largely responsible for the generation gap that seemed so much more evident between my American friends and my parents than among my South African friends. The times with my parents at meals were some of my most memorable times: We would share what we had done in the day, offer support, and discuss interesting and educational topics. In my experience, American children are so preoccupied with activities— tennis camp, summer camp, book club, hockey lessons—that they barely have time to learn the necessary tools in coping with being alone or in contemplating the significance of their experiences. Such a lack of time and an attempt to hide many of the realities of development involving sex, alcohol, and responsibility restrict maturation and result, I believe, in excessive, uncontrolled, and largely irresponsible behavior at college. Thus my American friends' behavior in South Africa drew attention not only to my respect for manners and tradition, but to many of the problems I was experiencing at Dartmouth. Not only was I from a different culture, but from a culture whereby I had come to understand and appreciate alcohol from an early age and where I was a product of a traditional family system in which my mother was a constant support and reinforcement in our family, providing stability and ensuring that there was always time to be together as a family.

When I first came to Hotchkiss School, I was shocked—as I was again at Dartmouth—by the students' handling of alcohol. Associated with the forbidden, alcohol was used to lose one's inhibitions in a new, unfamiliar environment. Coming from a culture and a family where alcohol was appreciated in moderation, I have found it extremely difficult to feel comfortable and happy with such apparently immature behavior. The current Greek fraternity/sorority system at Dartmouth College only encourages the lack of responsibility concerning alcohol. In many Greek houses there is not only an irresponsible attitude toward alcohol but a group mentality that seems to belittle outsiders, thereby preventing social interaction across gender, racial, and ethnic lines. Being a foreigner excludes one from the light conversation that evolves around common childhood experiences, American TV, or familiar places and people. As an international student and as a woman, I am often intimidated by fraternity mentality and feel that the houses discourage genuine intellectual conversations and meaningful communication.

One night I saw Sarah standing with a group of people in a fraternity house. I went over to say hi and was introduced to her friend Chad.

"Hey, George, how are you? Do you know Chad? George is from South Africa."

"No, I don't. Hi, nice to meet you Chad."

"Hi . . . So . . . you're from South Africa . . . um . . . ah . . . what's the political situation like there?"

He thought he was helping me by asking me about South Africa, but instead I felt even more isolated and alienated. Did he really care about South Africa or the political situation? Did he expect me to go into a long explanation, which would be necessary to begin to explain the situation? It wasn't like me to just laugh it off and give him a halfhearted response, so I went ahead and told him anyway. But five minutes after I had started, I could see him looking around—looking for a way out. So I saved him the embarrassment and quickly wrapped up my story.

Although I may shy away from constantly turning to South African politics as a source of conversation, I am pleased to talk to anyone who is truly interested in my country, anyone whose questions might stimulate new thoughts of my own. I am disheartened by people who are not really interested and use the serious and complex topic of South Africa's political and social problems merely to overcome an awkward situation. Such situations only reiterate my frustrations with being in a foreign country and in an environment where students tend to show an apathy toward true intellectual growth and educational conversations outside of the lecture room.

I often wonder whether I made the wrong decision in coming to Dartmouth, or even coming to America. I wonder if I would not have had as meaningful an educational experience at home—reading, being with my friends, mixing, and being a part of a changing South Africa. Instead, I have been exposed to a society of which I have, at times, been extremely critical. I have been a part of a campus whose social life is strongly dependent on a Greek system. I am shocked by the behavior of Dartmouth men and women in fraternity and sorority houses, and saddened by the group mentality that seems to prevent the growth of strong individuals. I have often felt that my confidence is slowly being chiseled away by the insecurities and homogeneity that is often found in a Greek house. During a time when we are going through so many changes and asking so many questions, I see many of my friends putting on false airs or developing eating disorders to overcome their own insecurities and cope with their developing minds. Thus I question the role of Greek houses in encouraging social skills and helping people grow, as opposed to providing a mere facade behind which to hide. My election as president of Kappa Delta Epsilon sorority has allowed me the opportunity to bring my concerns to the Greek organizations and attempt to encourage a support network and a reaching out to minority groups and diverse people from within the Greek system. Through my own experiences, whereby I noticed a distancing of myself from the international community after joining a sorority, I am sensitive to the image of the Greek system as an exclusive organization.

I also find many Americans apathetic about attempting to meet and understand international students. At the same time, I find many international students, like myself, largely critical of American society, and thus choosing to mix primarily within the international organizations at Dartmouth. Being a white South African, I did not, however, feel a strong link to the international organizations on campus. Not speaking Spanish, I felt alienated from the Latin group. Not being black, I did not feel a part of the African student group. I believe that my South African background—whereby we did not consider ourselves really a part of Africa, yet were too far away from anywhere else—made it hard for me to feel immediately comfortable with other Africans or with the larger international community. Having said that, I must add that I did feel a connection with the four black South African men already at Dartmouth. I had a number of interesting conversations with one of them, Alex, who helped me come to a better understanding of the plight and struggle of our country's black people and allowed me to ask many questions concerning my fears about our country's extreme political turmoil.

These encounters were limited, though, and I rapidly found myself becoming more involved with Americans and more distanced from the international community. Through my involvement with Americans, I have slowly been humbled in my criticisms of American society and have hopefully become more accepting of, or rather more open to, the ways in which I can learn from this society. My election as president of my sorority house was extremely important to me, as it represented my acceptance, and indeed my integration, into a society and a social system that I have mainly criticized to this point in this essay.

Through my sorority, I have seen a side of my peers that, at times, I had overlooked, and which is often ignored in the anti-Greek sentiment at Dartmouth. Weekly meetings have been a time of sharing smiles, tears, and insecurities. In a discussion of problems with anorexia and bulimia—problems that affect 15 percent of Dartmouth students, 90 percent of whom are women—I witnessed a sharing of experiences, a voicing of doubts and fears, an acknowledgment of womanhood, and a support network that I had never before experienced at Dartmouth. For the first time, I saw how necessary it was for women to have a place to come together and provide support for one another.

Most importantly, however, my sorority and my women's studies class have changed my attitude toward women. Although I should not be surprised, I am, in fact, impressed to see the way in which women come together to promote events and run an organization. Until this point in my life, my mentors have been men; my sorority and my women's studies course have provided me with an example of *women* who share my interests and ambitions. These women are successful and through their example provide very necessary encouragement. In a male-dominated society, sororities allow women to develop their leadership skills, find mentors and examples in their sisters, and turn to women for support. Perhaps because I come from a male-dominated society, I viewed other women as a threat when I came to Dartmouth, as competitors, as people I must compare myself to. How that attitude is changing! I now see many of my female peers as strong women whose goals extend beyond marriage and the family. Through them I see what I, too, can achieve, while still maintaining my identity as a woman.

Unfortunately, the peer pressure within fraternities and the emphasis on hard drinking and machismo tends to undermine the development of individuals in these organizations. I believe many Dartmouth men turn to the fraternity system for the security of a group mentality and male-bonding rituals. Such "escapism" does not, however, advance them in their own development or in their understanding of women. While Dartmouth was still a male-only college, a Dartmouth alumnus, Leonard Glass, wrote in the *Dartmouth Alumni Magazine*, "Fraternity life specified standards of hard-drinking imperviousness to hazing, to feminine reticence, and, often, to the need to be studious and serious. We wore our hair short, dressed like outdoorsmen, and viewed deviations with suspicion. . . .This hypermasculinity was a package solution to the lingering uncertainties about my own manhood that were alive and troublesome in early adulthood." Such insecurity and uncertainty are, I believe, even more visible in men today. The feminist movement has challenged and criticized men, and as a result they are even less secure of their manhood and their changing position in society.

This was brought home to me a couple of months ago when I accepted an invitation to lunch from a guy I knew. Conversation at the restaurant was a little awkward, and I could tell he was nervous, but we managed, and in the end it was actually pretty interesting. The check finally came, and the waitress put it in front of him. He made no attempt to pick up the check, and after about ten minutes asked if I wanted to leave. Not comfortable with the ambiguousness of the situation, I answered. "Well . . . um . . . don't we have to deal with the check . . . um . . . aah . . . well, d'you want me to pay or should we split it?" I said hesitatingly. "I'll put in ten dollars, and you can take the rest [the other ten dollars]," Bob replied.

I use this example to illustrate how the roles of men have changed and how, I believe, men are extremely unsure of what is expected of them and how to communicate with women in light of the strengthening feminist movement. A male professor once suggested that there were three stages of development that men went through in learning to communicate with women. In South Africa, a strongly patriarchal society, men are in the first stage of development, where they are expected to take control of a situation and are expected to pay for the woman's meal. The next stage is where I believe many Dartmouth men like Bob find themselves. They realize that paying for a woman might offend her or might imply some later commitment, which maybe neither individual intended. Thus they are hesitant about paying, and unsure as to how to address the issue. The third stage is when a man realizes the difficulties of a situation yet is completely open and honest in voicing his doubts and his concerns. Had Bob been similarly open about wanting to split the check, or had he voiced his concerns about the implications of his paying for my lunch, we might have both been more comfortable and understanding of the situation.

I realize that in light of the feminist movement, one might argue that the woman is equally responsible in addressing the issue of paying for the check. In such a scenario, I am still drawn to the traditional gender roles, whereby I would prefer the man to take the lead in addressing the issue (especially if he suggested meeting for lunch, as Bob did), even though I would be happy to split the check. In such a case, however, I question whether my opinions are based on gender roles or rather on a personality preference, attracting me to a more domineering, confident character who, having invited me out to lunch, addresses the issue of paying the check.

South African men tend to display such confidence in a way that the American men that I have come into contact with do not. On the other hand, I believe such security stems from the rigid gender roles still embedded in South African society and not from a better understanding between men and women. Many South African men and women are still unaware of the emancipation movement that attempts to liberate both men and women from the stereotypes into which they have been categorized.

South Africa is still a very male-dominated society. Among many of my female friends, I perceive a submission and a definite dependence on men. Very few of them take the prospect of a job seriously. Although I entirely support decisions to raise a family instead of becoming a career woman, I believe the social barriers and stereotypes are such that many women in South Africa hesitate to pursue meaningful careers even if they would like to. Men experience equally restricting stereotypes. As a man, one is expected to play rugby, be insensitive, unemotional, aggressive, and domineering. The sensitive man who chooses to stay at home as a father is, to my knowledge, very rare. Were a man to show any supposedly feminine qualities, he might be cast out by society as a homosexual who threatens other men's hypermasculinity.

I see evidence of such a characteristically masculine society all around me—in my family, among my friends, and specifically in my own personality. Throughout my childhood, I modeled myself on my father. Although I appreciated my mother's role in the family and the values she embedded in me, I always looked to my father as a model for my career and as a symbol of strength and success. Only recently did I realize that I had actually spent my life trying to be like my father. As a child I violated every feminine stereotype by refusing to wear dresses or to play with dolls; by insisting on being called George not Georgie; by having only boyfriends in nursery school; by playing in the mud and fighting with the girls in my class whom I saw as crybabies. I rebelled against the so-called feminine stereotypes as I strove to pursue a career and attempted to achieve a status of intellectual competence and personal strength.

Although I am still opposed to the "male-bashing" element of the gender emancipation movement, I have become more aware of the inequalities and the prejudices that do exist between men and women. When I came to Dartmouth, I would never have considered taking a course on women's issues, and indeed criticized those women who seemed overtly sensitive to simple fun. Now, however, I see the social pressure placed on women to look good, stay thin, and appear timid, or to denounce their femininity in their attempt to be respected as intelligent and competent students.

On a campus where many women refuse to accept such stereotypes, I have gained the strength and insight to question my own society. I am a woman with all the curves of a healthy body, but I am also intelligent and active and will not be restricted by societal myths that determine my fate as a result of my womanhood. I am indeed a feminist, or rather a "genderist," who is determined to free both men and women from the social stigmas that restrict and belittle them. We have a long way to go in South Africa, but what I am learning at Dartmouth is that strength does not require a suppression of the connected *yin* qualities within me. On the contrary, it requires a realization of the strength *within* these qualities and their enormous relevance to my changing and developing society.

In questioning my own development and beliefs in light of an American society committed to equality and democracy, I have also become more acutely aware of the ills of an oppressive society in which our servants call my parents "madam" and "master." Studying Chinese women in one of my history courses, I was forced to turn a microscopic eye toward South Africa and my own home. Our maids work all day, from 6:00 A.M. to 8:00 P.M. As they are the first to admit that they enjoy the leisurely pace and feel more a part of our family than mere employees, I had never stopped to question how they could be expected to provide the family foundation necessary to raise well-disciplined, good, honest children of their own under such working conditions. I look at my friends' treatment of black people, at my parents' paternal attitude to our servants in their attempt to justify our lifestyle, and at my own opinions toward South Africa through a new lens widened by my experience in America and my own changing realizations. Indeed, only through leaving South Africa and escaping from the confines of home could I truly experience such a journey.

Alvin Toffler, in his introduction to *Order Out of Chaos*, talks about reaching a "bifurcation point" in our society.

> In "Prigoginian terms," all systems contain subsystems, which are continually "fluctuating." At times, a single fluctuation or combination of them may become so powerful, as a result of positive feedback, that it shatters the preexisting organization. At this revolutionary moment—the authors call it a "singular moment" or a "bifurcation point"—it is inherently impossible to determine in advance which direction change will take: whether the system will disintegrate into "chaos" or leap to a new, more differentiated, higher level of "order" or organization which they call a "dissipative structure."

The South African elections marked this exact point at which the old order was challenged and a temporary state of chaos and confusion took its place. The violent resistance to the white government provided the necessary momentum to inspire such a political revolution.

True to Toffler's comments, I have held my breath and hesitantly followed such revolutionary change, afraid that chaos might, in fact, conquer over order and plunge our nation into a time of anarchy. An inexperienced new government faces the daunting task of educating eighty percent of the South African population, keeping promises made to black South Africans during the election campaign, and attempting not to antagonize a sensitive and fearful white populace. Economically, the country is sure to suffer. With the incredible brain-drain of educated white adults who are leaving the country, the political instability, and the land reform programs, South Africa cannot hope to keep up its economic growth rate.

However, as the new government gains its stride and peace continues to exist in South Africa, I am filled with hope that we are moving toward the establishment of a new "dissipative structure." The aftershocks of such a revolution can be seen and felt not only in the political changes, but also in every aspect of South African society, stretching beyond politics to a social and environmental reorganization and restructuring. Now is the time for me to use what I have learned to help create a new society committed to partnership and innovation, rather than stagnation and oppression.

In South Africa we have lived predominantly surrounded by the "blade" of a rigidly hierarchical, authoritarian society. This system has been largely defined by the political structure of a strongly xenophobic government resistant to change and threatened by different ethnic and racial groups. Such a system, in which tradition and authority reigned paramount, has reached far into the bosom of the familial setting and the gender roles of men and women in South Africa. As a result of his gender and his race, the white South African male has held power and control in the family as well as in business, politics, and in the shaping of our society, its values, and its myths.

The elections and the political revolution reflect current challenges to such traditional roles of gender and race. The empowerment of black people has shaken the roots of the hierarchical society in which the white man stood supreme over women and members of all other racial and ethnic groups. By challenging his power base, the black people have caused an entire paradigm shift, providing the necessary catalyst for the emancipation of all South Africans. In challenging the existing system, we have laid the foundation for a new, strengthened feminist movement; we are at a distinct "bifurcation point." As a white South African woman, I am in a position to facilitate the enormous social changes in which the patriarchal *yang* society can be replaced by one dedicated to greater interaction and connected ways of thinking.

As a result of my upbringing as a woman, I am increasingly aware of the connected thinking between men and women, between nature and human beings, and between our social system and the entire universe. For we are all connected—in our composition of atomic and chemical components, and in our mutual dependence on everything around us. As a woman, my blood flows with the changing of the moon and my spirit waxes and wanes with the ebb and flow of the ocean tides. Although we may have eaten from the tree of knowledge, we cannot escape the ecological cycle that facilitates the changing of the seasons and the harvesting of our next crop. I cannot ignore the tonal differences of my black brothers and sisters. I cannot ignore the different customs of the Zulu tribes, or the language of the Afrikaner people. Rather than attempt to destroy and defeat them, I can only hope to interact with them and allow such differences to provide innovation and creativity in a constantly changing and evolving society. This sense of partnership—a sense of connectedness and interaction that is embedded, largely by society, in women—has, as Carol Christ suggests in *Diving Deep and Surfacing*, the potential of overthrowing the hierarchical, dualistic society and replacing it with a more circular, holistic worldview. As she says, "Women's new naming of self and world often reflects wholeness, a movement toward overcoming the dualism of self and world, body and soul, rational and emotional, which have plagued Western consciousness."

Such a partnership stretches beyond racial, gender, and ethnic lines; beyond the dualistic approach to emotion and reason; and toward an incorporation of ourselves in the larger ecological system. As Chief Seattle once said in his response to an American president, "What is a white man without the beasts? If all the beasts were gone, man would die from a great loneliness of spirit. For whatever happens to the beast, soon happens to man. All things are connected." We have been takers from the white woman, takers from the black man and woman, and takers from nature. Now is the time to become "leavers" and to allow the creation to go on forever.

In South Africa, however, we are still far away from any such "leaver" realizations. While we wallow in the aftermath of our political and social revolutions, we need to be acutely aware of what responsibilities such change requires. Many of the black homelands lie littered with plastic bags and garbage scattered around the mud huts. In my home, we carelessly pack our shopping into endless numbers of plastic bags. We throw away cans, we waste food, we drain our water supplies. In a country where basic health facilities are scarce, where birth control is practically nonexistent, where education is limited, and politics are still unsettled, I often wonder what hope I have of reaching out to my fellow countrymen and -women to save that of which we are a part. But save it we must if we wish to preserve the beauty of the rolling hills and the rugged *bushveld*. And save it we must if we wish to preserve the evolution of the human race.

Last winter, when it rained for the first time in three months, I ran outside, dancing on the spikes that would become luscious and gentle with a few more showers. I felt the raindrops drip off the ends of my hair, falling onto my eyebrows, and rolling, slipping down my cheeks. I felt the wetness, the coolness, the eroticism, stirred within me by the drops of nature. They fell slowly at first—delicate, unsure, but gaining in confidence as they increased in numbers, gaining strength and fluidity from one another, until my hair was a mass of water and the water streamed down my face and my body, following the curves of my womanhood. I stood still, allowing the rain to engulf me until I was no longer separate from the water. My body was limp and my hair ran with the rain into the earth where it fed the plants and filled the running brook.

With the heat of summer, the rain meshed with my own sweat, flowing from within me to cool my body and protect me from the unforgiving African sun. I knew then that although I was indeed a part of everything—made from the same dust as the stars—I was, more than anything, a part of my land of origin. I knew what Shug, in *The Color Purple*, meant when she said to Celie, "It come to me, that feeling of being of everything, not separate at all. I knew that if I cut a tree, my arm would bleed. I laughed and I cried and I run all around my house." Again and again, I feel a deep love for South Africa that draws me back to the rolling hills of the Natal Midlands and the setting African sun.

My whole character has been shaped by the rivers, the mountains, and the *bushveld*, without which my spirit would simply shrivel up.

My friend James once wrote to me, saying, "Every year I expect you to have changed unrecognizably and am always relieved to find the same old person who still has a deep appreciation for all things South African. . . .Love for the place of one's origin and upbringing is a strange thing, but I think very powerful." Although the love for my homeland is indeed deep, had James looked a little harder, he would have found a very different woman than the person who left the dry, dusty *bushveld* four years ago: a woman dedicated to breaking down gender barriers and walls built between people of different skin color, different ethnic backgrounds, and different cultural practices; a woman sensitive to her position in the larger ecological sphere and committed to shaping a new society based on partnership and understanding rather than opposition and domination; a woman strengthened by her awareness of her own womanhood.

In distancing myself from South Africa, and in questioning the myths that shape and the stencils that remain within American society, I have been able to view my own society from a new angle from which my mind is more open to change and acceptance. For although I still love my country dearly, it is a love based on a deeper and reserved understanding, rather than that of a newborn baby's unconditional love of its mother. It is a love open not just to the voice of my own selfish desires or those of my family and my white, upper-middle-class heritage, but open also to the voice of the land and the people—all the people. For as Celie might have said, I think this world a whole lot simpler than we make it. When we come to "preciate" ourselves, everything and everyone—when we come to understand everyone and all the world around us—then we see the quality in everything and the God in everything. It is then that we come to love. I hope to take the spirit of these words and return to South Africa with the commitment to work with all South Africans. The commitment to have patience and understanding in the long struggle to rebuild our nation. The commitment to preserve the land to which I am tied. The land to which we are all tied.

In Search of My Voice

"Devneesh"

India

I was a complex ball of pride and insecurity as I passed through the immigration post at Boston's Logan Airport. I remember standing, bags and passport in hand, in a patch of sunlight streaming through a window, surrendering to the moment and feeling like the emperor of my life. I felt exhilarated. Liberated. Accepted. Welcomed. Now I could finally try to realize my dreams, I thought. But the truth is, I was running away, away from the shadowy patches in my memory. Ashamed of the person I knew myself to be, I was far from being the person I wanted to become.

I was alone for the first time in a strange land of beautiful, graceful white people. I was taken by how structured and controlled the faces around me at the terminal were. They all looked so smart and mature. So civilized and polished. I felt suddenly immersed in opulence. The abundance and obvious prosperity, however, struck me as being somehow cold. There was also a curious strain on these faces. What burden could these Children of Fortune possibly bear that would explain their placid, dispirited demeanor? They smiled out of habit and laughed occasionally, but it seemed their hearts were not in it. I figured people must just get bored when they have everything they could possibly want.

I was picked up at the airport by Sunil. My father and his had known each other for decades, and though we had met only briefly before in the security of my home in Bombay, I was delighted to see a familiar face and kept close to his heels. The cab we rode in was huge. I worried about how many precious dollars would be spent on this lavish form of transportation. I was beginning to feel the strain of my journey. My mind had been in a state of alert for quite a while, absorbing, observing, learning, unlearning, listening, tuning, and mostly worrying. Sunil was talking rapidly, about the rich history of Boston, his two years as a graduate student, and the developments in his research since we had last met. I could see him talking to me, but his voice began to fade away. My mind was fatigued, and I was getting weary of the adventure. I wanted to be in the comfort of my mother's presence, and I longed for the soothing smell of her saree.

Nevertheless, I was excited and anxious to meet my roommate-to-be. Jon arrived at Sunil's humble apartment the next day in a BMW, and we shook hands, expectantly. His palm enveloped mine, his grip was firmer than I was comfortable with. Although I had nibbled on some breakfast, Jon and I set out to grab a bite. I couldn't help but gaze in wonder at his brown eyelashes. His fingers were so fat. His manner so stiff and controlled. His voice so monotonic. And his expression so condescending. I soon found myself fighting the thought that to Jon, we were clearly not equals.

We zipped around Boston and came to a café he was obviously familiar with. I was taken by the name, Au Bon Pain, which I dared not try to pronounce. I followed him closely, picking up a tray and looking at the menus, just as he did. I was in for a shock: "What!! Two dollars for orange juice! Even more for a muffin. What the hell is a muffin anyway? You have got to be kidding. I don't want to spend that much, especially when I'm not in dire need of it." Resolved not to drain my wallet, I picked up a carton of milk, and sheepishly told him that I wasn't hungry. He was visibly irritated, and offered to treat me. When I declined, he was provoked further, telling me I had no reason not to be hungry, and that I shouldn't have eaten before, since we had arranged to have brunch together. His derisive tone left a strong impression. I would have liked him to be more understanding about my obvious embarrassment at not wanting to spend the money. No doubt it was an awkward situation for him as well, but there was clearly a significant difference between Jon and me.

I had thought about all the things we could do as roommates, exploring a new college setting for the first time together, making friends, playing games, and talking about women, but now I began to feel a little worried. He was asking me if my mustache was a "normal" thing for people in Asia. He was curious to know if I was a hero back home among my villagers, since I was coming to an institution that was obviously superior to anything within their reach. Surely, he surmised, I must come from one of the richest families in India to be able to afford an education here.

On the ride back to Sunil's we were briefly interrupted by Jon's mother calling him on his car phone. Later in the year, casting his caution away, Jon would joke to me about how his mother had asked him during that phone conversation if I smelled like curry. I did not suspect it at the time, and noticed only that he was uneasy and eager to denigrate his mother to give me the impression that he was less dependent on her than he really was. I wondered if Jon and I would ever grow to see each other as individuals, past the obvious differences that distracted us. In all my excitement about college and the wonders of partaking in the American melting pot, it had thoroughly escaped me that I might be an unwanted intruder, an alien entity from a backward planet, whom some Americans, out of generosity and magnanimity of spirit, had allowed to study and work here, and to marvel at their superior, evolved nature of being.

I was greeted in Hanover the next day by a brief respite of beauty, where these concerns receded again. The Environmental Orientation Trip was perfectly suited for a wide-eyed novice to nature who did not know what Gore-Tex shoes and sleeping bags were. Eternally thankful for every moment of the experience, I was taken by the untouched purity of nature around me—the clear river water, the age-cracked pines, and the cleansing mist in the mornings. The hope that the natives of such a heavenly abode might also be pure in their spirit of humanity seeped back into me. I especially liked my trip leader, and two others— a gentle Vietnamese girl and a quiet Puerto Rican guy. I was happy to have them as friends with whom I ate my meals, trekked the woods, canoed the placid river, and even did some good old-fashioned bird-watching. Rationalizing that they were both naturalized Americans, and therefore not too far from the people I would soon live among, my optimism that Dartmouth might indeed accept me grew stronger, and therefore more dangerous.

I met many people the next few weeks, attended many orientation sessions, and took many tests. Throughout the whole first week, Jon and I never managed to say more to each other than a polite greeting. We agreed he could take the bigger of the two adjacent rooms that made up 102 Sage. He brought in decorators, including his mother, to carpet his room, wheel in the television, VCR, and music system, and help him put up posters of cars, women, and all the different types of condoms one could ever want to use.

A lot happened that fall term; Jon positioned himself as J.J., and Devneesh shied away into Dev. Calling myself "Dev" eased the burden of enduring introductions, but I soon started feeling like a cheap imported car. I felt stared at and patronized in social gatherings, and learned to make clever excuses to avoid them. J.J. found a few like-minded males to bolster his image, and soon used alcohol and his critique of those things called women to pretend he was at ease. Ironically, he was seen as the mature, sensible guy who carried his wealth in style, and was magnanimous enough to bear the burden of living with "one of them alien types."

J.J. was a key figure in my process of adaptation. I would occasionally wake up to his morning mantra, "Dev's a fag." He introduced me to his buddies, who would poke and test my cultural beliefs. "Dev the Man, tell them why you don't eat meat." "Devdom, tell them about why you don't drink." "Dev, is it 'cuz it's bad Karma or something?" And they would chant "Karma Man" for painful lengths of time. I once retorted that I didn't need alcohol to bring down my defenses. "But don't you just wanna let go for a while?" they asked. Let go from what? I thought then that these defensive pink angels were all playing a game none really wanted to be part of, but that societal and parental expectations forced them to play roles from which weekend binges provided brief relief.

As J.J.'s pictures of his family disappeared from his room to save him the embarrassment of showing attachment, mine surfaced from the folder I had kept them hidden in, to keep me from giving up. I finally felt I could bear to see them without breaking down. Oh, I missed them so! But I couldn't let myself admit it, lest I shatter to pieces. I was working in the College Cafe, learning to flip omelets, make sandwiches, mop the floor, and run the dishwasher. When I would return from my shift on Friday nights at midnight, looking to sleep off the strain of the week, there would inevitably be a party in our suite. I would sob into my pillow while I held it over my head to muffle Axel Rose's disturbing "mother-fucker" and "bitch" and Nirvana's anguishing screams that made me shudder with fear. I would try to quiet my mind with a little prayer, and then lie awake wondering if at any moment J.J.'s friends were going to barge into my room and beat me up as a way to release some of the aggression their music seemed to breed. I would curl into my ten dollar polyester blanket and peer through the holes I had made in it.

I did not exist to J.J. and his friends. In the room that always had its door closed, there was no human being, no feelings that hurt, no intellect that mattered, and certainly no one who was being kept awake. Nothing. They could blare their music, flaunt their phobias about immigrants and "faggots," and all would be well. J.J. would tell me how he felt international students at Dartmouth—heck, in the whole USA—should all just go back home. They were leeches who took away valuable slots that local students were denied. They drained the financial aid that his parents were indirectly paying for. I, as an "import," was just getting in his and other people's way.

While peering through my blanket one night, the door swung open, and in walked a few of J.J.'s friends. They seated themselves on my bed, used my phone, ate my chips, and tottered around for a while completely oblivious of the curled-up bump under the blanket. They appeared to me to be shouting in argument about something, but that could just have been my fear exaggerating their intimidating presence. They left eventually, and I tried impotently to find relief in sleep.

When I expressed timidly to J.J. that I hadn't slept much the previous night, he said, "Dude, it's a party, Dude. Everything is cool." I desperately hoped I had appealed to his sense of pity, and scrambled away thanking him. Soon after, however, it happened again. I came back from the café, my bones feeling brittle and my nerves throbbing, to a smoky, noisy room of judgmental eyes. My confusion and fatigue gave me an extraordinary temper. I lay in my bed, fuming and humiliated, for a couple of hours. Then I picked up my courage, opened the door, and requested that they turn the music down. "Oh, sure thing, Dude," replied a sniggering voice, and after I closed the door, the music got louder.

"I have had it with you, J.J.," I raged to myself. I put on my jeans and rushed out of my room, heading across the green toward the campus police office. But as I got closer, my courage seemed to abandon me. By the time I crossed the green, I was contemplating giving them a few more hours to enjoy themselves before I went back. After all, I reasoned, I was only an import. They had a right to their fun, and there was no sense in my getting in the way.

So I curled up on a bench and tried to snooze away the growing lump in my throat. A black dog with a red collar sauntered around the green and soon settled itself comfortably near me on the ground. Though I have been afraid of dogs from a very young age, this dog felt like my soul mate. He understood me. He was me; I was he. My position at Dartmouth College was like that of a tanned dog that walked on two legs. When my owners, the college trustees, pleased, I would walk around, parading myself, contributing to their vision of diversity. In return they paid for my college expenses. The humiliation and worthlessness that I felt that moment on the bench still make me very angry. I had reduced myself to a state in which I was glad just to be patted on the head, fed now and then, and allowed to wander freely, as long as I didn't bother anyone. The indignity numbed me. I curled up, defensive and weak, too empty for tears.

But I asked myself a fundamental question. Why did I let them do this to me? They are not to blame, really—I am. I let them taunt me. I didn't have the courage to face them, to ask for what I deserved: basic respect, not for special accomplishment, but for the simple reason that I was a human being. And something changed in me that night. I saw myself for the proud, arrogant, overachieving geek that I was. I deserved every bit of the abuse I had gotten. What a coward I had been. In my desperation to make America my home, a place where I would be accepted, I was giving in too much. But I was going to take it no more. The lesson was learned, and it was time for me to raise myself up, for my own life, my own happiness, my own free will.

I returned to my room feeling empowered. It was deserted, and I slept. The next morning, I firmly told J.J. there would be no more parties in our room. And to my amazement there were not. I slowly began to change my accent, listening intently to those around me and practicing my American voice in whispers. I put on a mask of the stoic male that I felt would keep the curious at bay. My classes became the focus of my attention. It was time to start bridging the gap between who I really was and who I wanted to be. I had reached the nadir of my existence, and now felt cleansed and ready to undertake a process of building. For the remainder of freshman year I erected my scaffolding for this ambitious construction project that I intended to last a lifetime.

While I struggled to handle my roommate's bigotry, I fought another battle—a crush on a woman I imagined would be the answer to all my problems. One of the first acquaintances I made at Dartmouth was with Farha. On the first day of fall term, I was eating alone in the dining hall, contemplating a bland salad and wondering if I would be able to sustain myself as a vegetarian much longer. When I got up to surrender the dirty plates, my eye caught someone else sitting alone at another table. She looked Indian, and I was struck by the radiance of her face and her shiny black hair.

I excitedly went over to her table, trying to appear casual and comfortable, and introduced myself. She said she was Farha from Iran. To me she was Sunshine from Good Land. She spoke with almost childlike mannerisms that betrayed her full bright red lips and big shining teeth. I shook her soft Vaseline hands and helped myself to a chair across from her. We talked about simple things, like adjustment difficulties, and she responded with the most sympathetic eyes I had ever seen. After I left, Farha grew on me, like a fungus.

I thought of her constantly, using the memory of her soft manner to bolster me during the first few difficult weeks of that fall. In my imagination, I told her my deepest fears and secrets, and confessed that things weren't really as good as I pretended they were. When we finally did get together, though, I would tell her she was naive and unrealistic and portray myself as experienced and practical. I looked upon her with disdain as a mere romantic who wouldn't survive in the real world. But when we played pool, I would stand at a distance looking at her, wondering if she would ever see through the masks that I skillfully put up to distract her. Would she ever see the aching, sentimental, romantic part of me? I fired a spear at her now and then that punctured any desire she might have had to try and get closer to me, and sure enough, she stopped trying to understand me altogether. I thought less of her for having let me win in the battle to defeat myself. I gave up the hope that Farha and I would ever be close friends. J.J., in sympathy with my failed hopes, explained that I needed to find myself an American woman who wasn't going to hassle me with "all this Islamic shit."

J.J.'s bigotry, Farha's rejection, and a growing feeling of academic incompetence made me miserable that year. I vividly remember one afternoon in that first winter, when I went down to the river, lay on a hammock, and contemplated walking onto the frozen river, not caring if I would fall through and freeze. As I lay there, I asked myself a key question: "Why should I go on—what is there for me at Dartmouth, or anywhere else?"

I don't think I was serious about doing anything drastic to endanger myself, but it was the possibility of suicide that spurred me to think of reasons to live another day. I was working hard, plodding away at physics and math classes that I did not care much for, and also working grudgingly at the café. What was it all for? To graduate from Dartmouth and work myself up the ladder so that J.J. and I could one day sit at the same table, drive the same cars, and live in similar houses? I knew that, beneath my insecure shell, material respect was not what I craved. The overachievers and super-competitive people at Dartmouth that I lived and worked with were not role models for me. And if their lifestyle was all that my time spent in Hanover was leading up to, then I didn't really care if it ended or not.

As I lay there, my mind wandered into the depths of my latent childhood memories. Although it felt like I had come such a long way from places I had once called home, in another sense I was still facing the same conflicts. I remembered that there were actually a few times when I had pondered taking my own life. These times came invariably when I did not meet the standards that I or others had set for me. My right to live in this world, I thought, was earned every day by my achievements, failing which, it only seemed natural and fair that I should forfeit that right.

I think I must have made the connection between parental affection and high achievement during my first few years of schooling in Bombay. Report Card Day was easily the most important time of the year. It surpassed birthdays, festival days, and certainly vacation days. There was a ritual that I practiced every Report Card Day. I would be playing in the street outside my house, growing excited in anticipation, waiting for sight of my father returning home. Just as his car turned the corner, I would abandon my game and my friends to race home, wildly, and hide under my bed, clutching my brown report card. As he entered the house, exhausted and hungry, he would hand over his briefcase to my mother, Amma, and with a twinkle in his eye would play along with my game, asking Amma where I was. She would call out for me, and I would emerge from my hiding place, pretending to be afraid to face my father, hoping to mislead him into thinking I had done poorly. I would look down at my feet, report card hidden behind my back, trying to act grief-stricken. Amma would tell him it was Report Card Day, at which point I would unveil my hidden treasure, flashing the gold star pasted on it that indicated I was first in my class, the passport to my father's affection. He would chuckle in satisfaction, beckon me to him, plant a noisy kiss on my cheek, and shower me with a string of nicknames. They made little sense, but they made my year worth living.

This annual ritual was altered one day when I stayed indoors on Report Card Day, shaking genuinely with fear. I had gotten a silver star instead of gold, and was at a loss as to how I could possibly face my father. Would I be beaten? Or perhaps just bitterly scolded, which was usually worse. Maybe he would cast me away, disowning me, and renouncing his ties to a failure like me. Instead, he simply washed up, sat down for dinner, and conferred the title of "The Second One" on me. I was taunted and teased for being "The Second One," and the newcomer who was first that year became my prime target of hatred and competition. I held him responsible for taking away my father's loud kisses and nicknames, and made sure that I never relinquished my gold star again. After that year I never heard "The Second One" again.

The thought of losing my father's attention and affection gave me the motivation to achieve and earn my parents' pride. I also saw my achieving as fulfilling my *dharma,* or duty, as the way to assure them that their generous investment in me was not in vain.

When I was younger, my father ruled the house with firm discipline. The hierarchy was very clear: The decisions were made by the head of the household, my father. My mother had the right to voice her views, and my sister and I had the right to voice a suggestion, but it was my father's firm nod of the head that made legislation. I loved my father dearly, and longed to be strong and wise like him someday. He had no qualms in showing affection and would often make me laugh by playfully wrestling with me, dancing around most awkwardly, and making faces impossible for me to replicate. I relished his barrage of affectionate nicknames and squirmed with delighted embarrassment when he got into those affectionate moods. And I felt that on each Report Card Day, I extended my lease on the right to be his son for yet another year.

Soon, though, my father's scrutiny extended into everything else in my life. He felt he needed to correct my habits, my etiquette, my speech, my English, my posture, my behavior, my temper, my style of handling situations, my need for tact, the volume of my voice. He helped me develop an introspective view of myself, to know how to identify my weaknesses and improve upon them. That trait helped me a lot when I found it necessary to stop, take stock of a situation, evaluate where I was headed, and then make the changes I felt necessary, all without inflicting too much pain on my bloated ego.

However, my father's constant vigilance also made me very self-conscious. I had to put up the front of being the ideal son in his presence. When we moved to Malaysia after my seventh birthday, I came to associate this "ideal" identity with my academic performance. Indigestion before exams was my measure of sure success. My other Indian friends chose to keep a distance from me, as I became unpleasantly competitive in every field. On Report Card Day, I beat all my enemies, as well as all my fears and insecurities. I earned the bronze medal for my class every year, and prided myself in being the top Indian student.

The Chinese believed they were naturally a superior race, and established themselves as the hardworking, deservedly prosperous ruling majority in Malaysia. The darker races, Malay and Indian, were lulled into a submissive role as lesser peoples and accepted what little came their way. But I was never an easy person to suppress. I had a mouth too big and a voice too loud, which made many people uncomfortable. I was spurred by parental pressure as well as by the need to champion my race. I built my life around competition and achievement.

In sixth grade I was faced with a mammoth challenge to these aspirations. My parents had set their sights on St. Joseph's Institution (SJI) as the best place for my secondary education. Now it was up to me to work toward getting into it; I hated that whole year. I had nightmares for months before the nationwide exams that determined who got into which school. I spent the majority of my time at my desk, mostly worrying. That year, my indigestion gave me little comfort that I would be able to succeed. I needed something alternative to fall back on in case I failed to get into SJI. For years I had walked across a bridge over a canal on my way to school. I decided that if I was not accepted at SJI, I could easily climb over the green sides of the bridge and put myself at the mercy of the cars and the canal below. The thought of thus escaping facing my father comforted me at night, and I waited for the day of the results. As I went to school that fateful day, I marked the spot on the bridge that would be ideal to jump from. But I had indeed gotten into SJI—the premier secondary school for boys in Malaysia.

Until then I had largely been ignorant of my life as a pawn in the success story that my parents had designed for me. But now, as I approached age thirteen, I was beginning to understand more of the world around me, and came to realize that for the most part, that world did not include me. I saw that I was entrapped in this game of parental expectations, but did not have the courage to try and change the rules.

My first week in St. Joseph's was spent in admiration of its traditions and its hundred and sixty-odd years of high achievement. In my first year, I was initiated into the various conflicts that plagued the remainder of my years in Malaysia: fighting for my space, defending my race against the Chinese, struggling to relate to the other Indians who were of a different worldview, trying to sustain myself on a vegetarian diet, and struggling to live up to my father's expectations.

My Indianness centered mostly around classical Carnatic music, vegetarianism, and my newfound interest in meditation. The other Indian boys, because of their different interests, stuck together, spoke in their slang, idled on the stairs, and did badly academically. Although I found myself defending them to the Chinese, I didn't really identify with them either. I found myself rationing my time and efforts among all the groups, not wholly respecting or belonging to any one, but trying to fit in with all of them.

One aspect of my lifestyle that set me apart was my *mridangam*, a drum that is played in classical Carnatic music. The tradition is strong in my family, and many relatives hoped that I would follow suit and become a famous Carnatic percussion player. In Malaysia I began taking lessons. I enjoyed the first few years, and basked in all the attention I got. I performed on stage and on TV and radio a few times in Malaysia. However, once I entered SJI, academic excellence became my foremost concern and *mridangam* was relegated to a mere hobby. In my second year at SJI, I got tired of making excuses to avoid the required two hours of daily practice. Complaining that schoolwork was just too hectic, I turned away from *mridangam*. My father soon came to accept my change of heart, although he predicted that after I grew up I would look back and regret having quit.

My father was right. I do regret it. I could have grown to relish cooking up rhythmic patterns in my head, to revel in expressing my creative energy. But there was one glitch that made me stop. I had tried hard to get the exercises right, but it wasn't easy. I would practice till my hands bled on the rim of the drum, but I just couldn't seem to get it right. The thought that I could try so hard and fail at something was devastating to me. I had built the illusion of being a super-achiever.

Everything else came easily to me, and *mridangam* had to as well. When it didn't, I decided to pack it up. My father bestowed on me another title—"The Quitter."

My father came home soon after with news that when I finished the school year we would have to relocate to India. We had lived in Malaysia for nine years, and it had affected my view of my homeland. India, with its lackluster economic performance, was a frequent butt of jokes in Malaysia, where material success was the all-important element of survival. Even to the local Indians, I would try to defend India, talking about its history, its benign nature, the endearing humanity of the people, and so on. But now, faced with the idea of going back and living in Bombay, I found myself quite opposed to the thought of ruining my career prospects, stuck in a rut in an unknown corner of the world.

Knowing that I was going to be gone soon, my ties to friends became stronger and more sentimental. I cried through my entire farewell ceremony at SJI. When our departure day came, I was touched to find twenty-three of my friends at the airport to see me off. As I walked to the plane, I turned to take a last look and saw a line of dark faces lining the windows of Gate 34, making me feel like the most loved person in the world. They gave me the confidence that I was indeed ready for India, and I tried to look forward to my first breaths of winter air in as long as I could remember. It would be a stark difference, I told myself, and I must try to make the best of it. In retrospect, I am glad that we moved to Bombay. The tough streets of Bombay were an ideal classroom to have my identity and core beliefs bolstered in preparation for my giant leap across the continents to an American college. In the two years there, my own voice grew louder and more confident both within my family and in school; indeed, Bombay ultimately helped show me who I was.

We landed in Bombay on January 9, 1989, almost ten years after we had left. My initial reaction was one of simple shock. We landed at night and were guided through the airport and the streets to the hotel. I still see the images: a mass of dark oily faces pressing themselves on the glass windows of the airport; the taxi cab, an arcane remnant of the 1960s; the empty, narrow, dimly lit streets of Bombay; and the hotel room that served as our home for a month as our apartment was renovated far behind schedule. It was a tough experience for all of us, and tensions grew.

One evening my father returned from the office and noticed that I had left my sweater unfolded on his bed. The smoldering volcano finally began to spew lava. He began shouting at me about how I was completely irresponsible, uncooperative, and an utter pain in his rear. Finally I emerged from the bathroom, fed up with the abuse. I don't know what came over me, but I just didn't feel like hearing my father's inconsiderate noises any more. "It's not fair, Appa. I'm only sixteen. There's a limit to what I can take, too," I answered back.

For the first time I had found my voice and stood my ground, though fleetingly. We argued about the sweater for a while, and then I let him have the last word. He then asked us if we were ready for dinner. We normally alternated lunch and dinner between a Chinese restaurant in the hotel and a South Indian place farther down the street. The latter was my father's favorite, as it was the closest place he could get to home-cooked food. But being quite tired of the same Indian fare, I asked if we could eat Chinese for dinner instead. "Old Faithful" vented his steam yet again. "Don't you talk back at me. You always want to eat the same thing. Over and over. You either come with us, or don't eat at all."

I retorted, my voice quivering in fear, "It's just not fair. Not fair. We have our problems, too, you know. It's tough for all of us. You're the one who got the transfer to Bombay, and you go to the office and that's it. I have no idea what's going to happen from here on. I'm scared too. You're not the only one with problems."

My father gave me the look of a predator, too angry for words. He was beginning his strongest attack on me yet when the phone rang. While he talked, my sister said that it was all over for me, and that the only sensible thing for me to do now was to apologize to father after he got off the phone. "Apologize for what?" I asked. And she said, "Just tell him you weren't thinking." He got off the phone and there was a cold and uncanny silence. I walked over meekly and told him I wasn't thinking. He looked up, and with his next words raised himself from being a mere policing benefactor to an adored role model. "That's not true. You were thinking. And you're right. It is tough on all of us. We'll go eat Chinese."

My sister couldn't believe it. My mom, glad to see the storm pass, bravely went up to my father and placed a supportive hand on his shoulder. At that moment, I loved my family. I believed that we were now ready to take whatever lay ahead for us in Bombay, for we were finally beginning to act as a unit that shared its fears and respected one another's needs. I understood, and even felt, my father's pain: He was scared, too, of what was going to happen to all of us. That incident represented a remarkable victory for me. I had taken a big risk in speaking out for something I felt strongly about, and the reward was quite sweet. I had been scared out of my wits, yet had taken a leap of faith, trusting my instincts that the just outcome would prevail. This incident, though minor, stuck with me thereafter. It flashed before my mind before I finally confronted J.J. at college, and again before I mustered up the strength to express my feelings toward Farha.

In the next couple of years my father and I became good friends. My sister attended university in Australia, and that left just three of us at home. My father had his frustrations and his lessons in adaptation at the office, and I had my daily trials at school. We brought them to the dinner table, where we shared our thoughts and grew to respect each other more. Knowing that I was trying my best to adapt and survive in school, my father didn't pressure me as much. I was discovering a confidant and a role model in my father.

Father also made no attempt to hide his pride in his son. He was happy with the way I was flourishing and maturing, growing in stride with the incremental measures of freedom given to me. I know that my growing older must have had something to do with it all, but I'm convinced that it was the softening of my father's nature that made Bombay bearable. Gaining his approval and making him proud of me, for who I was, for my ideas about people, for the way I dealt with situations, gave me tremendous encouragement and confidence.

Bombay went beyond just being a catalyst in the changing relationship with my father; it shaped my understanding of myself, and of the people around me. It's a tough thing, becoming disillusioned with people. And I was disillusioned, over and over again, by the people who I came into contact with in Bombay. It was especially hard, since I had looked to India to fill a void that I felt in my identity. I went back to India thinking I was finally among my own people. We would understand each other, and we would be better accepted for the values and common faults we shared.

In short, I had been convinced that I would meet more like-minded people in Bombay, that I would develop strong connections that complemented my connections in Malaysia. I just had to! It was my culture—I was Indian, wasn't I? I had read the Mahabharata and

Ramayana, hadn't I? I was initiated and reasonably religious, right? Put together, in my head, that meant that India and I shared a common "culture." I was to learn, much to my dismay, that culture goes beyond books, food, song, and religion. It strikes at the core identity of a person, and Bombay and I were clearly not cut from the same cloth. The educated middle class in Bombay seemed to be caught up in living for societal approval, mainly by accumulating piles of money. I saw a society that was immensely cynical in its fatalistic surrender to suffering, and surprisingly aggressive, given its nonviolent modern history.

I soon found myself at Bombay Public School (BPS), the most expensive private school in Bombay. What I saw at BPS was nothing short of appalling, and it did not reassure me that I would soon fit in in Bombay. The students would sit quietly and attentively when "Sir" or "Ma'am" was around, but the moment the authority figures left the classroom, mayhem broke loose. Chairs toppled, bodies clashed, as the boys, all younger than I, got together to play a game that they had invented, hitting a tennis ball against the back wall. There was absolute pandemonium at the back of the class where I sat.

A large part of my time was spent worrying about the state of affairs in Bombay. The education system, with its blind emphasis on pure percentage points and admissions tests, coupled with parental pressure, was wreaking havoc on the character of the students. All anyone cared about was grades. Character mattered not; as long as a student had the grades, every misdemeanor in the world could be justified. This bothered me a lot, for many reasons. What were these boys going to be like when they grew up? What kind of a society were we going to have? It was such a shock that I was going to be living with people like this; I was terrified that in a couple of years I would grow to assimilate and take on characteristics that I did not respect. Even if I didn't want to, the pressure to perform, given the yardsticks that others measured me by, would demand that I cheat on exams, and take every opportunity to push someone else down in order to climb a little higher myself. The survival game, played by trees and insects in the Amazon, was being enacted "live" in Bombay Public School, and I was probably the only person there detached enough to see it.

I had to do something. Anything. I stood for elections in my class and became a representative of the Students' Council. I decided to start with the smallest unit—my own classroom. I convinced my classmates to be more organized in maintaining and caring for our classroom. Soon they got the desks put in orderly rows, the floor swept, chalk for the teachers, and we started to actually feel proud being Class 11–F. Spurred by my success, I ventured into other classes. Soon thereafter I was walking up the stairs from recess when a group of boys "escorted" me into the bathroom; there they beat me up. "Just who the hell do you think you are? Just go back to Malaysia or Hong Kong or wherever it is that you came from. This is India, okay, and we like the way things are just fine." I was able to stare down their leader, again finding a determination that I did not know I had. This boy then actually apologized for the "misunderstanding," pulling something straight out of a Hindi movie. "Hey, man, we could use someone like you in our group. Why don't you join us? Here, take my hand in friendship." Although I turned down his invitation to join their gang, he went on to buy me a mango drink, apparently convinced that I was worthy of more respect than he originally thought.

After that, though, my attempts at organization slowly fell apart. I had hoped that the momentum of my early successes would inspire others to join in and start contributing positively. Instead, as my energy waned, so did the condition of the classrooms. I was attracting more cynical derision than I was inspiring, and I soon learned to bear down and start working toward my escape from what seemed to me like Alcatraz.

The first year of Bombay, with its encounters with prejudice and closed-mindedness, took its toll on me. I grew cynical and aggressive— emotions that I felt I needed to get by from day to day. I also picked up the important Hindi expletives and managed to keep a few friends happy once in a while by buying them drinks during recess. I met up with some of the more sophisticated girls, and was invited to dance parties; repressed and socially unknown as I was for so much of my time in Malaysia, I thoroughly enjoyed the popularity I received in Bombay. But that was the public image of Devneesh in school. On the way home, I would release my tension and anger at the hopelessness around me by punching and kicking the back of the seat in front of me. By the end of the two years, that bus endured a lot of abuse from me— the metal seat was dented and mangled by the time I graduated from BPS.

I should say, however, that I was a markedly different person at home. I thought about each day, satisfied that I had pulled it off.

Whew! I saw myself as playing a role in school to survive. It wasn't really me. Oh, no. The real me had to be securely hidden away. I nurtured myself at home, in the evenings, by meditating, in private, with the lights off, floating away to a distant place buried deep within me. I was amazed at the extent to which I learned to perfect the art, and soon grew to look forward to the two or three hours in the evenings when I sat by myself and worked diligently, toying with my thoughts, emotions, and beliefs. Meditation helped show me my strength and nurtured my idealistic beliefs, just as BPS helped to show me how low I could stoop.

I didn't really live in Bombay or go to BPS after that. I was distant from almost everybody I met and soon retreated into an inner shell where nobody was allowed. I rarely spoke in class and liked to spend recess on my own. There were not many strong connections of my liking to be made in Bombay. Taking the SATs and running away to an American college or university seemed like my only real option. Dartmouth was the only college for which the early decision deadline hadn't passed when I received the forms, so I put all my effort and prayer into that application, and waited for the decision. When I was notified that I had been accepted, I shouted and jumped in my house for twenty minutes nonstop, for this represented an escape from Bombay and what the city had come to represent for me.

It is difficult to put into perspective the influence that Bombay had on me. It gave me a lot of strength and confidence in myself, as a person with mental ability and social skills. However, it also took away from me a certain mirth I had. Life became an endless struggle against suffering and disappointment. Defending myself against the challenges that faced me every day, I also learned to broaden my views about other human beings. I had never before been exposed to such magnanimity of spirit, or such depravity of morals. In Bombay, my ideas about what humanity and suffering meant gained broader, deeper definitions. But it had become clear to me that Bombay would not nurture the person whom I thought I wanted to become.

As I flew over western Asia and the Atlantic on my way to Dartmouth, my excitement and anticipation grew. Dartmouth was my final chance, my final hope for finding a place where I belonged. Turning away from Malaysia and now India, I looked to America to fill a void of identity and acceptance. Would I find a home? Would I find friends? Would I both give and receive love and respect? I admit it was a lot to expect from a new land, but Dartmouth was to be my very own unhindered opportunity to realize my ultimate goal—to know myself.

Which brings me to that afternoon in the winter of my first year, when I went down to the river, lay on the hammock, and contemplated walking onto the frozen river. In the calm of the frozen riverside, where the trees were laden with snow, I vaguely remembered a song from what seemed a long-forgotten distant past. During my second year at St. Joseph's, the senior assistant used to lead us singing:

If I can help somebody, as I pass along.

If I can do my duty, to a world upwrought.

If I can spread Love's message, that the Master taught . . .

Then my living shall not be in vain.

That song had always made me feel happy, and it did this time, too. It made me think about what use I could be to society and about what really gave me happiness. If I could make a difference to somebody or someplace, sometime, I thought that would make me so happy. It would satisfy my need to do something lasting and productive. I could go on at Dartmouth, doing all the things I was supposed to, obeying the ingrained habits of my upbringing and my present company, but secretly hoping to make a difference, in my own private way, in my own private time. In doing so, I could perhaps both know myself and be happy with what I knew.

The Devneesh that had been bred to succeed and achieve, for security and recognition, finally allowed another Devneesh some space to breathe and grow. The second Devneesh wanted to do what made him most happy—to try to live unconditionally. That day a small battle started between my two halves—one side accountable to my parents, seeking their approval, and the other stressing my independence, accountable only to itself and the few selected people that it respects.

Foremost among the select was Michael, who was my closest American male friend. I looked to him for a gateway into American life, and he always explained as patiently and sincerely as he listened. He did it without being condescending, as though he recognized that it was an effort for me to adjust. I wondered how Michael came to be so different from the other males that I had met. He was the reverse image of J.J., and I was eager and hopeful that our budding friendship would grow with time, and that we would continue to respect each other as we came to know each other's strengths as well as weaknesses.

I longed to be seen as an equal by Michael, for I saw that he was a good person and I wanted to have him accept me as such as well. I couldn't identify it then, but we shared a common thread: Both of us had been through times that were painful and that made us look beyond the immediate, requiring us to grow and shape ourselves to deal with the pain. Perhaps both saw ourselves as outsiders at this college: he, a Jew from Texas, and I, a Hindu from Bombay. As a result, we both had a certain measure of confidence and respect for ourselves, which not only enhanced the quality of our conversations, but also made us look to each other for understanding and empathy.

Friendship with Michael was played by strict rules. And I often worried that words spoken during a disagreement or in a bad mood would permanently come between us. There were many times when Michael saw me in one of my more insecure and defensive moods. He would see me put on airs to impress someone, or be rude to a mutual acquaintance. He saw me be socially rough around the edges, and saw me make my blunders. Sometimes he would say something about it: "What was that all about, Dev? I didn't really understand why you did that." Caught in the act, I would find myself scrambling to hide my nakedness. Realizing that defensive explanations, regardless of how creative, were probably not going to fool him, I'd find myself discussing my faults with him. As a result, he got to see me more completely, and the fear that he would reject me for my faults was assuaged slowly.

The other person who has commanded my enduring respect is Farha, who has since evolved from being a "fungus" in my imagination to becoming a part of my every day and night, my daily thoughts and feelings, my anger and my tears, such that I feel incomplete when she's not around me. I love her dearly, and she has given me what nobody else has before—honesty, trust, and respect. And she had brought out the same qualities in me, which I never really gave anyone else before either. She has become the active part of my conscience, which keeps me in check. She gives me the warmth of a mother, the support of a friend, the attention of an equal. We learn every day from each other, as we grow to understand each other more.

Yet as I explained earlier, it wasn't always like that. Our present relationship, cordial and occasionally intimate, began in the fall of my junior year, after I returned from a summer internship in San Francisco. After our dismal interaction during freshman year, we had hardly met or spoken to each other during the fall of our sophomore year. That winter, though, I decided to take the initiative to break the ice. It worked, and we cautiously experimented with getting to know each other as friends. Because of my friendship with Farha, I threw away an application for transfer that I had requested to MIT. There was too much I could potentially lose, I felt, if I left Dartmouth now.

After reuniting with Farha I got a summer internship, and the next few months turned out to be the most important three months of my first two years at college. It gave me relief from Dartmouth—from its fraternities that I felt excluded from, and from the constant competition and politics that plagued me there. It also gave me a chance to be alone, working hard, earning money, resting well on weekends, and cooking my own food. For the first time I started to feel I had a niche where I was cozy and comfortable. I also learned a most important lesson that summer.

It was a Saturday that summer, when two friends and I made a trip to Mount St. Helens. As we hiked up to the volcano, we soon came to a point of the trail where a patch of snow lay dead in our path. If we were to go on to get a glimpse of the open top of St. Helens, we'd have to cross that patch and walk on for about an hour more. I looked down and saw that if I slipped while trying to cross it, I would slide for about a hundred meters and then fall right off the face of the mountain. I could feel my legs preparing to mutiny. I wanted so badly to get across, but was entrenched in the belief that I couldn't do it. I would fall. I would slip. I would die. I would look like a fool. I couldn't do it. It was a dumb idea. What would father say? He'd say it was a dumb idea. He's right, he's always right. Turn back now, and there won't be any trouble. No risk. No danger.

I wasn't going to look like the coward to my friends, though. Halfheartedly, I started to try to cross the iceberg. One step, left foot forward. That was okay. Next, move the right foot. Good. Now, move the left foot over . . . Oops! . . . My foot slipped, and I panicked. I still had my right foot in place, and so I dug my fingers into the icy slope to keep myself from falling. Then my fingers started to freeze, and I realized I had to do something fast. This was it. I was going to die. I began to run through a list of the things that I thought I would regret if I were to fall from that cliff. I wouldn't realize my dream of helping India out of its poverty, and I wouldn't live to give Farha the silver ring that I had made for her birthday. I remembered my parents, and thought to myself that they were going to be heartbroken at my death. One of my friends steadied me, and we inched our way backward off the snow. I was only too glad to be on firm ground again and thought that it was best to give up and head back.

We reluctantly turned around and started walking back, and I faced head-on the realization that I had given up on myself. It was my fear that had enlarged a simple patch of snow, not much different from those abundant in Hanover, into an imposing iceberg. I realized I was running away from an opportunity to do something that was within my reach because I was inhibited by my fear. And that patch symbolized many fears: my fear of never being completely independent of my family, my fear of failure, my fear of letting down those important to me, and, yes, my fear of not being able to face Farha without worrying about rejection.

I decided to try again, trying not to think of my fear of falling. I instead recited the Gayatri Mantra to calm myself, to remind myself of who I really was. I pushed away other thoughts, inhibitions, warnings, and fear signals, and just thought about getting across. Much to my amazement, in my newfound courage, the patch appeared no greater than a harmless speck on the ground. Before I knew it, I was across, and so were my friends. We went on to get a wonderful view of the side of the mountain that had been blown open, and I was amazed at how easy the whole thing had been. On our way back, we came across it again. There were a couple of middle-aged women trekking across it. Ashamed as I was that such a simple thing had almost gotten the better of me, I vowed that once I got back to campus, I would give Farha the ring, and I would tell her all there was to tell, tossing my defenses to the wind.

And that is exactly what happened. I told Farha quite plainly that much of the person I had shown her in the past two years was a hoax. I revealed that I had been scared of letting her see me in my natural state, lest she reject me. Vulnerable though I now was, I felt my affection for her flow through me. Farha, who had never been intimately involved with a male before, took some time to get used to the idea that she was interested in a guy. Given her family's strict objections to her being in a relationship, especially with a non-Muslim, it took inordinate courage on her part to take the steps that she did to get to know me better. She ventured out of her cocoon, and we spent days and nights finding out about each other, and finding ourselves in the process.

My upbringing was not geared toward taking risks. I am from a traditional conservative background that would have been only too happy if I had turned out no different from the generations before me– mild, passive, salaried, educated, and none too ambitious. But the events in my life, coupled with the impulses of my soul, ended up taking me out of that cozy cocoon, so much so that to go back would be akin to incarceration.

All through my adolescence, I have been struggling to find a community outside my home, struggling to find my own voice, to define my own dreams, carve my own path. My parents will always be a part of me, even after they are not physically around to comfort and guide me. However, I still am looking, in earnest, to build a community of close friends who understand and stimulate me.

I struggled in Malaysia through my first ten years of schooling. Just as I was beginning to adapt adeptly, just as I was venturing out of my shell, learning the rules of the society vastly different from that in my home, I moved to Bombay. I thought I'd finally be home, but that too soon turned out to be a mirage. Unwilling to give up looking for a nest, I came to the United States, attempting to find that elusive community that would nurture me. Have I found it here in the four years that I've been looking? The answer perhaps lies in the fact that I know I can't go back to either Malaysia or Bombay now. I couldn't give up my links with Michael and Farha. I couldn't give up feeling hopeful again that my goal is still reachable. Here, in America, I am free to chase my goal of growing endlessly. I am free to give my voice freer reign than it ever had before. And as a result, I am the least cynical and unhappy that I remember ever being.

Still there are times that I feel America will never really be home either. I can be happy that I am around friends I love, but to most people I meet, I will always be a "legal alien." Alas, the age of the immigrant is over in America. A community of English-speaking Europeans have lived here long enough for their indelible cultural stamp to dominate. I fear I will be a member of a minority group wherever I go. Such is the life of a wanderer. Some enjoy wandering, and may look upon my state with envy. I, however, am tired of wandering and want to feel a link to the land I am in, to the people I am with, and even to the air I breathe. I want the words I voice to be familiar to people around me, to have a deep relevance to their core being.

I want to feel like I helped build this American community. Helped it grow. Helped shape it so that it is better off in the future. I want this for me. I was born too late to fight in the American Civil War, too late to struggle in a sweatshop in New York during the Great Depression, too late to work alongside Gandhi while he built modern India. But my generation will also have its struggles, and I am perfectly poised to contribute a lion's share in the drama of the twenty-first century. So I continue in pursuit of this mirage, except I am, for the first time, enjoying the chase, relishing the risks, and loving scoping out the next opportunity that will give me a strong sense of connection with the people around me.

Trying experiences help one see oneself and know oneself better. My experiences have helped me get to know and love myself, and I'm more capable of respecting and loving others because of it. I know I have my own battles, my own challenges, my own red devils in the night, my own snow patches on cliffs, my own childhood fears and inhibitions, but I'm trying to grow out of them, one at a time, painstakingly moving toward a more fulfilling time, as I know and respect myself more. I am trying. I am doing it with a certain honesty and courage. And I can't give myself a better compliment than that.

A Little Voice from My Heart

"Misun Kim"

South Korea

I am back. Unfamiliarity still bewilders me. Why do I feel this way? I have been here for almost three years, so this place should not be so unfamiliar. Yet every time I return after a break, I go through a painful ordeal of readjustment. I have to force myself to fit in because I feel so different from the mainstream. I feel like I am wearing something that does not quite fit me. I am like Hesse's Steppenwolf—the eternal outsider. This "outsiderness" is reinforced whenever I come back to Dartmouth. Being an outsider does allow me a certain degree of freedom; if I don't like something, I don't have to force myself to: I can always leave. However, being an outsider also inevitably means that I am not one of "them," whoever "them" might be.

I refer to my dorm room as "home," yet I find it ironic that the place I call home reinforces my sense of being an outsider. Do I feel this way because I am a foreigner? Is this another story about a culturally confused and shocked foreigner who doesn't quite understand American culture? Perhaps. But I want to emphasize that this is also the story of a person who struggles to escape her stereotyped identity while struggling even harder to keep her "difference" in order to define who she is. It is my story, and my version of the truth.

Who am I? A skeletal answer would be that I am a twenty-one-year-old female Korean-almost-American student at Dartmouth. I was born and raised in Seoul, Korea, and I came to the States eight years ago, at the age of thirteen. These are the basic facts about me. However, there have been many Misun Kims created and re-created—the Misun Kim who is typing her autobiography now is considerably different from the Misun Kim of fifteen years ago. I look back at my early childhood with mixed emotions; it seems untainted, perhaps the happiest period of my life. I was innocent and the world looked rosy; I was confident and comfortable with myself. I was liked by people the way I was; I did not have to please others to have them pay attention to me.

Everything changed when we came to the United States. It will always be the most important change in my life because this was when I became an outsider. Many regard "change" as improvement, but change can also be painful and backward. Sometimes the pain is like a sharp pang that penetrates into the deepest part of my bones.

My family decided to move to the States when I was thirteen because of my father's business. The first painful change I experienced here was that our family no longer belonged to the "typical upper-middle-class intelligentsia." It was not simply the stepping down in economic and social status that brought me such pain, but also the awareness of the value U.S. society puts on such status. When my family lived in Korea, we were not rich, but I had always felt that my family belonged to a certain privileged group. Both of my parents graduated from the top universities in Korea, and most of their friends were at least at the same socioeconomic level. It was all lost when we came to the States; my sense of belonging to a particular group and my understanding of where my family fit in was forever lost.

My sense of personal inadequacy and of being lost in space was reinforced during my high school years. Those five years at a U.S. public high school reshaped my personality, reconstructed my perspectives on the world, battered my self-esteem, and tempered my pride. One episode, apparently trivial, captures my sense of alienation.

It was the third day at my junior high school in America. I was in physical education class. The azure sky was clear on this crisp, early autumn afternoon. The field—a huge green carpet—was unrolled in front of me. Little did I know that this was only a prelude for the indignity that continues to haunt me. Our gym teacher put us in two rows, and pointed at two girls. They stepped forward, and each received a soccer ball. Then, these two girls turned around and started to pick one person at a time. At first, I had no idea what was going on. However, after two or so were picked, I began to get the picture. These girls were the captains of the gym soccer teams, and they were picking people for their teams. "Madness! What kind of humiliating process is this?" I thought. "Is this real? I cannot believe this is happening! It is like a slave trade!" One by one all others were chosen; I stood isolated, the last to be selected. Everyone seemed to be laughing at this pathetic-looking Asian girl who couldn't understand English. I wanted to run away, but my body was riveted to the ground; I felt light-headed with the sorrow that slowly filled me. The Misun Kim I had known until then ceased to exist.

The irony of the incident is that I had thought the PE class would be a golden opportunity for me to show people that I was not mute and stupid. I had thought that once I surmounted the language barrier, I would be like one of them. It didn't even occur to me until then that I also had physical barriers that prevented people from getting to know me. The pain I felt was like an acid being poured into an open wound. I couldn't even become indignant. I completely lost the sense of who I was and who I was supposed to be.

I began to dislike myself, especially my physical appearance. I wanted to be tall. I wanted to have a big smile all the time. I wanted to be thin and have long legs. I became very introverted. It was the first time I realized I was the outsider, the odd ball. But I could do nothing about my features: I did not have blonde hair and I could not have blonde hair. Why was I being punished for what was beyond my control?

Since I realized the power of physical attractiveness and the value bestowed on appearance, I had to do something to compensate for my physical features. I studied until I cried from exhaustion, both emotional and physical. I was in a constant battle with myself because my ability to express myself in English was nowhere near my intellectual capacity. I was quite literally trapped in my body. If it weren't for my father, I would have accomplished nothing; he was my voice and my ears. He helped me with my homework every night and went over my papers, faxing corrections to me even when he was in Korea for a business trip. To me, studying was more than mere learning and absorbing knowledge. It was the only way to prove to people who considered me stupid that I was not stupid. When I came to the States, my English was about the level of a three-year-old. My high school classmates mocked me for being antisocial, and at the same time, they expected me to speak flawless English and know every "cool" thing an American teenager should know.

Time is the best remedy for many problems. As time went by, I was dethroned as the resident imbecile, and even gained the awe, or at least respect, of my classmates. The triumphant moment came when I graduated as class valedictorian, a bittersweet moment for me. I felt vindicated when I looked down at my classmates from the podium; I had climbed to the top academic honor and proved to them that I was not the dumb, muted Asian girl they had once thought I was. "Congratulations, Misun Kim," I said to myself. However, after the initial surge of pride and fulfillment, I felt quite hollow. What exactly did I gain? Was this all the compensation I was to receive for all the pain I had gone through? Then I would rather have returned it. I wanted the untainted Misun Kim back.

My quest for my lost self became even more desperate when I went to college. I came to Dartmouth with such high hopes. I had thought that since it had an excellent reputation, the people here would be very much like me. Wrong! People were not what I had expected. They were all too similar to the students at my high school: shallow, superficial, typical, conventional. Americans kids with high I.Q.s and even higher egos. What made it even worse was that when I was in high school, I could choose to ignore most of the people because I was smarter than they were. That situation no longer held true.

My freshman fall at Dartmouth was an ongoing nightmare. I was not smart enough to breeze through classes but was too "cool" to study all the time. I felt trapped with a big ambition and a small brain. My standards still demanded I get golden grades, but I wasn't smart enough to earn them. It bit. It hurt. The self-confidence that I had been building for five years was once again assaulted. First of all, I was angry that the incentives (grades, in my case) didn't even reflect a tiny fraction of the effort I put in. Raised in an academic environment, I had been held up to other people's expectations. I was always referred to as "the smart one." I was "good" at almost everything, though not excellent at anything. Nevertheless, academic achievement gave me the most motivation. I am not sure whether I enjoyed academics because I was good at them, or if I was good at them because I enjoyed them. Academically achieving was also my way of surviving hard days in high school, the only way to prove to people that I was worth something. I was a small wonder, and I thought I was quite smart. However, here at Dartmouth, not only was I the average one, but I also had to accept the fact that these beer-guzzling airheads got better grades than I did.

I also began to distinguish the difference between intelligence and intellectualism, and came to the conclusion that Dartmouth lacks intellectualism. The students here are definitely intelligent, but that does not necessarily mean that they are intellectual. I think that intellectualism is what constitutes being human; if anyone insults someone else's intellectualism, I interpret it as most offensive. I do not understand why so many people at Dartmouth are afraid to reveal their intellectualism. They are closet nerds who are afraid to admit that they study. Why do they try so hard to establish a facade of being geniuses who just happen to get good grades?

Since the incentives (grades) were no longer adequate motivation for my academic pursuit, I lost all interest in studying. I did not enjoy school and hated the social scene. I felt occasionally that I was accumulating knowledge when I found a course that attracted me, but spent most of my time figuring out the purpose of my existence at Dartmouth. I had an ongoing, endless debate with myself. My emotional self would ask, "Why am I here?" My rational self would answer, "I am here to get a good education so I can become an M.D. or a Ph.D." Then my emotional self would ask again, "Is it worth going through this hell to become successful? No, I would rather return to Korea, where I am appreciated and welcomed." My rational self would become impatient. "I can't have everything I want. I must give up for the higher goal. Don't question and just endure."

I couldn't even seek solace from my parents, because my father had advised me to attend college in Korea, but I flatly rejected his offer and came here. It was solely my choice. I now had to be responsible for my decision. It was ironic that when my parents dropped me off at school freshman fall and were looking around the campus, my father apologized for wanting to send me to college in Korea when this was where I wanted to be. He said he was very happy that I would spend the prime of my life in such a beautiful place. I couldn't, then, tell my complicated problems to my parents. It would have broken their hearts. They had done everything for me, and I couldn't be a baby anymore. The only joy in my freshman year was crossing off days remaining before my return to Korea for the summer.

Life in Korea in that summer was good; I took two terms off, and worked as an English tutor for Korean college students. I was also reunited with all of my friends and my family. I was like a fish jumping back into water; I was revitalized. Familiar faces reassured me that I belonged, and I was not alone anymore, though I knew it was only a six-month stay in that utopia. When the time finally arrived, I was not ready to return to Dartmouth. Physically, I returned from Korea, but my mind was still there, floating. I had nothing to look forward to in my return to Dartmouth.

Indeed nothing had changed when I returned to Dartmouth; it was still an unwelcoming and unfamiliar place. Yet a crucial revelation occurred as well. When I halfheartedly complained to someone about my difficulty in choosing classes, he suggested moral philosophy. I was indifferent; I just needed something for my third class. So came my fateful encounter with philosophy. It was interesting and challenging in a way that I had never experienced before. It teased my brain. It forced me to think critically. It was fascinating and subtle.

I realized that I actually liked to study philosophy for its own sake. It was a major revelation, and I wanted to learn more; my intellectual thirst was unquenched. I applied to a foreign study program in Edinburgh, Scotland, and took three philosophy classes at the University of Edinburgh. I was proud that I was learning the thoughts of such philosophers as Hegel, Hume, Kant, and Heidegger. However, it was also heartbreaking to discover that I was not particularly gifted in what I so enjoyed. There were some very bright people in my class who grasped these concepts more quickly than I did. During discussions, I was often intellectually intimidated by my classmates. Philosophical readings are more difficult to understand than other readings, and being a nonnative speaker adds one more row to the wall that seems already too tall to surmount. Indeed, I still struggle with English when I write papers. With my Asian background and way of thinking, I often find it difficult to construct an argument the way traditional Western analytical philosophy requires.

Despite all these disadvantages, I cannot extinguish the little flame that's burning inside me. It keeps me going. Philosophy is a subtle seducer. The beauty of philosophy, it seems to me, is that it reminds me of my existence as a human being. It teaches me to become not just a person, but a good person—honorable, intellectual, thoughtful, and caring: the essence of being human. It is the source of my inspiration and the cause of my pain at the same time. I am the heroine in this tragic love affair: I am afraid to commit myself because I might die of a broken heart.

If philosophy defines me in the realm of intellectualism and individuality, interacting with others would be another way to define who I am. We gain our consciousness and self-consciousness through others; we realize our existence through others, although this issue is more philosophically profound than how I have just stated it. Despite this importance of human relationship, my misanthropic tendency often makes me shy away from forming relationships. I am also an Epicurean who believes that the road to happiness is to remove the source of pain, and one way to achieve this goal is to prevent oneself from encountering the source of pain.

Most of the relationships I have observed here seem ephemeral and superficial—based only on physical attraction and self-consciously cool attitudes. I would say physical attraction is the most important factor, especially in male-female relationships, and this seems to apply cross-culturally as well. Both in Western and in Eastern cultures, males love beautiful women and vice versa. The question then becomes, "What is beauty?" While standards of beauty vary among individuals and cultures, there seems, as Hegel stated, to be a universal convergence of feeling—approval or disapproval—for particular subjects.

A traditional beauty in this culture has blonde hair, blue eyes, a slim, tall, and athletic body, and a huge smile with snowy white teeth between two voluptuous lips. This is the image of a beautiful woman—an image I can never ever fulfill. That is not to say that males do not acknowledge other beautiful women who do not fit this description. The point is, rather, that this particular image has been a persistent norm for a beautiful woman. When I was younger, I often became distressed by the fact that I did not and could not have these features, and hence could not be a beautiful woman. Even in college, at a fraternity party, where the majority of relationships are born, I often cannot help feeling as though the compliments made by males to those who have these qualities are indirect insults to me, because I do not have them.

But what about Asian women? Aren't many attractive and exotic Asian women without blonde hair and blue eyes still considered beautiful? A stereotypical Asian beauty has a slender, willowy, helpless-hopeless figure, and long black hair. Her pronounced cheekbones and slanted eyes add to her exotic quality. These Asian women are the lotus blossoms who melt the toughest guys' hearts and make them feel that they are the studs who can protect these blossoms. The stereotypical images of Asian women being docile, obedient, and submissive are tantalizing for many males, who would choose their macho masculinity over their lives. The image of Madame Butterfly still lives in the hearts of many Westerners.

Yes, these features are also deemed attractive, but do I match them? Perhaps this anecdote may serve as answer. One day, a friend and I were talking about someone who was going on a blind date. As her willowy figure disappeared from our sight like a dream, he commented, "She really worries me." I looked at him with a what-are-you-talking-about expression, and asked, "Why?" He replied, "Can't you see? She looks like a rape magnet. She looks so helpless and fragile. Guys like girls like that, but they also often have wrong ideas, you know." Then he looked straight at me, and said, "Whereas, YOU, Misun, look like a type of person guys would NOT want to mess around with." Helpless and fragile I apparently am not.

A truly attractive person can only be developed from inside. Although personality and other qualities such as elegance, attitude, humor, and intellectualism make up a person as a whole, these qualities are not often discovered immediately. You discover them after you have gotten acquainted with a person. However, how do you ever get to know what the person is really like unless you are attracted to them in the first place, since the physical attraction often precedes these other qualities? How would anybody be attracted to me and thus be able to discover my true self, when I do not fit into the images that attract them? So I often coil back into my shell.

Someone may criticize me for blaming my unhappiness on my imperfect physical features, and cite a lack of discipline and weakened self-esteem. "Why don't you exercise and lose twenty pounds? Then you will have a willowy figure yourself. Why don't you grow your hair long? Why don't you change? All these women are running to be in a great shape; they never allow themselves to indulge in luscious food. They feel great and look great. Why can't you be like them?" I try. I try my best to look great. I use calculus and an Ivy League education to figure out all these calorie charts and other complexities behind the newest diet. I acknowledge that it does give me more confidence and self-esteem when someone compliments me on my physical features; however, I can feel a suppressed anger inside me—anger at myself for being vain and superficial—and yet I still obey the system. I feel vulnerable that others dictate how my body should look. I loathe the implications behind this willowy image of Madame Butterfly. Who sets the standards anyway? Who derives pleasure from watching these great figures? Not women. We women think we do because others approve of these figures. Would we still be concerned about willowy figures if others no longer judged our bodies?

At this moment in the women's bathrooms across the States, women are sticking their fingers down their throats to induce vomiting in an attempt to void the guilt and shame for eating even a scoop of ice cream. These are women who have been stripped of their own sense of who they are because of the pervasive Barbie model of womanly perfection. How dare you deprive me of my pride like this? Adapting myself in such ways is as futile as screaming in a vacuum.

It may sound contradictory, but as much as I am profoundly suspicious of human relationships and feel contempt for so many human beings, I respect human dignity and am fiercely loyal to people whom I consider my friends. Respect for human beings rarely allows me to make false or casual promises to others, since I believe that once I make a promise, I am obliged to keep it. I also have stringent requirements for people wanting to be my friend. I am straightforward and brutally honest, with very clear opinions about who should be my friend and who should not. I expect others to fulfill the expectations I have of them as friends, as I fulfill mine as their friend. I finally have come to understand we all have different expectations of one another, and I should not force my view on others, but I still feel pain when my friends disappoint me.

I used to rationalize such conflicts and problems as being a part of an inevitable cultural barrier between the West and the East. However, when I went to Scotland on my foreign study program, I realized I oversimplified the issue. I felt the medium—the feeling of valuing the same ideas such as open-mindness and concerns for others—through which I could express myself. I felt connections with people, especially with the family I stayed with. My host mother and I became especially close because I shared my problems with her. I could feel that she was sincere, and she really worried about me. I knew she was genuine in her interest in me, and I told her about my problems. Typically, one of my American acquaintances would only have said, "Oh, sorry. Well . . ." Instead, she comforted me, listened to me seriously and tried to understand me. If even a mere acquaintance is willing to understand your problems, how comforting and trustworthy would it be to have them as friends?

I believe my emphasis on the value of friendship and the importance of genuine human relationship comes from my Korean background. Koreans regard friendship and obligations of various kinds as a quintessential part of being a person. The Korean notion of individualism, at least what we used to believe before Westernization, is collective individualism. There is virtually no notion of "I," and the "we" feeling is instead embedded in our minds. I suppose this is due in part to the fact that Korea is a 99 percent homogeneous society. Our sense of "we" is inevitably associated with our sense of belonging. You belong to your parents, you belong to a society, and you belong to a country. It is a reciprocal relationship. By belonging to something, you have an obligation to fulfill the duties assigned to you. In return, you will be protected and feel a sense of togetherness. This is the common medium.

One might argue that within such an environment, individualism, creativity, and a sense of independent identity would not thrive. I do not deny this, and when I was in Korea, in some sense I relinquished part of my individualism in order to belong to the whole. However, I did not think that I was losing a sense of my identity so much as gaining a different identity as part of "we." I was happy being "we"; I did not have to prove to anyone that I was different and individualistic. I might eventually have yearned for individualism and a unique identity if I had not left Korea, as I might have felt confined in this intricate web of life, wanting to escape. Still, I felt a connection and self-identity when I was in Korea and Scotland that I rarely have felt in the States.

This is not to say, however, that I have found no true friends at Dartmouth. A proverb says, "A person who has made three true friends in his life is the most fortunate one." Since I seem to have found one friend here—a friend whom I have learned from, who has influenced my thoughts, and who shaped who I have become—I am a third of that most fortunate person. I met this friend on my freshman trip. I was one of many freshmen eager to meet other people and make my way here at Dartmouth. I did not notice any particular faces, but when I looked around I saw a serious-looking Korean girl. I instantly recognized that she was Korean; there was a mark on her face like that of Cain's. All I could see were her incredibly dark and thick eyebrows, and a shiny forehead accentuated by a yellow hair band that held her long hair back from her face. She looked dominating. As I tried to hide from her, she started walking toward me. I fled. She hunted me down, and asked me, "Hi! Are you a Korean?" I answered, feeling quite petrified, "Yeah. Are you?" She said. "Yes. My name is L.P. And yours?" That was the first of many encounters.

She told me that she was a second-generation Korean born in Georgia and raised in a very Korean atmosphere; her Korean was surprisingly fluent, and she told me that her family visited Korea about every two years. My initial hostility slowly disappeared, and by the end of that day, we were joking and laughing like little girls. Although there is no doubt that our Korean background provided a grounding for our friendship, it was not the sole foundation for it. L.P. is simply a good person: deep, intelligent, intellectual, funny, compassionate, passionate, and respectful.

In freshman year, I was on the verge of falling off the cliff, not sure of who I was. L.P. was like a branch sprouting from a crack in the cliff offering me a place to hold on. And I held on to her tightly, trying to save my precarious existence. She was virtually the only one I could talk to. I needed a person to whom I could unreel my pent-up frustration with the academic indifference and social disappointment of Dartmouth. I needed a human being who respected me enough to sympathize with my problems. Her being Korean assured that she could understand anything and everything about my life and the problems I had. But like any truly valuable thing in life, our friendship did not come easily. Her friendship was another source of emotional entanglement because I felt insecure about our friendship, felt that I was putting an emotional burden on her. I truly appreciated her friendship, but I was also prepared to be disappointed because I did not want to be hurt.

I think our friendship crystallizes our experiences, emotions, and sharing. When we came back from our fall term away (L.P. was in Korea, and I was in Edinburgh), we were more mature, and her experience in Korea had broadened the areas of our understanding. We now talk about our dreams, our filial obligations, and families. We talk about our identities as females, Koreans, and minorities at Dartmouth. We are often amazed at the similarities in our experiences and our feelings about our circumstances, our future—even our love for certain Korean food! I feel at home when we speak in Korean; there are certain feelings and expressions that can only be adequately expressed in my own language. It makes my day to know that in this emotional wilderness, I can talk about the joy of eating kimchi-chi-gae (a simple Korean dish) with someone. I find myself through her friendship. I do not have to be somebody else. We still laugh about our first fateful encounter.

If I identify part of my "self" in my friendship with L.P., then I depend on others for self-definition as well. I think that my struggle to define my identity is connected to my questions about the purpose of my life. If someone asked me why I live, I would answer, "Because I was born." If someone asked me for whom I live, I would say for my parents' sake. Living my life for someone else? Isn't that absurd? Maybe. My strong sense of filial obligation is the amalgamation of my love and respect for my parents and family, and the Korean tradition. This is the vital force in my life: my own notion of filial obligation, a lot stronger than what is conventionally understood. It is complicated and emotionally charged and very taxing. However, it is my sense of obligation to my parents, not my feelings for them, that is most taxing.

I have tremendous respect and love for my father. He is an incredibly talented man. His perseverance and dedication to his family are extraordinary. The depth and range of his knowledge impress me as well. I do not think the world has been quite kind to him. He stepped into the wrong career, but his difficult and hardworking life has been the source of my motivation.

My feelings for my mother have changed, especially since I went to college. I think that she could have been, or even should have been, a great pianist, had she not married and instead pursued her career . She often tells me that she is where she is because she didn't try her best, and she was too proud to compromise. Of course she always ends with the same phrases: "I am happy as I am. I have you and your brother. Also, I am married to your father." Her comments are like pebbles being thrown into a pond, though, making only ripples—little sad ripples. She pushed me quite hard, and when I was in high school, I defied her fiercely. Now we understand each other much better, and I feel that I am finally old enough for my mother to depend on me as I have depended on her. Now I begin to understand her not only as a mother but also as a woman whose path I am walking in right now.

Besides my deep love and respect for my parents, my culture demands that I fulfill the most fundamental filial obligation: to stay alive and well until my parents' death. It may sound ridiculously basic; it has not always been that easy for me to fulfill. I think almost everyone basically lives for themselves, but I am afraid I can't say the same thing about myself. I want to challenge people's notion of life. Most people believe that life is good, or at least, that it should be good. But is it good, or do we merely want to believe it to be? Moreover, can one bestow such values on life itself? It is a subjective statement that life is good, yet we believe it to be objective, and tend to label people as social deviants, or at the least to have psychological problems, if they do not conform to such a view. I think it is unfortunate that people, without any critical evaluations, force their own view on others. When there is no objective guideline for deciding what is good or bad on certain subjects, for example, life, your belief is as valid as anyone else's. If you don't think life is good, then it is not, regardless of what other people think. And I do not think life is fundamentally good. I think that the evils we encounter and endure far outweigh the pleasures we enjoy; hence, life is not as "good" as many believe it to be. It seems to me that people tend to overlook the pain they go through; they just brush difficulties aside as being aberrant because they firmly believe that life is good. If others believe that, it is fine with me. However, do not judge my views on life based solely on conventionality, because it is not an absolute measuring rod to gauge the quality of life.

My sense of filial obligation dictates that I be successful, that I become a doctor. I don't remember when I made a final decision to become a doctor, but perhaps it was when my parents and I agreed that it would be a suitable profession for me. I have a strong sense of morality and feel an obligation to help mankind; I am good at memorizing and other brutal academic atrocities. Thus, I came to the conclusion that I would go to medical school. My mother was not very receptive to the idea and asked me why I wanted to make my life more difficult than it needed to be. I did not really understand her question. At that time I wanted to be successful, not for just my parents, but for the sake of success. I didn't realize the implication of the ordeal that lay ahead.

Once my decision became clear, word traveled fast. Everyone around me was more excited about my going to medical school than I was! Once the cycle begins, you cannot really see the end, and don't know what you've gotten into. I took all the excruciating pre-med classes faithfully. I hated every one of them. Not only was the subject matter uninspiring, but most of my pre-med classmates were willing to sacrifice their sense of integrity and dignity for good grades. I felt as though I was contracting an incurable disease of unnecessary aggressiveness and lack of humanity by associating with them. I decided I would quit to save myself.

Then there was a little voice from my heart: "You can't really give up. You can't let your parents down. You are obliged to fulfill their expectation. Nobody made you become a doctor. It is your decision. You created this chaos, you finish it." Sometimes I am amazed at my ability to swallow so much. For two and a half years, I have had a battle with myself every single day. The moment I wake up, I have to tell myself why I am leading the life I am leading, and why I'm not directing myself in other ways. I cannot find myself in the chaos of endless doubt.

And this doubt comes from a polarizing force that pulls me another way: philosophy. I want to become a philosopher. I look at female philosophy professors with admiration and jealousy. I daydream about lecturing about Hegel and Kant. Would I live a passionate and desirable life as a philosopher? I think so. Can I make it? I am not sure. Do I have a talent? Enough to get by, but not enough to become someone significant. Am I willing to take this risk, or, rather, can I afford to take this risk? I become more skeptical. Most importantly, can I disappoint what I imagine to be my parents' expectations? A constant battle between self-assurance and self-doubt drives me insane. When I go home to see my parents, I realize how silly my problem is. Of course I'll become a doctor. However, as soon as I come back to school, the "forbidden passion" of philosophy always gets refueled. I cannot stop. I am being torn between two diametrically opposed forces.

Basically, I feel I must be successful to make my parents proud. The irony in all this is that my conflict is another form of self-inflicted pain. I don't think my parents are aware of my self doubts, as I have never discussed the matter with them. My mother keeps telling me that this is my life, that I have to live for myself. "But Mother, I do not have my life. I cannot live my life for myself. I don't know how to do it anymore. Don't you understand?"

This June will mark my ninth year in the States. Soon it will outnumber the years I lived in Korea. I feel that my life here has been a history of denial: my own denial of this culture and the reaffirmation of my denial by others who do not accept me, and treat me as a perpetual outsider. For all this time, I have never felt that I belonged to this place; I will always be an outsider. Steppenwolf.

Perhaps my persistent self-denial, my position on the margins, has been partly a defense mechanism. You may lead your life peacefully as long as you bury your pain and ignore your heart. You can eradicate painful memories and embrace only the good ones, as pain only begets more pain. However, I think I have grown to recognize that by denying perhaps the most crucial stage of my life, I will never know who I really am. Pain and loneliness have been an integral part of me, the very qualities that have defined me. Now I am transforming this pain into passion and a sense of obligation to reach higher goals.

This process of recognition does not come easily. Sometimes the pain is so intense and acute that I just want to quit, to leave everything behind. Sometimes I feel like a handful of ash consumed by my anger and frustration. I have to remind myself who I am and why I exist. The reason for my existence is not ontological. My recognition of my presence in this culture has also created a new obligation that I would like to fulfill. While my view of this country has not been quite rosy, that doesn't mean that I do not appreciate what I have received here; I do feel fortunate and grateful for all the opportunities I have enjoyed, the opportunities that have been available to me only in this land of promises. I admit that I could not have accomplished what I have through my own desire and inspirations alone. The structures within this country have been lenient enough to allow me to achieve my goals. I have been fortunate enough to experience the best and the worst of both education systems. Moreover, whether or not I like to admit it, the fact is that I have received many opportunities and have used them to the full extent. My Korean background shaped me to value what the American education system offers me, and it has offered it generously.

After all these stories about my lost identity and the evils I encounter every day, it would be a contradictory statement if I said I wanted to live here for the rest of my life. No, I don't, but I will not leave this place, or better yet, cannot leave this place, because I have my obligation to return the opportunities and the support I have received. I cannot say I have always enjoyed this good fortune. It came at a price, and mine was very expensive. I had to renounce my life in order to receive this fortune, in order to complete my obligation to my parents and everyone else to whom I am indebted. Although it might not be what my heart desired in its darkest moments, I chose to become a human being with a definite set of purposes, and in an ironic sense, I am grateful that all these obligations and pain have taught me to realize who I am.

I Sing the Unsung Songs

Yu Chen

China

At Dartmouth College, people often ask me how I came to be interested in women's studies or how I became a feminist; they seem surprised, considering the fact that I come from the People's Republic of China. The first time I was asked it caught me off guard: "I was born a feminist," I responded, though of course that is not true. In fact, it was my early years in China that shaped my feminist insights, which have been sharpened during my time in the United States. The unfulfilled dreams and regrets of the women and girls whom I loved back in China prompted me to come to America, in hopes of one day speaking for them.

Twenty-four years ago, in a small town called Dafeng in southeastern China, Mother brought me to this world on the fourth day of a Chinese New Year that had been spent in starvation. We suffered a desperate shortage of both food and attention from her uncaring husband. Mother said she would never forget that New Year: She was about to deliver me; her old single-roomed home provided by her husband's "work unit," the electric factory, was freezing; the briquette in the stove was cold and smokeless; she was starving; her husband was out meeting friends and playing cards; and her four-year-old son, my brother, was crying.

Had Mother known that, twenty-four years later, her daughter would be living a relatively carefree life and receiving a good education in one of the most prestigious colleges in America, would that have brought her some comfort in the midst of poverty, starvation, and cruelty? Maybe. But I know what would have brought her greatest comfort, had she known it: that I would remember all she had gone through as a girl and woman; that I have made an asset of her life stories and remained true to them; and that she is the greatest reason why I am the person I am. Through my studies in college, I have come to appreciate how girls and women, such as my mother, my female friends and classmates, have shaped my life and aspirations. And I have felt the urge to sing their unsung songs for them: songs of frustration, forbearance, courage, and determination.

I grew up with many girlfriends in the village schools. Our friendships often extended beyond the classrooms to the dusty roads, stone bridges, and fields and rivers of rural China. I remember sailing with a friend in an oval wooden tub down the narrow river beside her house while we picked fresh green water chestnuts (*lings*) from the river. I also remember how girls from my class taught me to dredge up water plants with a string bag attached to a long stick and feed them to pigs; how to fish lobsters from the river with frog meat as bait; and how to identify edible wild herbs in the fields, which made very good dumpling stuffing. I once brought home so many edible wild herbs that my mother despaired of ever cleaning them. But she eventually made all of them into stuffing so that my work would not be wasted.

I have always been extremely close to my mother. I slept with Mother at night, because my father and brother lived away from our village. My father started teaching at a high school in town, which my brother also attended. We went to bed very early every day, at around 7:30. She would sit in bed knitting, while I sat in front of her with my back against her chest. We would stay like that and talk for half an hour every night before I fell asleep. I don't quite remember what we talked about, but I remember the warm fuzzy feelings that we shared (I am sure she felt the same way I did) as I sat rested against her arms and legs.

I grew up listening to Mother telling me her stories, which often filled my heart with awe and sadness. Mother was born in the civil war, fought between the communists and the *Guomingdang*. She was born in a haystack amid the rumble of gunfire and under the attack of hovering fighter planes. Mother became parentless at one year old because her father had been shot by the government before her birth for saying something "antirevolutionary" (he said that the communists might not win the civil war) and her mother remarried and moved away. Great Gram brought her up. They were very poor, and lived on what Great

Gram could earn knitting fishnets and making clothes by hand for other people. My mother often told me she would never forget Great Gram working late into the nights in the dim light of oil lamps. During the hot midsummer nights when Great Gram was working, Mother would frequently slap Great Gram's legs with a fan to drive away the mosquitoes. Watching Great Gram, whose legs were as thin as the stem of a romaine lettuce, made Mother sorrowful. She would often take over the fan to drive away the mosquitoes for her. Their income was very little; nevertheless, when my mother turned six, Great Gram managed to send her to school. In return, Mother shared as much of Great Gram's work as possible after school. When she was not doing her homework, she helped disentangle flaxen thread, knit fishnet, and sew strips of buttons made of cloth. She learned to do these chores and worked hard. She did not have a chance to have fun and enjoy a carefree childhood.

When Mother started high school fifteen miles away from her village, she could not be home to help Great Gram and tried to be very thrifty. For a whole term, all she ate was rice gruel and the cheapest vegetable soups. Every month, when it was time to go home, Mother would walk instead of taking the bus; this would take her four hours each way and save her fifty Chinese cents. When a new term started and she had to carry luggage, she would take the luggage to school the day before with a borrowed bike, leave her luggage there, ride back to her hometown to return the bicycle, and then walk to school again the next day. She would make three trips just to save fifty Chinese cents, which was enough to buy her half a month's soup. The harder Mother's life became, the stronger was her will to study and excel. Mother thought that if she could go to college, she would be able to get a permanent job, which would help improve the family's condition. She would then be able to repay Great Gram for all her kindness and nurturing.

Despite Mother's hard work and excellent academic performance, she suffered harsh discrimination throughout her school years (which were during the Land Reform and Cultural Revolution) because of her "antirevolutionary" father. The teacher would always say, "Children of antirevolutionary parents must pay special attention to reform themselves." In order to "redeem" herself, she worked very hard in "labor classes," where students worked on the school's gardens. Once when she was lifting water, the bucket scraped the skin off her heels.

To top off all the discrimination, she was not allowed to go to college because of her family status. So instead, after high school, Mother took any job she could find. She once worked at the rate of twenty Chinese cents for every hundred pounds of radishes she cut for a food company. Within a few days she became the fastest worker; she cut over five hundred pounds every day! After toiling like this for a dozen days, half of the nail on her left thumb was rubbed off by the knife, leaving only flimsy skin covering the red flesh. But, Mother did not complain; she felt happy because she was earning money and no longer sitting at home. She worked temporary jobs like these until March 1966, when she was told to substitute for a pregnant teacher. She then started to sub in many schools, and teaching has become her occupation ever since.

I have never known Father's motivation for marrying Mother, as he never seemed to care for her. At the time, Mother felt she didn't have a right to pick and choose, and she married Father shortly after they had been introduced. Before long, she started to see that he was having relationships with many women. He had a well-paying job in the army, but never sent money to my mother even after my brother was born. Mother was feeding herself, my brother, and ill Great Gram on twenty nine *yuan* (approximately three dollars) she earned each month teaching in various places, while father had over fifty *yuan* every month.

From a very young age, I knew that my parents did not get along. Mother was always laboring in the household, but Father never laid a finger on household chores. He was very picky about Mother. She told me that when we were young, she used to wash clothes by hand at noon when my father was taking a nap. If my brother made any noises, my father would become irritated and criticize her. He would criticize her for not keeping the kitchen organized enough, or for leaving some threads on the floor after sewing. I often felt, and still do, that poor Mother is living like a frightened rabbit, always on her toes and running in all directions at once.

When I was in first or second grade, Mother discovered that Father was having an affair with a seventeen-year-old girl. Mother became very sick, angry, and desperate. She cried so much it frightened me. I could not stand seeing her swollen eyes, because I had looked up to her as a mighty person. After all, she was taking care of all of us! How could she be down? They sometimes quarreled in front of my brother and me, and then I would cry. Mother would accuse Father of having been betraying her all the time, and he would try to justify his betrayals. During this chaos, Mother was still somehow washing all the clothes and feeding us on time; she would not delay even one meal. But I knew she was dragging herself on; she was doing this only for us, my brother and me. She would have divorced my father if not for us, for at that time divorce was such a taboo that everybody believed that it would disgrace the children. I knew she was hurt, fragile, and could break down at any time. Indeed, she weighed only eighty pounds!

I think the reason Father has never cared about Mother is that he thinks she is not worthy of him, since she did not go to college. Once an old schoolmate of Father's visited us, and Mother prepared a feast. When the guest, my father, and I were sitting at the table and Mother was busy serving, the guest praised my mother's cooking. Father said, after my mother had left the table, "One thing good about a wife who does not have a college degree is that she cooks well." Afterward, my mother told me that she hated it when people said she cooked well. She said she wasn't made just for cooking.

Not being able to go to college had been an eternal regret for my mother. Her life would have been different if she'd gone to college; she might have felt equal with her husband and been able to stand up better for her rights. When she and Father quarreled, she would often sigh and tell me with intense regret that, in her sleep, she still dreamed of taking college entrance exams. I always felt so sorry for her.

However, Mother now has an achievement she is very proud of. When the government implemented policies to remedy the persecution of people with a family background like my mother's, Mother was able to take exams and become a formal teacher. Only two people succeeded of the twenty-three in the county who took the exams. This change brightened Mother's life, and she told me when I was still in high school, "That was a pivotal point in my life. I was able to live with my back straight and head up now; no matter which school I taught at, nobody could bully me anymore. I could even speak up for the weak. I think life is fair." It was this optimism that helped me more than anything to succeed in an educational environment that expected my failure.

I say this because my high school was quite demanding and competitive. Many people thought my scores would drop as school got harder, because I was a girl. There was a prevailing distrust of girls in our school. If I slipped on one quiz, people would question my ability to keep on top. But I managed to stay on top of my class in almost all exams. I remember a teacher in my seventh grade who always praised and encouraged a boy in our class, who invariably came second to me. She frequently said to him in front of the whole class, "Look, you are so smart, you have the potential and should compete with Chen. Why can't you beat her?" And in ninth grade, a math teacher wrote a problem on the board and said, "This is a difficult one. Only boys can do it." His words hurt me badly.

Throughout high school, I felt the pressure of skepticism about me because I was a girl. I can imagine that girls doing less well than I must have encountered far more serious skepticism and might well have been hopelessly weighed down. A very good friend of mine, Siling, was a victim of such skepticism. She was very literary and I liked her for that. I learned a lot from coauthoring antithetical couplets (a kind of word game), coediting small newspapers, and collaborating on blackboard designs with her (we had a blackboard for colored chalk designs and writings on the back wall of each classroom). She had done well in junior high, but her family made her apply to an elementary teaching school instead of a senior high because they didn't think she could make it to college. Many other girls experienced the same treatment in my high school.

In contrast to these popular prejudices, Mother has always trusted girls absolutely. Once a colleague of Father, whose son was a top student in a neighboring class, compared his son with me when he was visiting our home. My father tried to be modest and said, "She is a girl and her grades will drop as she grows." Mother immediately looked up from the celery she was sorting and said, "Don't say that." When I was preparing for the college entrance exams, she would come to my desk and tell me with an assuring smile, "I know you will do well."

And she was right. I did do well and got into Beijing University. It was 1989, right after the Tiananmen Square movement. The government decided to send all the students admitted to Beijing University to a military school in another city to be brainwashed for a whole year, because Beijing University students had been especially active in that movement. I was among those sent to the military school for our upper-class fellow students' "mischief."

My year in the military school was marked by friendships with girls. I lived through the loss of freedom, endless formation drills, political study sessions, and verbal abuse by relying heavily on my friendships with my nine roommates. I believe it was the same for everybody else. The ten of us did everything together: sleeping, eating, walking in lines, going to classes, standing in drills, wiping and shooting guns, and even taking showers together. We lived like one person: We cursed the military most of the time and cheered when somebody received a letter or had a visitor from outside the stifling school. The first person to receive a letter from home treated every roommate to some cakes. We all looked forward to one another's birthdays. In my first letter to my parents, I wrote, "My classmate Hongjuan and I made an appointment to cry together, and Wang Hailing said she'd join us." That year was the first time I had been away from home and lived with other girls. They helped me overcome my homesickness, and I gained a lot from our strong bond.

I also was determined to continue to succeed in my academics. Although the military school despised reading, I tried my best to find bits of time to read. Sometimes I tried to memorize English words when lying on the wet ground and practicing aiming guns. Due to my perseverance, I was able to do well later in the placement exams at Beijing University.

The university has a poetic campus, with its famous "light of the lake and shadow of the tower," its pink lotuses covering the lake "spoon sea" in the summer, the massive golden leaves from the ginkgoes on the ground in the fall, as well as cobbled trails along the lake. I lived near this lake with five roommates from my university class, again all females. The room was narrow, and barely big enough to accommodate six bunked beds and a table. For a little bit of privacy, we each circled our beds with curtains that we made out of colored cloth. When all the curtains were drawn, the room was separated into spheres of pink, blue, white, green, and light purple. Every night we slept in our small spheres surrounded by different colored curtains, through which conversations went in all directions.

Not surprisingly, these conversations often explored relations with boys. We girls were experiencing even more gender polarization than we had in high school, and we were becoming more aware of our differences from guys. In high school, we were all pretty single-minded; all we thought of was getting good grades and getting into a good college. (In China, once you are in college, you are basically guaranteed a job when you graduate.) Now that we had been accepted into a college and the pressure and motivation for hard work was mostly gone, we needed to think on our own about our life purpose. We quickly realized what we learned in high school was only geared toward exams, and that we had very limited knowledge about the world at large. Most importantly, we didn't know about politics. On the other hand, Yang, the first of our group to start dating guys, knew politics well. We felt dwarfed.

In talks at night, in our room, we discussed women's inferiority. Yang really stressed how smart guys were, "They know about politics and sports. . . . My boyfriend is better than I." I found her words jarring. Yang had impressed me as a responsible vice monitor and treasurer of our class, and she planned all the activities almost single-handedly for us. Whenever we had an outing, she was the one who checked on transportation, and bought the tickets and food for us. On the other hand, her boyfriend, a classmate, did nothing for our class. He made unwelcome and "insightful" remarks when we happened to make a mistake and failed to buy classmates birthday gifts while everybody else did. We all felt he was a self-centered guy. I could not see why Yang felt he was better than she.

I also disagreed with the majority opinion of my roommates that women weren't as good as men. From my own experience in my family and in school, I was never that impressed with men. More importantly, I was ambitious myself and was doing very well in class. I had no difficulty staying on the top of my class in exams, and found no reason to admire men more than myself. Instead, I was very upset at the inferiority complex in our room.

Our opinions about relationships also disconcerted me. We put too much premium on a happy marriage. We were worried about not marrying the right person. Most of us thought that life would be perfect if we married somebody gentle, understanding, humorous, capable, and rich. Stereotypes of motherly or childish/trivial women played a large role when we talked about relationships. For example, when Yang felt like a nurturing mother, she would say something like, "Cai [her boyfriend] is so silly; he is like a kid. He always mistakes the conditioner for shampoo. Oh, boys just don't care about these trivial things. I sometimes feel as if I were his mom." At other times, she would play the childish role and claim, "Girls act childish; we want to be doted on."

Being doted on was understood as being loved. Yang's theory, which we all more or less agreed on, was that if a guy loved you, he'd try very hard to dote on you and please you, and do whatever you wanted him to. I think this idea resulted from a sense of insecurity about relationships. The girls in our room tried to get the upper hand when we started dating, but that often resulted in frustration and a sense that we could not really win, unless the man happened to be very nice. We felt ineffective in relationships with men: we threw our tempers at them; we shed tears in front of them; we raised hell; or we acted like spoiled children. For their part, the men responded apologetically if they were nice, or they would brush us off. When we heard our friends say, "He was mean" or "He was nice today," we knew who had the upper hand.

I did resent the stereotypes of women as either "motherly" or "trivial," but I felt the same insecurity as other girls, especially for fear of being stuck with the same kind of marriage as my mother's. When I started dating, I would compare my boyfriend with others' and say, "Yang's boyfriend allowed her to mess up his room, but my boyfriend wouldn't let me—he does not love me as much." Later as I sat in my women's studies classes at Dartmouth, I would remember this insecurity, with disbelief that we had let our lives spin around men.

I might never have gained this perspective, though, were it not for Lisa Stearns, an American Fulbright scholar who inspired me to come to America. I became friends with her during my sophomore year at Beijing University, after taking one of her classes, Law and Women— the only seminar and the only feminist class I ever had in China. In contrast to my other classes, where I had to listen and take notes, Lisa's class gave me the chance to think, question, and speak up. Instead of always giving a definitive answer to a question, she would open it up and let students discuss it from different angles. For example, to illustrate unequal relationships, she would ask us to talk about relationships in our families and communities, instead of telling us stories from texts. She asked us who made decisions and who did chores in our families. She would also meet students at a café or hold free discussions over lunch at her home. Her fun-filled educational style amazed me.

The most exciting thing about Lisa's class was that I found my voice there. I had been a latent feminist, but I first learned the word "feminism" from her. I remember she once asked us the following question: "Under what circumstance do you think a man can beat his wife?" Some students said, "If she is adulterous," and other students said, "If she does not treat him with respect." I said, "Never." After every student had talked, Lisa said, "I would agree with Chen Yu." Though she did not put it in a conclusive way, her endorsement of my opinion was extremely encouraging. I felt for the first time that a professor had cared about something closest to my heart.

I also remember when dealing with labor laws, Lisa mentioned the fact that women's work inside and outside their homes was often unrecognized, undervalued, and underpaid. She thus helped me put into words the problems that I had seen in my family and in the society, and putting the problems into words meant challenging them. Her class made me come to see feminism as the answer to the problems in my parents' relationship, my high school teachers' discrimination against girls, my roommates' inferiority complexes.

Lisa represented the lure of America for me. I started to see America as a place where I would be allowed to discuss ideas freely and where feminism was widely understood. At Beijing University, I was assigned by the school to study Burmese language and culture, having no personal say in the choice of major. I decided that if I came to America and specialized in women's studies, I would become powerful enough to effect change. So alone among all my classmates, I applied to American colleges and was accepted at Dartmouth.

I have always been ambitious. I had aspired to be the best in whatever career I pursued. I remember the words of a country's president, whose name I have forgotten, "I wanted to be a writer, but discovered that I could not be the best writer, so I chose the second best profession for me and became a president." Being the best at something was the most basic standard I chose to live by. Mediocrity was unbearable and unthinkable to me. I often said to myself, "How could I stand being a common person? I would rather die if I had to live like everybody else." My aspirations to be the best had not been much hindered before I came to Dartmouth. I studied with relative ease in high school and got into the best university in China; there again, I breezed through most examinations with flying colors. The professor in charge of our Burmese class said that I was the best Burmese student he had had since the Cultural Revolution in the 1960s. My roommates all agreed that I had a knack for languages. But my luck changed after I came to Dartmouth.

It is one thing to study languages, and it is another thing entirely to study other subjects in a foreign language and compete with native speakers. Back in China, I spoke better English than most people; I even believed I could speak fluently. But after arriving in America, I became conscious all the time that I was not a native speaker. I would hold back comments or questions in classes because I was worried that I could not speak as eloquently as American students. I had also expected that people would at least show some interest in my background, only to find out that most people were not interested in where I was from and that they took my ability to speak English for granted.

Classroom performance was just one of my problems. I also felt alienated in this new country. Even my dormitory room looked too new and unwelcoming to me. On arriving on campus, I was immediately impressed by the modern design of my dormitory, the brown carpet that ran up the stairs, and the spotless walls. Far exceeding my expectations, my room—my own single room—was bigger than the one that my five roommates and I had shared in Beijing University. When I casually pulled out a desk drawer, I was startled to discover that there was some kind of device under it that made it slide out at the slightest pull. I thought, "Wow, the Americans are so clever and luxurious. They know how to make life comfortable." I even had a bathroom, which was stunningly beautiful: It had a big mirror in front of the snow-white sink, a shower with a stainless white plastic curtain, a clean toilet, and two lights!

Everything in my room was dauntingly new. After hanging my clothes in the cabinet and putting away everything else I had brought, the room still looked pretty empty and huge: The measly belongings I had brought were simply not enough to fill up the room. In contrast, my suitemate's started to look packed an hour after she arrived, accompanied by her mother. The first thing she asked me was, "Hey, I am going to buy a fridge, do you want to share it with me? It's a hundred bucks." I hesitated a little and said, "Well, hmmm, I don't know if I will have enough money after buying textbooks. I need to buy books first." In the next two years I was to experience frequently the subtle embarrassment caused by the fact that I am from a third world country. My friends would kindly ask me if my parents were coming to the "freshmen parents' weekend," assuming that my family could afford the trip.

I have certainly also experienced people's misconceptions about my country. When the janitor, Barbara, showed me how to use the laundry machine, she told me to bring four quarters. I was puzzled: "Four quarters of a spoonful of detergent? Why not say a spoonful?" I followed her to the basement with a box of washing powder in my arms. The basement was like a labyrinth to me, with hallways leading to other dorms, study rooms, and TV rooms. I was almost afraid I would not find my way back when we arrived at the steamy laundry room. When Barbara found out that I did not bring the quarters, she asked, "Don't you have washing machines in China?" I said, embarrassed, "Well, yeah, but they don't take money." Later I quite often met people who either assumed there was nothing, not even things like washing machines, in China, or that people lived in the same way as in America, neither of which made me comfortable. After turning on the machine, I stood beside Barbara, not knowing whether to chat a little with her or leave. She saw my awkwardness and said jokingly, "You are excused." She must have found me as wooden as a dummy.

I also discovered sadly that the English I had learned was not adequate in an American college. I found that I hardly understood anything outside class because students' language was full of slang. I remember walking with three freshmen one day; supposedly we were having a conversation, but after introducing myself, I soon lost what they were saying. All I knew was that they were talking excitedly and loudly among themselves. I felt left out. Finally I overcame my shyness, and interrupted them: "What is 'bullshit'?" The girl beside me replied, "Oh, just an expression."

A lack of familiarity with idiomatic expressions was not the only reason I did not fit in with my classmates. My UGA (undergraduate advisor) group was a bunch of happy people, for whom laughter came easily. I wanted to laugh with them, but it was just not so easy. When they talked about TV or some other culture-specific things, I didn't quite understand. I wanted very much to learn more about them and participate in their conversations, but as I sat at Ben and Jerry's ice cream store with my UGA group and watched their endless motions of waving hands, grinning teeth, tossing back their heads and laughing— all of which did not hold much meaning to me—I felt lonely and awkward.

I also did not immediately pick up the ways people do things. In Beijing, I made connections effortlessly with the girls in our class through our bedtime talks; here, I came to realize that you have to "do things together" with people in order to connect. For example, when my roommate asked me to join her and her friends for dinner, I failed to take it as a sign of reaching out and told her I had eaten. Most perplexing to me was their high enthusiasm for sports. During freshmen fall, the football season, several people asked me if I had seen the previous weekend's football game. When I said no, they cried out, "No? You are missing a lot, Chen!" Out of curiosity, I went to one of the games, and it turned out to be one of the most painful hours in my life. It was a damp, late-fall day, and I nearly froze sitting on the outdoor bleachers. People around me, however, were very excited, jumping, waving, and yelling. Some of the people even had green paint on their faces, and several freshmen with paint on their bodies ran across the football field. I couldn't understand the excitement, let alone feel it. I didn't even care which side won. Instead of the excitement I wanted to feel, I felt sad. I thought I was missing my life, because I was not feeling as happy as everybody else. I came home before the game was over, and asked a Chinese senior over the phone, "What's wrong with me? Why is everybody else excited while I am not?"

Being new, lost, and feeling inferior at Dartmouth was painful, but most painful of all was being away from Tony, a man I had dated for two years back in China. He was a foreign student from Sierra Leone. I missed him every minute. Whenever I felt stressed, I sought the best release: I would sit in front of the window, take up a pen, and write a few lines to Tony. I wrote him all the time, telling him how much I missed him, and how I looked forward to seeing him at Christmas. (He had promised to come see me then.) I asked him to please write me, and waited anxiously for his letter. I waited and waited, often standing in front of my mailbox, but I had to wait a long time.

One night my UGA group was playing games in the hall, and people were going wild, even painting their faces and hands. Loneliness struck me so hard that I could not stand it anymore. I burst into my room and picked up the phone. I had refrained from calling Tony because I knew if I started I would never stop, but I could not stand it anymore. Despite the laughter in the hallway, I fell on my knees and cried over the phone, begging, "Tony, please write me."

The long-awaited letter finally arrived, and it was to paralyze me emotionally for almost a year. In this letter, Tony told me that he was going to marry a woman who was his former girlfriend, a daughter of his parents' friends who had done many favors for his family, who now insisted on marrying him.

How do I describe my feelings after reading that letter? My heart, mind, and body felt empty. I had to work my student job at the cafeteria, but I could not hear any instructions from my supervisor. As I mechanically placed can after can of drinks in the cooler, all I could think was, "This is the end of the world. Tony has left me. Why do I still live? How could he just leave me?"

During the next weeks I was in turmoil. I desperately wrote and called Tony, begging him to take me back, to "save" me. I would cling to the slightest hope and make all kinds of propositions to save our love, but in vain. My depression was to last most of my whole freshman year. When I was stressed, whether because of work or my inferiority complex, I would think, "If I had Tony, everything would be fine. How nice the days with him were!"

Two years have passed since I was so desperate, and thankfully my perception of my love for Tony has evolved. When I look back at those dark days now, I am struck by my begging for his love. I am struck by how much I romanticized our relationship and forgot about all the frustrations I had had with him in China. I am surprised that the days I spent waiting for his letter at Dartmouth did not remind me of those evenings in Beijing when he stood me up. He had often been very late for our appointments and would make me wait outside his room for hours. He never understood my frustration with his lateness, but I was so attached to him that I continued to see him. I had placed him at the center of my life and planned everything to fit his schedule, but he had not treated me in kind.

Now I can see how unbalanced our relationship was. I can see that I was so attached to Tony because I had been socialized in a society where romance between men and women is everything, especially for a girl. I fell prey to this socialization, like so many other women. When I waited for his letter, I was living a fairy tale: the girl in distress waiting for her prince to rescue her.

I see this all now, though at the time I felt only the pain of separation, a pain exacerbated by what I was encountering in my course work. The first book I read at Dartmouth was Milan Kundera's *Immortality*, a novel that explains the futility of the search for self. I read it at a time when my self-esteem was being painfully eroded by Tony's betrayal and my cultural displacement, and my ambition to be unique was at risk because of low self-confidence. *Immortality* convinced me that individuality could be only an illusion. I then started what Erik Erikson calls a moratorium stage in my life, that stage in which a late adolescent actively searches for people or ideals to make commitments to. I kept asking what I should live for if not for greatness, uniqueness, and immortality.

I now consider *Immortality* a little too cynical in its attitude toward individuality, but it is not strange that I was bewitched by it then. In China, communist propaganda places no value on individuals and stresses individuals' sacrificing for the great collective; paradoxically, however, it also emphasizes "realizing the value of the self," that is, contributing to the social good through altruistic achievement, which in turn brings fame and immortality. I had noticed that all the Chinese monuments to its martyrs say "immortality." The emphasis on achievement is not an invention of the West, as many people imagine; the Chinese simply place more emphasis on altruistic or intellectual achievements than on self-serving or material achievement, or at least this was true in times past. The communist propaganda is overwhelming and leaves many people no time to think for themselves, to consider whether they agree with it or not. High school students, moreover, don't get the chance to think about their life because they are usually so deeply enmeshed in academic work. College students are usually assigned their majors and jobs, so they feel there is no point in much reflection anyway.

It was not surprising, then, that I would find *Immortality* both refreshing and disturbing. It was refreshing because it made me think of life in new ways. It was disturbing because it uprooted my deepest belief in my values. There are many ambitious people in the world, but I was ambitious in a way different than most. For me, piling up money or wielding great political power was not important; these were ambitions I considered too common to be great. I wanted a lot more individuality, though I did not know exactly what I was looking for.

During my years at Dartmouth, I have often been paralyzed by the two fundamental questions posed by *Immortality*: What is my life for? Why am I here? Having no answer upsets me. In my first year here, I cried a lot, not only for the loss of my boyfriend, but also for the meaning of my life that went with him. I had identified with what Tony had seen in me, my intelligence and specialness. Now, not only had the cultural displacement undercut my self-confidence, but the flattering mirror Tony had held up was now broken. I blamed men for their fleeting passion—a blame that stemmed from witnessing my parents' relationship. On the other hand, my desire for romantic relationships was insurmountable. I was feeling so lonely that every night I would spend hours on the phone talking with every acquaintance I could think of, including all of my Chinese friends. What I really wanted was a person to talk to intimately, and I continued to try to find a meaningful self through the attention of a lover.

My women's studies classes, though double-edged in the combination of challenge and exhilaration they offered, gradually empowered me and redirected my focus in my search for self. Like *Immortality*, women's studies classes continued to push me out onto the path of the moratorium stage. On the one hand they made me think a lot about the relationships between men and women and about issues of social justice. They provided me a sense of my worthiness as a woman and a person, as well as insights into human relationships and the problems of the society. On the other hand they were deeply frustrating, because talking about injustice often filled me with rage and depression. The problems talked about in class reminded me of my own and my parents' problems. I wished that my major was not so intertwined with my personal experience, and I longed for a break from "problems."

Immersed in thoughts of injustice, I was also too quick to blame men in general for my personal problems. My mistrust in men is the most deeply rooted feeling inside me, resulting from my parents' relationship. This mistrust permeates every level of my consciousness and seems to ooze out of my pores at times. This mistrust, aggravated by my women's studies classes at Dartmouth, intensified my frustrations: Although I still longed for a romantic relationship with some man, I didn't see a way out of the power imbalance between men and women. I was even rather disgusted by men, particularly after my dependence on Tony. I could not reconcile my hatred and desire for men.

Toward my junior year, I started to understand my women's studies classes differently, and learned from them a different view of romantic love between men and women. Two books in particular enlightened me on this issue: Toni Morrison's *Sula* and Alice Walker's *The Color Purple*. In *Sula,* the title character became a role model for me, a woman who cared not about a man's love but about a woman's friendship. I began to see that a man's love was not essential for my happiness. That realization helped me break free from my concern about not being able to win a man's love.

The Color Purple affected me deeply, too, especially the relationship between two black women, Shug and Celie. Shug had been in love with Celie's husband, but when she discovered that he had been tyrannizing Celie, Shug took Celie away and began to live with her. When people asked the formerly docile Celie what she and Shug did together, she replies: "We make love." It is such a beautiful and convincing story; it portrays a lesbian relationship as it is—fulfilling and normal, normal in its own terms, not in terms of being the same as the majority. As I started to think less and less of men, I also started to see women as real potential partners for women. Am I indicating that frustration with men has pushed me toward lesbianism? No, for that would indicate that women are secondary choices. But I have started to think that women have only been deceived into taking men as our first choices. We have been deceived by traditional romance movies, novels, and, above all, fairy tales. After reading *The Color Purple*, I can envision more fulfilling relationships with women.

Not to deny that I still desire men once in a while, not to deny that I still feel lonely for lack of a significant other by my side, not to deny that I need love. But, the word "love" has taken on a new meaning for me over my past two or three years at Dartmouth. A man's affection is no longer the arch-love I seek, nor is my own blind attachment to a man. I have discovered instead the significance of female friendship and affection in my life. I suppose that most people feel they need some kind of love and affection, but I have also learned, through the two novels that changed my concept of love, that love is a social construct: Women have been taught by heterosexual propaganda whom to love and whom to expect love from—men. Now we can relearn how to love, to love women, and to expect love from women.

My growth over the past three years has been an intersection of two paths: my quest for self and for love. Have I found my self and confidence? Have I found a great meaning in life? Have I learned what love is? Have I succeeded in finding self through love? Have I learned about love through my understanding of self? My answers to these questions are not crystal clear, but I have come a long way in my struggle for positive answers. Participating in classes, discussions, and numerous social events, traveling in Europe, meeting new people, and gaining friendships in the United States have all given me more and more confidence. My women's studies classes and readings have played a great part in my evolution, for better or worse. Despite the initial frustrations mentioned earlier, they have enlightened me: They have taught me to question the realities and social norms, and they affirm my quest for social equality and my wish that nobody live as tragically as my mother was forced to by her society and her husband. Since I can relate myself to the honorable cause of equality, I am not so caught up in the concern about how great I can be personally. Questions about the meaning of life have become less significant for me.

On the other hand, I am not ready to give up my ambition to be a great achiever. An elderly friend once told me that maturing is the process of discovering your limits: Many people have great ambitions when they are young, but lose them as they age. I refuse to accept this kind of maturation. I have always had big dreams, and I have learned that I can realize these dreams only if I don't give them up. Many people think that my biggest dream, an equal society, is impossible, but my mother tells me never to place limits on my potential. I would like to expand her advice and say that I should not place limits on humankind. As Priscilla Sears, my closest women's studies professor, says, "What is difficult can be achieved now; what is impossible takes a little longer."

By teaching me how important it is for a woman to take control of her life, Mother long ago sowed the seeds of feminism in me. Her courage and forbearance have demonstrated to me the possibilities of great strength in a woman. Her unreserved trust in my ability has also led me to refuse to be confined by social norms and prejudices. Since I started school, I have often had to fight against prejudices, and have also witnessed my female friends' own struggles. Even in Beijing University, where people were well educated, I had to face my roommates' inferiority complex. I longed then to fight prejudice, but found my voice only in the more open environment in America.

As a person who values emotional connections, I have sought to discover my self in the reflection of a lover's eyes, to the point of losing myself in blind love for a man. At the same time, I have often acted defensively with men and felt powerless, like my female friends at Beijing University. It is the generally more progressive atmosphere of the United States, compared to China, that has taught me to stand on my own feet again. It has helped me reject my former obsession with men, along with the system that enforces it. To counter the general pattern of male dominance over women in our society, I have consciously chosen to bond with women. I am relishing female friendships and love, and am discovering my self—my voice, my soul—through these relationships because they respond to where I am from and where I am going. My self lies in my love for women: my mother, my female friends, and myself. I live to sing the unsung songs for these women, and now live with my back straight and head up.

Re-Viewing Identity

From the Death Line to Dartmouth

Almin Hodzic
Bosnia

Serbian soldiers circled the front of my house, screaming and firing rounds in the air from their automatic weapons. Finally one of the soldiers broke the main entrance of my house with one kick of his boot. "Everybody in this house, get out and stand in line!" he shouted. My mother looked at us as if she wanted to say something, but in the last moment she could not. We exited the house to see soldiers who appeared dirty, smelly, unshaven, and tired. Dressed in black and dark blue military uniforms, many of them wore masks so they wouldn't be recognized. All I could see were their bloody eyes and dry, broken lips. They carried automatic rifles, which seemed like they could not wait to spit their seeds of death.

When one soldier asked where my father was, my mother replied that he was working outside of the country. The soldier's reply was, "Too bad, ma'am, that he'll never see you again." When my mother asked what he meant by that, he responded, "My dear lady, don't you see I am going to kill you? Don't you see I am going to kill *all* of you?" My mother burst into tears, and he demanded that we sing "Who Says, Who Lies That Serbia Is Small," the Serbian national anthem. When we started singing, he repeatedly shouted, "Louder, louder, you Muslim bastards!" I was standing at the end of the line next to my old neighbor who did not know the song. But she still opened her mouth, pretending to sing. I tried to be as loud as I could to cover my neighbor. Suddenly the soldier blurted out, "Stop, stop, I don't want to hear any more." He turned to face the other soldiers. "I think I am gonna finish them off. Don't you think we should finish them?"

As I realized that my life was going to be over soon, an incredible peace came over me. There are some things in life that a person cannot control, and this was one of those situations; my life was in the hands of another man. When that dirty, smelly soldier made me sing, doing all he could to humiliate me, I felt not like a human being, but an animal that had to obey orders and stare at the ground. I had done absolutely nothing to this Serbian, who was an Eastern Orthodox Christian—I did not even know him. But for him there was one wrong thing with me: My religion was different from his, and for that reason alone I was an animal in his eyes, an animal to be exterminated. Just because he had a gun and I did not, he was master of the situation. We were not two men—we were man and animal. And I was momentarily going to be shot. I was an innocent little fourteen-year-old farm kid who had never harmed anyone, and there I was in the hands of a monster in whose eyes I had no right to exist. In that moment, everything was stripped from me: my pride, my childish wishes, my dreams of the future.

My eyes were faced toward death. The soldier readied his gun, screaming, "Who wants to die first?! Let me hear it?" At that moment another soldier, masked, entered my yard and demanded, "Stop, I want you to go on. I will take care of these puppies." Without hesitation, the other soldier responded, "Yes, captain." My death had been at least postponed. The captain pointed at my mother and me, "You and you, come inside the house with me and open the doors." (They took this precaution so no one could surprise them from behind a closed door.) When we entered my house, the soldier pulled off his mask, and there, to my shock, was my karate instructor, whom I had known for a long time. "Coach, what are you doing here?" I asked. "Don't ask too many questions, son. I would like to give you advice: Take your family and head for the concentration camp. There you will have a better chance of survival. You can't stay here. As soon as we leave, walk toward the city and go straight to the camp."

Going from the death line to Dartmouth was something that I never could have dreamed up. My experiences in Bosnia showed me that life is a journey that holds extraordinary challenges. Coming to Dartmouth was another challenge where I had to face a new world, a world in which I felt myself different. How was I going to reconcile my war experiences with the tranquillity of college life? How was I going to fit in when I had a different accent from everyone else? How was I, a nondrinker, going to feel at home in a school where alcohol seemed to be the key ingredient for making friends? How was I going to interact with a roommate whose background would be so different? How was I going to act in front of women? Was Dartmouth going to shape me into an American who wants to become independent and successful even if it means living away from his family—an American to whom freedom means nothing but the word? Or was I going to be able to keep my Bosnian heritage, thereby distancing myself from American culture and preserving values such as family, religion, and hard work?

I did not yet know the answers to these questions when I came to Dartmouth, but I was leaning toward embracing American culture. It meant becoming an American, but one who has mixed values, both American and Bosnian. It meant that I had to find a balance to fit in and be accepted. But I knew that to be the good man I have always wanted to be, I had to keep in mind what I learned when I was a Bosnian during the war, which is that the best way to live is to love and respect all people, no matter what their color, race, religion, or nationality. I could never forget this lesson. Dartmouth, I knew, was going to bring many challenges, but none comparable to waiting in the death line. My traumas had given me an inner strength to face all obstacles. I was determined to succeed: It was time to figure out how to do so in the world of Dartmouth, a quest that would challenge many of my assumptions and much of what I learned while growing up in Bosnia.

I was born and raised in the medium-sized industrial town of Prijedor, where children were taught to value three things: hard work, honesty, and respect for elders. Besides working in paper factories, many people from Prijedor were farmers; most of them worked morning shifts in the factories and worked on their farms after completing their shifts. The predictability of our lives made change seem unlikely. Every day people came from the factories, fed their animals, milked the cows, had family dinners, and went to bed. Every spring they sowed seeds; every summer they picked hay from the fields; and every fall they picked corn. Year after year, the cycle was repeated. When they completed their harvests successfully, they looked at their barns with pride; on the other hand, when things did not go well or the weather would not cooperate, they would look to the skies impatiently. After hard work during the season, it was a great feeling to smell fresh wheat and corn.

In my family, my dad was an industrial painter, and most of the time he was away, working in different countries. Although my two younger brothers and I missed him, we knew we were in good hands with my mother. At times I thought that she was the strictest person in the world, but I knew she had the biggest heart, too. She raised my brothers and me in a way all parents should raise their children; she was strict, determined, kind, generous, hard-working, and, most importantly, strong. In a society in which males made the decisions, she was the decisive one in my family. Taking care of our big family farm and a big family store, which she owned, she was a very successful woman.

She never appeared tired, but I knew she was. There were times when she would go to bed and I would hear through the walls her deep sighs, but because of her pride she never admitted her exhaustion. She was determined to show her children that with hard work you can do anything. At age ten I already knew everything about farming, although there were many times that I wish I did not! When all the kids from the block were running in the fields and enjoying themselves, my mom felt that it was more important for me to learn to grow tomatoes and potatoes. I was angry a lot of the time, but if I were to experience my childhood again, I would not change a thing. Nothing made me more happy than waking up in the morning and seeing a beautiful sunrise or large white flakes blanketing the fields. Nothing excited me more than surging out of the house and running through the endless fields of golden wheat. Being away from the world of drugs and crime, life on the farm was unbounded happiness, brought about by calm, peaceful surroundings.

Besides working on the farm, two other things were crucial to me: school and religion. My mother always insisted that these things are necessary to be a good person. She often asked, "Is the farm really something that you want to do for the rest of your life? Do you really feel that this is a good life?" It almost seemed as though she did not want me to stay there, or maybe she believed a farmer's life was not really for me. In my heart I knew that I wanted to be a doctor, engineer, or lawyer. I did not want to follow my ancestors' traditional path, get my share of land, and continue to farm. I did not want to be a farmer, period! I wanted to experience a different world, in which I could learn about something more than milking cows. It just seemed like the right thing to do. For this reason, school was always the most important thing in my life. Invariably, I carried books with me, and many times I ended up at the top of my barn, reading books as I inhaled the beautiful smell of dry hay. My love of books, and learning in general, has always existed, and learning has always presented me adventure.

As long as I can remember, my religion has been important to me. Even though we had some Christian family members, I was raised a Muslim, and as I grew older, I learned more and more about what it is to be Muslim. I remember my first day of fasting during the month of Ramadan, in which you can't have food or drink from sunrise to sunset. I was so excited after I completed the fast that I wanted to do it for a full month. Even though my mother tried to convince me that I was too young, I did it anyway. I think that believing in God helped me to get through difficult times, particularly during the conflict that took place in my country. Even though I was raised a Muslim, I will always call myself a Bosnian, a Bosnian who knows what his religion is, but also a Bosnian who is ready to share his heritage with others.

Before the war, Bosnia was a model of diversity and multiculturalism. In Bosnia there are three main religions, or cultures: Bosnian Muslims; Bosnian Croats, who are Roman Catholics; and Bosnian Serbs, who are Eastern Orthodox Christians. We are all southern Slavs and we all speak the same language. In the towns and cities, especially in Sarajevo, which was the capital of Bosnia, intermarriage was quite common. In my family, we had friends who practiced different religions, so we shared their holidays and they shared ours. I played soccer and practiced martial arts for nine years, all with friends who were of various religions. I remember that after hard practices we all used to go to a place called Cuko, a favorite teenage hangout, to get soda or ice cream. There was never any distinction between my friends and me, no matter what our religious beliefs. We were simply friends.

To understand the horror that engulfed us, I need to retrace the steps that led up to the aggression. In April 1992 we had an election in which the majority of Bosnian people voted to change the communist system to a more democratic one. At the same time, people had to decide whether to stay part of former Yugoslavia or become independent. As communism crumbled and Bosnia became independent, Serbian president Slobodan Milosevic changed the constitution and united the power from the six separate republics that made up the former Yugoslavia. He seized more and more power for himself and for the Serb-dominated army in Belgrade (the capital of Serbia). For this reason, two former republics, Slovenia and Croatia, seceded from Yugoslavia and became independent. Bosnia was left alone in Yugoslavia under Serbian domination until it followed Croatia and Slovenia's examples and became independent. The Serbs in Belgrade were particularly opposed to Croatian and Bosnian independence, because of the large number of Serbs living in these countries, as well as their large amounts of natural resources. They wanted to create a "Greater Serbia," with all Serbs living in one country. For this reason Serbs attacked first Croatia and then Bosnia. The air was full of expectation. The ultimatum given by the Serbs had run out. They threatened first to bomb my village, and then attack it with infantry; they wanted us obliterated. The only reason for their attack was that they did not want us around; they did not want to share holidays with us or accept our religious differences.

All of this intolerance led to horrific and inhumane acts of violence, such as the frightening scene that begins this essay. The night of the first bombing of my village was a beautiful summer night. I remember that on nights like this, we children would go to a nearby action park. After the rides, excited and happy, we would run home to tell our experiences to our parents. But this night was different. Instead, my family, together with my relatives and several neighbors, had to find protection in the dark, stinking basement of my house. The younger children did not have the patience to sit in one spot inside, so I was excited when my mother sent me upstairs to get cigarettes, which was the only way to pass time. As I entered my mother's room, groping for the drawer with the cigarettes, the darkness of the night was suddenly painted white with the bright flash of a fired Serbian projectile. The whole house shook from the detonation of the bomb, and I was thrown to the floor. As I crawled down the corridor, I could feel the vibration of the house and hear the music of the windows that was caused by the reverberation. I could hear the wreckage flying all over the place, hitting the ground and buildings. Dogs howled and whimpered, as if they sensed that the devil had arrived. Indeed, the devil of war was here.

I was scared and confused. I asked myself if what we were going through was anything like the wars that I learned about in history class, wars in which people die, wars that don't bring anything good, wars in which there were no winners. Another bomb came in and hit my neighbor's barn, setting it into flames instantaneously. The barn was very old and made of wood; the combination of old, dry wood and the hay inside the barn made for a spectacular plume of fire. This was real—this was a nightmare come true.

More projectiles landing in our neighborhood reminded me that it was time for me to seek protection in the basement. Edging into the basement gave me more proof of the reality of war. The small candle in the middle of the basement lit the room enough that I could see everybody's eyes—eyes filled with fear. Family and friends sat in neat rows on both sides of the basement; they huddled so close to each other that they seemed to seek protection under one another's skin. Even small children seemed to sense that something terrifying was happening, and their mothers gently put their arms over them. My aunt was crying in the corner, and her three-year-old son, trying to move her hands from her wet eyes, repeatedly asked, "Mammy, please tell me, why are you crying?" Trying to console her, he said, "Please don't, I promise I'll be a good boy. Mammy, please don't cry." I felt like crying, too. Somewhere at the far end of the basement, I could hear noises made by rats that seemed joined with us in terror.

After endless bombing, the Serbs tried to break the village's line of defense with infantry. The fighting continued for two days, during which we never saw the light of day. Suddenly, a neighbor came to our basement and urged us to run away because the Serbs had broken into the village and were killing everybody in front of them. Panic began to spread. We did not know where to go or what to do, surrounded as we were on all sides. One man suggested we head for the forest, which was about three miles from my house. Since nobody else had any better suggestion, it seemed like the only thing to do. As we fled the basement I could smell fresh gunpowder and sense stray bullets whizzing over our heads. Women, children, and old men were running—trying to escape death. Mothers were carrying their children, and in case they could not carry all of them, they grasped their hands and dragged them forward. By the time we arrived in the forest, a few thousand Serbs were already in the village. They began to burn one big part of the village. They torched our mosque and tried to destroy every sign of Muslim culture. Since the forest that we stayed in looked over the village, we could clearly see spectacular flames reaching into the sky. Stunned, we watched our homes burn, and saw everything we had worked so hard for disintegrate. It seemed that the villagers would rather die than witness this spectacle.

After spending four days in the forest, we ran out of food. We had no choice but to go back home, regardless of what would happen. When we straggled home, nobody was there and our house, surprisingly, remained standing. The Serbs were in the part of the village they had burned and destroyed. People who lost their houses stayed with those whose houses were intact. We tried to capture animals to feed ourselves. During the next month, Serbs came to our houses and took our possessions. In many cases they threatened to come back the next day, expecting to extract money from each person. "We are going to come back tomorrow, at which time you better have money and gold," they would say. "If you don't, I'm going to kill you and your children and burn your house." People that did not have any money had to go find money from someone else or they had to run away. In most cases their houses were indeed burned.

During the nights, the Serbs fired endless rounds from their automatic weapons to show their power; one morning, though, everything was very quiet. After a long time of very loud days and even louder nights, I had almost forgotten what silence was like. I could hear the songs of playful blue jays that were standing on the nearby tree. It was a beautiful summer morning. I thought that perhaps the Serbs were finally going to leave us alone, but unfortunately that was not what happened. Suddenly grenades exploded and shots resounded. Serbian soldiers were coming from all sides, marching in neat rows. After realizing that they were going to be at my house soon, we all huddled into my basement once again. We figured that soldiers could not kill many people as easily as a few.

That was the time we were saved by my karate coach, and if you believe in luck, we were certainly lucky then. But others were not as lucky as we were. That day, two thousand people near Prijedor were killed in one hour—two thousand innocent people, mostly men between age fifteen and sixty-five. The rest of the men were taken to several concentration camps. Once the soldiers exited, people who were left in the village, mostly old men, women, and children, started walking toward the city. Most of the people killed were lying dead on the side of the unpaved road that led to the city entrance. There were groups of three, four, five, or even more corpses. By the time we entered the city, we had gotten used to seeing dead bodies. Even though my mother insisted that I avert my eyes from the twisted corpses, I could not help but look. From the way the dead bodies were positioned, their arms tucked under their heads, it almost looked as if they were asleep. Most of them were already hard to recognize; it was hot and they were covered with flies. That night we slept among the corpses.

The next morning the Serbs sent us buses, but only a few of them. They put more than a hundred people on each bus. I found myself under one of the seats. In that moment, I felt an incredible relief that I was still alive. By this time there were so many moments when I could have been killed, but it hadn't happened. When we arrived the next day at camp, I could see an enclosed area of wire netting with thousands of people jammed up against each other. In my case, the concentration camp was a high school in Trnopolje surrounded by barbed wire, soldiers, and swamps. After the Serbs gave us several general rules (one of which was that males had to sleep outside on the ground, and women and children were to sleep inside the school), we were taken inside the camp. There were people who had been there for several months already, some so skinny that I could see their ribs clearly. Some were in very bad shape, not only because they had not eaten in days, but because they had also been severely beaten during interrogations. Some lay helplessly on the ground, while others sat with their heads close to their knees, as if in prayer.

During the first three days at Trnopolje, there was no food or water. I felt very hungry for the first day or two, but I got used to it by the third day. People ate grass, insects, and worms. The biggest problem for me was the thirst, and since there was only one water pump, it was hard to get any water at all. As the oldest son, I would sometimes wait for an entire day just to get a gallon of water. Also, since I was old enough, I was separated from my mother and brothers: While they slept inside of the school, I slept outside on the ground. Besides not having water, there were no bathrooms; the stench of human waste was unbearable. Somehow, after a while, I got used to even that. Although my stomach constantly reminded me of its emptiness, I tried to ignore it as much as I could. My youngest brother was so hungry and thirsty that he would bite his fingers to moisten his lips with blood. Even though my mother was unable to provide us with food, she did not want to show us how much this was hurting her. She desperately tried to keep her tears inside, but at times I could see her wipe her face with her long-sleeved shirt.

After three days, the International Red Cross discovered the camp and made the Serbs give us some food. To provide us with food, the Serbs went through villages and captured and butchered stray cows. This food was by no means enough for everyone, so the men made sure that women and children got their portions. People divided the smallest pieces of bread among their closest family. I considered myself very lucky when I got a cup of pasta and a piece of bread. From my days at the concentration camp, I will never forget the torture people endured. Every day, several prisoners were taken to the interrogation room to be questioned. The Serbs always found a reason to beat them. Some of the prisoners never came back because they were beaten to death or killed by shotgun. Others came back, but they were beaten so badly that they cried in pain. Some of them pleaded to other prisoners, "Please kill me. I can't take the pain anymore. Please kill me." The Serbs used different torture techniques such as building fires on people's chests, cutting off their ears and reproductive organs, and beating them with baseball bats. They committed the most horrible acts a person could possibly imagine. My blessing was my young age, as I did not have to go through interrogation.

The most terrifying moments were when Serbian soldiers came into the camp looking for women, who were taken to the nearby motel and raped. Every time soldiers came inside, searching with their bloody, drunken eyes, I knew that they were looking for women. I was always afraid they would take my mother. I did not know what would happen if they took her; I always thought I would rather die than see her taken away. Luckily, though, she was never selected. Many other women were not so lucky. Something that I will never be able to remove from my memory is when they took a twelve-year-old girl who lived near me. In my country it is a great dishonor to have sex before marriage; it is particularly dishonorable in traditional families. This girl was from one of those families, and after she was raped by ten Serbian soldiers, she was returned to her mother. Somehow she survived, but she was both mentally and physically sick. Since in her mind she had been dishonorable, she was constantly crying, "Mammy, I am sorry. I did not want to do it. Mammy, I am so sorry. Please forgive me." Even though her mother kept assuring her that there was nothing to forgive, the girl kept crying. I felt an incredible anger inside of me and wondered how human beings could be so cruel.

After twenty days in the camp, the Serbs decided to release most of their prisoners. They did not have the means to kill everybody in the camp, and they did not want to feed everyone. They took women, children, and old men and put them into big trucks, which were packed to overflowing, and drove us to a Bosnian army-controlled settlement in Bosnia. Because the place where the Serbs let us go was on a dividing line between two sides, we had to walk for about ten miles to finally be free. Reaching the line was an ecstatic feeling. I remember tears flowing down my face, and even though I did not want anyone to see them, I could not stop crying. I just felt like hugging my mother and brothers and never letting them go. We were finally free. After spending three weeks in the town of Travnik, we arrived in Croatia, where we were finally reunited with my father, who had barely survived three months in one of the worst concentration camps in Bosnia. Seeing my father was one of the happiest moments of my life; after six months apart, my family was finally together again. Though my father got his job back in Croatia and we began going to school, my parents quickly realized that the future there was not very promising. We wanted to get away from the war zone and go where we could start over again. That place turned out to be the United States, where we were sponsored by three churches in Greenwich, Connecticut.

Our adaptation in the first six months of our stay in the United States was complicated by language problems. No one in my family spoke any English, and we had to first learn the basics. At times it was frustrating when people tried to talk to us and we did not know what they were saying. I remember my first social studies class (they had put me in the sophomore class based on placement tests that I took during the first few days of school), in which my well-meaning teacher took me in front of my class to explain what was happening in Bosnia. I did not know where to start. It seemed that she asked too much. Where do I start? The firing line? The concentration camp? What do I tell them about me? Even when I finally figured that I should explain the history of the conflict, I did not have linguistic skill to do it. Finally, I decided to draw on the chalkboard a picture of the city encircled by Serbian soldiers. But since I did not know how to say "surrounded" I just repeated, "Serbs around, Serbs around and then boom, boom." I used my whole body to try to explain. Even though my teacher constantly smiled to indicate that she understood, I was sure that the students had no idea what I meant. I could see their confused faces, wide eyes and open mouths. I just remembered that I was in a sweat after this class, and even though I was extremely frustrated, I still smiled. Inside, I was ready to cry. Perhaps I felt this way because this was the first time I ever looked back at my experiences during the war or perhaps because I had an uncomfortable feeling of being different. Maybe I just did not want to be put on the spot and made to talk. Or maybe I just wanted to keep my memory of the horrors inside of me.

Since I took mostly sophomore classes and school was quite easy, I took the opportunity to work at four different jobs to support my family. My parents, in their turn, seeing the opportunity this country offers to those who make an effort, worked extremely hard— determined to give their children everything we asked for. Being the oldest son in the family meant that I had to grow to become a man much sooner than I expected. Because my English was improving day by day, I was the one who had to answer the phone, make arrangements at my brothers' schools, and pay the bills. Even though I was invited many times to parties, I always had to give the same reply, "I am sorry, I would really love to come, but I have to work." The jobs ranged from washing dishes to delivering food, from landscaping and catering to working in an animal hospital. Even though at times I thought that I could not take all of the pressure, I knew that this was for the good of my family. If I were going to make the American Dream come true for all of us, it meant working all the time at any job that was given to me. I had to take that responsibility, and because of it, I had to skip the time where I could just be a normal, carefree teenager.

In time, we adjusted. We turned more to American food, drank espresso instead of strong Turkish coffee, and even decorated our house in an American style. It seemed that every day my younger brothers became more American and less Bosnian. Traditional Bosnian music was replaced by American pop rock, my middle brother began to play the guitar, and they both began wearing baseball hats, most of the time backward. The idea that my younger brothers were becoming more American did not surprise me much. The process of assimilation seemed to be happening more quickly for them than for me, but then I had lived in Bosnia much longer and had had time to establish my Bosnian roots. This did not mean, however, that I did not try to connect with my peers. I am by nature open and outgoing, and that has definitely helped me connect with others. By my senior year I was a member of several clubs, one of the top soccer players in my school, and, most importantly, the head of my class. I had friends who were whites, blacks, Hispanics, nerds, and dummies. Even though at times I really wished to have a best friend, I did not mind knowing many people and being moderately close to all of them.

Throughout my first two years in the United States, I found most American people friendly and understanding. But I was disappointed in how little Americans know about the world. In many ways, American people are very self-centered and the American government acts only out of its own self-interest. For instance, in today's crisis with Iraq they are considering punishing Iraq on its own. The interest of the United States in this kind of country is clear: to ensure that oil, an important aspect of the American economy, remains obtainable in the Middle East. During the war in Bosnia, the American government did not let my people defend ourselves, since French and Russians disagreed with the policy that would let my people get weapons to defend ourselves. While the people of my country were dying, the Western world merely watched, not risking involvement because there was no real profitable interest in a country like Bosnia. I was surprised when I talked to some people who had no clue that there was a war in my country or even where my country was located.

One time at school a girl asked me where my accent comes from. I told her that I was from Bosnia; she commented that I had a cute accent. I thanked her for her compliment, but then she asked, "Where is Bosnia? Isn't that in Russia or something?" She was very embarrassed when I told her that Bosnia was located in the Balkans and that it was part of former Yugoslavia. In some way this unconcern angered me, but I knew that I had no right to blame American people for this ignorance and that I had to look at myself first. Even though I was generally informed about conflicts in the world, when I was home in Bosnia I was not troubled that so many people were without freedom, food, and health. I wish that I never had to experience what I did to learn the lessons of freedom. The fact that so many Americans took their freedom for granted bothered me, and even though I wanted to forget about my past and look toward my future, I decided to start talking about my war experiences to wake them up from the dream that the world is perfect. Speaking at schools, churches, mostly in front of young people, I felt a great satisfaction when young people came to me and said, "Mr. Hodzic, thank you so much for your speech. I learned a lot from it. Yes, I do take so many things for granted." I knew that I was doing a good thing. Freedom is the most precious thing a person can have, and I am determined to use my experience to teach Americans its value.

Of my college acceptances, my acceptance into Dartmouth came last, and I knew it was my first choice. There was something about Dartmouth and its people that made me believe that it was perfect for me. A beautiful campus, friendly people, a great academic institution. When I read my acceptance letter, I was so excited that I ran around the house several times yelling, "Yes! Yes . . . I got in." To make things better, they gave me a financial aid package that was nearly a full scholarship. My mother cried, and my father and our American family friend who helped me with college applications were smiling so that they would not cry. I hugged them all, one after another. The beginning of a good dream had begun. It was time for me to discover a new world, meet new people, and learn about different perspectives and different cultures.

Spending four days in the New Hampshire wilderness on a freshman outing trip gave me a chance to make my first friends at Dartmouth. To get to know each other better we had to talk about our backgrounds. At first I was a little uncomfortable telling my story, but eventually I felt almost privileged to tell these people about Bosnia. As I informed them of my culture and my world, I felt an incredible joy and pride, particularly when my peers appeared fascinated by my story. I was happy because my peers seemed to want to meet someone unlike themselves. I felt that I was already contributing to Dartmouth. It seemed that after this trip I was even more excited about this college. Meeting my roommate, an event I was anxious about, turned out to be a very positive experience. He was from the South, and he told me about the politeness of southerners, and proved it by the way he listened to me and was genuinely interested in my stories about Bosnia. After a few weeks, my roommate and I became close friends, and we would talk about everything, including women.

I was very interested in finding a girlfriend when I came to Dartmouth. After all, I thought Dartmouth was nothing like high school, and women here were much more mature. I was hoping to finally find someone who was looking for a nice guy instead of a macho man! Every time that I had someone particular in mind, it seemed like the same thing always happened: I would see her in a fraternity basement, drunk to the point where she could not stand. Even though it might sound picky, I never found women attractive who drink to the point that someone can take advantage of them. I also must admit that I attributed my lack of luck in dating to the fact that I was from a different country and that there was something I lacked that native-born U.S. men possessed. I had a cute accent, but that was about it. It seemed at first that the only thing to do was give up and just be friends with everyone.

I first visited a fraternity on my first weekend at Dartmouth. Even though freshmen were not allowed in them in the fall term, I got in without a problem because I am relatively large and I went with a sophomore. I found it interesting, though, that my size, strength, and muscularity were advantageous. I felt that females, and males even more so, had much respect for my strength. I was known all over campus as "Big Al." Entering the fraternity, all I could see was a basement packed full of people. They all looked drunk, and the noise level was so high that there was no doubt that most of the students there were intoxicated. In the corner of the basement there were a couple of large guys, who were, as I was told, football players. Suddenly they began yelling something and threw a trash can at the wall. This scene of large men hitting the wall and screaming was enough—I knew that it was time for me to leave. This was the Dartmouth that I did not know about. Even though I knew Dartmouth had a bad reputation for alcohol consumption, I had tried to ignore that fact. That night I could not sleep, and I don't really know why. Maybe it was because I never saw anything like that in my life, or maybe because I was just very surprised with the number of people who were drinking.

I have never tried alcohol in my life, and the idea of getting drunk has never impressed me much. When I went to alcoholic parties, at times it seemed like I did not belong. I kept going, though, because it was the only thing to do. I did not want to be the exception or not be "cool" because I did not party. In fact I went to one fraternity much more often than others. In it, alcohol wasn't such a big priority, and there were even other people there who did not drink. I guess drinking is one part of American culture (and specifically Dartmouth culture) that I refuse to accept. From all I have learned and everything I have seen about alcohol, I have come to the conclusion that alcohol doesn't bring anything good to people's lives. Given that Dartmouth's social life is largely based on alcohol, I am determined to be different in this regard.

Blending socially, however, was easier for me than finding my feet academically. I was so excited to be at Dartmouth that I embarked on many things, and I did not have time to concentrate fully on any one thing. It seemed to me at first that everyone around me was so much smarter than I was. At times I was very impressed with what people had to say, which made me wonder if I was at the right school. This is where my determination to succeed came in. I could not give up, I could not disappoint myself and my parents. It was time to show my mental strength and determination to succeed. By hard work I was able to show everyone that this was the right place for me, and that I deserved to be at this college.

Although many students had intelligent things to say in the classroom, at times I was surprised by how little they knew about the world outside of college. For instance, when we talked about moral reasoning in my men's studies class, "The Masculine Mystique," I was amazed to hear the type of moral conflict that a student chose to discuss. A major conflict of his was whether or not he should allow his roommate to copy his CD collection. I said to myself, "Is this really something that he sees as a significant dilemma, a critical challenge?" It seemed to me that he must never have experienced anything that would represent a true conflict. He always had everything in his life and he had never seen another world, the world in which there are hungry and homeless people, the world of wars and natural disasters. One doesn't learn these things at places like Dartmouth, a college that is academically prestigious and mostly white, where an example of a worrisome problem is underage drinking. All I hope is that in some way, I and others with similar experiences can teach those people who know very little about the imperfect world that there is much more to learn.

Part of that imperfect world comes back to haunt me no matter how hard I try to put my past away and move on to the future. In a newspaper headline, in conversations at the family dinner, and particularly in dreams, memories of Bosnia flood back—sometimes I am striding down Prijedor's main street with my friends, a phalanx of young men, brimming with life, laughing at girls who catch our eyes; more often, nightmares of the concentration camp with its screams and despair jolt me awake.

At home in Connecticut last Thanksgiving break, my parents showed the family a tape made of my cousin Subhija's wedding five or six years before the war started. The groom's family had come to collect the bride; most of the villagers attended. The party took place on the first floor of my uncle's summer home set on a flourishing fruit farm. The floor was just an open space and perfect for the festivities.

As they readied themselves for the film, my father and mother sat huddled together on the sofa. Once the tape began to roll, none of us spoke a word. The screen was blank for a few seconds, but we could hear traditional Bosnian folk music played on the accordion and guitar. Usually, I love this music, but now I felt strangely sad and apprehensive. When the picture came in, we saw happy villagers dressed in their best clothes—men in suits and ties, women in beautiful long dresses. Some of them sat at tables, eating and toasting each other with their glasses—full of *sljivovica*, a strong brandy made from my uncle's juicy plums—held high. The other villagers danced or stood around in clusters. On the screen was vibrancy and joy; in our living room was silence and sadness. It seemed all of us were staring at the television without blinking an eye. I noticed that my mother was on the verge of tears, and my father took her hand in his hands. She was able to keep from crying until her twenty-year-old nephew, Fikret, came into view. The image showed him close up, singing lustily, his arms raised high in joy. My mother broke down: "They killed him! They killed him! And he was so innocent and young! Those bastards killed him!"

I didn't know what to say, but felt that if I didn't say something, I too would break into tears. As I asked, "How was he killed?," I felt the vibration in my voice, and it was as though pieces of iron were piercing my throat. My father answered since my mother couldn't. "He was killed in front of his house with his mother and father watching; he was shot in the neck from a distance of a few inches." Pretending that I had to go to the bathroom, I left the room. I went outside because I desperately needed fresh air. While I tried to inhale as much air as I could, tears streamed down my face. I wasn't strong enough to hold them in. I had to cry. No, it wasn't fair for my cousin to die so young and innocent. No, it wasn't right that so many other innocent people like my cousin died—died for no reason. And I, now exactly the same age as he was in the film, am somehow alive.

There are two highlights in my Dartmouth career so far: meeting my girlfriend and being a member of the crew team. Both of these have made an incredible impact on me as a person and helped me in my acculturation. As I mentioned earlier, I never really had a single best friend. Meeting my girlfriend, Heather, gave me a best friend, and also a friend who was always there for me, ready to listen. From the beginning I knew that we had a lot in common: We were raised in similar ways, we both had the same respect for our parents, we were both competitive and hard-working, and neither of us drank. She was special in many ways, but the fact that she did not drink really made her truly unique. Once I met her, I did not care anymore about my past, in which I was unsuccessful in dating. All that mattered was her. At times I wondered how I found her, someone who is so caring, funny, hard-working, focused, and beautiful. At times Heather reminds me of my mother: There is nothing that can stop her when she wants to achieve something. She is a very strong woman, something that I admire very much. I adore her and know that she loves me for who I am. Heather is one of the best things that has happened to me, and I look forward to our future together.

Before meeting Heather, I wondered what it would be like to date someone from a different culture. At the beginning of our relationship, I did not know how Heather would react to my differences, so I did not tell her much about my past. I asked myself, "How is she going to react to the fact that I am a Bosnian Muslim, that I don't eat pork and don't drink? How was I going to explain my fasting during the month of Ramadan? How were her parents going to react?" So when Heather became interested in learning my language and told me that she would not eat pork, I was very impressed, for this meant that she wasn't just interested in Almin the good-looking athlete. Heather's approach to me meant that while I was adopting a more American way of life, I always had that option of calling myself a Bosnian.

And Heather's parents see me as their daughter's boyfriend, who is very good to her. Since the time I met them they have always respected me and my differences. They admired me for not drinking, and they were interested in my religion. In fact, one time after I had fasted for a whole day they prepared a large meal for me, which meant the world to me, for it showed that not only Heather, but also her parents, accepted and appreciated me for who I am. In our relationship, I have discovered things about myself that I never realized before. I have, for example, realized that I am a very emotional person. Even though I look strong and tough, I don't have a hard time crying in front of her. Being next to her I find a safe haven, where I can express myself the way I feel.

The other highlight of my Dartmouth experience so far is being involved in sports. I played soccer in high school, but I did not know if I was good enough to play at Dartmouth. Because of my size, the crew coach was determined to have me try out. Since then, crew has become a way of life. Being the strongest on the freshman team helped me become one of the most powerful rowers. Crew gave me a chance to make some close male friends, to become physically and mentally stronger, and to enjoy teamwork. This year, as a sophomore, I am on the varsity team, and that makes it more challenging and more fun. Crew is much more than a sport; it has taught me many things, such as determination, persistence, and how to push myself to reach goals I never thought possible. And although I cannot be as open with my friends as I am with Heather, I feel my best male friends to be members of the team. After losing my closest friends in Bosnia to death and disappearance, crew practice means the stability of being surrounded by my teammates, my friends.

I am now more American than Bosnian. Or to be more precise, I feel more American outside, while inside I am holding on to the Bosnian values my parents taught me. I am perfectly happy with the way I have accepted American culture and incorporated my Bosnian values. Embracing American ways of life has helped me to adjust here at Dartmouth, and keeping some of the Bosnian values has helped me to view things from a more neutral point of view. I think that by integrating two cultures, you learn more about yourself, about the people that surround you, and about the world in general.

My opinion of Dartmouth has changed in some ways; I don't have that perfect image of it anymore. Although my relationships and experiences with crew have made my Dartmouth experience incredible, I realize that this college is just a part of the world we live in. Alcohol abuse, sexual abuse, and rape all exist here, no matter how much I don't want to admit it. But in the end, I consider myself lucky, and I think that every person at Dartmouth should feel fortunate as well. My experiences have taught me that as long as you have your freedom, you should consider yourself lucky. I went through a war and many situations near the brink of death, yet here I am—getting a superb education, sharing a wonderful relationship, living with good friends, being a successful athlete, and being accepted for who I am. I could not ask for more.

Where do I see myself in ten years? I hope to achieve my American Dream. I want to be a successful businessman, have a white house with a pool, and a happy family with whom I can share the positive and negative lessons I have learned from living in two cultures. This partially means raising my children in the American way, but also letting them know about the different world that I have come from. I am grateful to this country for giving me freedom, and I'll be glad to call myself American in a few years, but I'll never forget being in a firing line and starving in a concentration camp. I'll never forget my endless running through wheat fields. I'll never forget milking cows and being a farm boy. These are things that will stay with me as long as I live.

Finding Solace in the Familiarity of Myself

Lai Heng Foong
Malaysia

I no longer feel connected to a particular race, culture, language, or background, but to me and myself. My discovering this was simply a recognition of who I am, or rather who I have come to be. It was a reaction to feeling rejected by my own country and wanting to find a sense of belonging and permanence in my new home overseas. I have always been self-reliant, which, as I have felt my way around unfamiliar environments, has helped me define the sphere in which I could feel totally comfortable and self-assured.

The reflection on my identity began in response to questions that were put to me when I first stepped foot in a foreign land. I spent two years in Canada, and then moved to the United States, where I have lived for the past four years, except for a year spent abroad in different parts of the world. Everywhere I have gone, I have been asked where I come from, what my background was, my ethnicity. As I began to incorporate and assimilate the cultures that I was exposed to during my travels, I realized that my response to those innocuous questions became more complicated, and found that I could no longer give a simple answer. I began to question my ethnic, cultural, and national identities, which were constantly evolving as I settled into the lifestyles of these "foreign" people. I started to address issues of race, socialization, politics, and gender roles in a more concrete manner, which was imposed by the structure learned during my sojourn abroad, so that gradually the borders between foreign and familiar became blurred and undefined.

The circumstances that led to my dislocation from the familiarity of my home set a precedent that was to shape my subsequent years. Initially, I had to develop my own sense of security since I was so far away from home. Many people feel that language helps provide security and reassurance when they are in an unfamiliar environment, but having gone through four very different education systems in three languages of instruction, I feel that language has never offered me any permanent solace. I was fluent in English when I arrived in North America, so language was not a barrier to my settling in there, but my competence was not always positive; it allowed me too often to pass as Canadian or American, even when I felt most excluded.

I am always stumped when I am asked my mother tongue, a more frequent question than I would wish. The truth is, I do not have one. My parents spoke different Chinese dialects—my father Cantonese and my mother Hokkein—so they communicated with each other in English. I spoke Hokkein to my mother and Cantonese to my father, so if both of my parents were present, there would be two languages going on at the same time. My siblings and I conversed in Hokkein, because our mother was with us more often than our father. When I went to Chinese primary school, I learned a third Chinese dialect, Mandarin, which was the medium of instruction.

From the Mandarin school I moved to a Malay-language secondary school, where I was immersed in a completely different language once again. My close friends, however, spoke English, not Malay, and although I am most fluent in English, I did not start learning this language formally until I was age nine. However, I have long felt an affinity for the language, probably because my parents spoke to each other in English; they never truly learned each other's dialect throughout their marriage. I feel even more attached to English now because I have reached adulthood in English-speaking countries; it has become the language of my dreams. I have been asked about my mother tongue so many times that I am beginning to get irritated by the assumption that I will give a simple answer, which is not possible because of my complicated background.

It has been easy to convince myself that I have left my background behind. Although I appreciate my past for having shaped me, I no longer feel an intimacy with it. Perhaps I have merely put my past into a back closet in my consciousness, but I no longer turn to it for assurance. There is a large gap between who I was in Malaysia and who I am now, which sometimes makes me feel alienated when I visit home.

Through having to sort out my conflicts of identity and the paradoxes of my self-definition, I have learned it is easier to live in the present when one is unencumbered by the past. To understand this, one must understand the past I have moved away from. I was born and grew up in Kuala Lumpur, the capital of the island state of Penang, Malaysia. My ancestry is Chinese, but I have never really felt all the cultural and racial implications of my ethnicity. In school, I always had Malay, Indian, and Chinese friends. I never thought that I was "different" from my friends of other ethnic backgrounds because of my different skin color, or that my facial features somehow reflected a fundamental difference in my abilities or personality.

Politically, however, I have not been so unaffected. Malaysia, on the surface, appears to be a racially harmonious nation with three major races—Malays, Chinese, and Indians—but personal experience has shown me otherwise. Although racial discrimination has never been documented, I have experienced direct discrimination that has not been and probably will never be recognized as such by the authorities. Malaysians have always struggled to define a national identity, but trying to cross ethnic barriers has been difficult, primarily because one group has dominated all the important decisions. I always felt that I lived in a society divided into a few cultural subgroups whose identities remain distinct.

My own knowledge of the situation in Malaysia has been shaped in part by the outlook that I have gained in North America. While filling in applications for American colleges, I was struck by the fact that stating one's race on the application was optional. In contrast, we are required to state our race on all official documents at home or they will not be processed. Thus we are constantly reminded of our race and ethnicity. As we grow older, we begin to notice that we are "different," not simply because of our facial features, language, or religion, and these differences become actual barriers to opportunities that we rightly deserve. The Malays call themselves *bumiputeras*, which means "people of the land." In a country that claims to be a multiethnic society, that name suggests the actual political climate that non-Malays find themselves in. In the Malay-dominated society, I am constantly reminded that I am Chinese. I am a foreigner in my own country.

This racial divide is a legacy of Malaysia's history of British rule.

When the British began to relax their hold on their Asian colonies, the nationalist movement in Malaysia took shape. Because the Chinese and Indians were not yet firmly established, the Malays were the prime movers in the struggle for independence. The Malays believe that this justifies their claims to the right to govern the country. Several special privileges for Malays were written into the constitution as part of the settlement for independence; since then, the Malays have maintained their stronghold in the political arena and have introduced policies institutionalizing many privileges for themselves in property, business, and education. These policies caused repercussions for me at the end of my secondary education.

I had a very rigid education. The school system in Malaysia thrives on competition; parents encourage it, students put up with it, and the system perpetuates it. Looking back now, I realize that I was lucky to have come out of the experience unscathed, but I also know that I was one of the system's success stories. My success was due in part to my ability to adapt well in different situations, and to rely on my own inner strength. Many students are not as lucky.

My primary school in Lai Meng demanded an astonishing level of conformity. I always had a ponytail tied back with blue, white, or black ribbons. Girls were required to wear a dark blue pinafore that could not be more than an inch above the knees, a starched white shirt underneath, white socks folded to the ankles, and clean shoes polished white as snow (or as we said, "blancoed"). Tedious chores such as polishing our shoes had to be completed every week, and prefects in Standard Six (equivalent to grade twelve) checked that these regulations were complied with. We also had to stand when the teacher entered the class, greet her, and then recite the multiplication tables. These rules were intended to instill a "sense of conformity to authority" at a young age, as in my culture, respect for authority is considered an essential childhood acquisition. A child is taught never to question the authority of elders. Nothing short of a revolution could create individualism to counter this conformity. I have hated white shoes ever since.

In my subsequent years of secondary school, I learned how to survive on the borderline of the rules, while thriving on the competition that permeates the school system and excelling in my studies. My education in Malaysia can be best exemplified by my determination to succeed in everything I did, which was the only way to gain recognition and separate myself from the masses in a system that thrives on conformity. This determination allowed me to leave my past behind, and begin a new life in North America.

The catalytic moment in my decision to leave my past was my first direct experience with racism. As a result of the racially based selection policies in education that I alluded to earlier, universities have quota systems for the different races. Some programs exclude certain races, and I was the victim of this policy. When I applied for a university, I found that ethnic Chinese were denied entry into the matriculation programs at local universities and that scholarships for foreign universities were also dictated by race.

I was one of the top students in my city in the National Examinations, and was full of confidence and hope for the future. I wanted to be doctor, and although I had heard that the matriculation program for medicine at the University of Malaya and other local universities was racially exclusive, I wanted to apply anyway, if only to dispel these rumors and satisfy my own curiosity. I was so idealistic then. Armed with this optimism, I applied to study medicine at local universities and in Britain. I was rejected outright for both programs, with no explanation. In the meantime, I discovered, to my dismay and frustration, that friends who had not performed half as well as I had secured places at local universities or, even better, obtained scholarships to study overseas.

I could not believe it. After years of denial and disbelief, I had to accept that racial discrimination is a very real phenomenon in Malaysia and that I was its victim. How else could I explain the rejection of my applications when friends whose results were less impressive had managed to obtain places in universities and overseas scholarships? At first, I could not face the reality of discrimination, because I knew deep down that doing so would give me the impetus to leave the country. It was easier to blame myself.

I also was not ready to leave my family and all that was familiar to me, yet destiny was already leading me in that direction. I found an opportunity to leave everything behind—my frustrations, my disappointment, and my life at home. An advertisement in the newspaper offered a full scholarship to a chain of schools called the United World Colleges, established by a German named Kurt Hahn. Hahn envisioned that bringing students of diverse cultural and social backgrounds from all around the world to study and learn together could deepen their understanding of each other and help promote peace through this process of mutual learning. These aims spoke directly to my own nearly shattered idealism and rekindled my hopes. Determined to put my past behind me, I applied for the scholarship and was accepted at the Lester B. Pearson United World College in Canada, with a full scholarship from the Canadian International Development Agency. This is how I ended up in an idyllic high school on the western Canadian coast.

I left Malaysia with a sense of relief, because I no longer had to deal with the alienation I felt at home and I could be released from the bitterness of being rejected by my own country. And so, with these emotions whirling in my mind, I boarded the plane bound for a faraway land. I was immediately able to relate to the more relaxed and personalized approach to education in North America, which is tailored to the needs of students at all levels of instruction and abilities, and allows for more flexibility in the curriculum. The North American system also encourages more self-expression, something that is sadly lacking in the Malaysian system.

Despite the feeling of exclusion I had felt as a minority in Malaysia, the interethnic experience that I had been immersed in there did serve me well in my life overseas, specifically in Canada and the United States. Perhaps my disappointment and frustration at the treatment I had received from my own country and my desire to search elsewhere for opportunities that were denied me at home also helped to cushion the "culture shock" I was told to expect when arriving in a new land. I eased in to my first "foreign" experience in Canada almost painlessly. I must admit, though, that, in retrospect, the environment at my new home made me feel more welcome than if I had gone to a "normal" high school. When I first arrived at the Lester B. Pearson United World College, I thought I had found paradise.

The college sits on the southern tip of Vancouver Island, on a piece of land along the waterfront. The buildings are nestled among coniferous trees, and the place has a feeling of seclusion and peace. I found solace in the tranquil surroundings, even more than in the school's physical beauty. I felt it was a welcoming place in which I could begin my new life. I was eager to leave my past behind—the disappointment, the pain, the alienation. The peaceful surroundings and the welcome I received from my roommates gave me courage to sever my spiritual ties with my country, and though I missed my family, I was not homesick. There were so many distractions and exciting adventures that I couldn't dwell on sentimental feelings of being separated from my family.

I was immediately excited by the prospect of sharing classes and activities with people from different parts of the world. While I was at the school, the student body was made up of two hundred students from seventy-two countries. No one group could be singled out as a minority because we all were minorities, except for the Canadians. I was thrilled at the chance to meet people from all around the world, though it was quite overwhelming at first. I could hardly remember the names of the students' countries, some of which I had never heard before, let alone the students' names!

The next two years proved to be a blissful, stimulating period of exposure to other cultures. This gradual immersion in diversity inculcated in me the value of not associating skin color or nationality with inherent personality. I became convinced that a common bond holds us together—our humanity—which transcends all barriers. I learned to appreciate the true meaning of love, peace, and international understanding. Although we sometimes made fun of these oft-used words, we understood them as the means by which our life paths had become intertwined.

At Pearson, we were taught to think for ourselves and to formulate our own opinions about different issues. It was here that I gained a deeper understanding of the cultural and social biases that shape one's opinion of the world. It was also here that I started learning philosophy, and my humanistic leaning, which had been suppressed by years of a science-based education, finally found expression. I had always felt stifled in school in Malaysia, where one is not taught to form opinions, but to follow the teachers' views. Even in history, a subjective discipline, we were never asked what we thought in our exams. We only reported what historians thought or our teachers' interpretations of historical events. I never questioned the validity of my teachers' views. The knowledge gained at Pearson, however, was always supported by a self-reflective perspective, which deepened my understanding of many subjects and relationships.

What I found exhilarating about Pearson was that every day was a new experience. Suddenly I felt I could do whatever my heart desired; there was no code of behavior that I had to abide by. My newfound expressiveness not only helped me academically; it also helped me establish closer friendships and ties. My imagination and adventurous spirit were finally given free rein. I learned to do many things that I would never have dreamed of, among them scuba diving and rock climbing. I felt that I was exploring potential that had lain dormant for many years. I was so intent on discovering my hidden potential that I did not even have time to dwell on the fact that I was in a foreign country, so it was relatively easy for me to adapt to my new environment.

At Pearson, I became more aware of events outside of my own little world. Being an international group, the students were an excellent resource for information on world events. When the Berlin Wall fell, for example, the German students gave a presentation and held a celebration afterward in our student and faculty common room. World issues ceased to be just reports from news channels; we felt connected to the issues because we had friends who were affected by them.

This sense of connection was heightened during a trip to Europe in between school years. This trip was a significant turning point in my life. I learned much from my West German boyfriend about the rich traditions and history of the places we visited, and we stayed with other Pearson students, which personalized the experience even more and increased our understanding of cultural nuances. We traveled through England, France, Italy, Yugoslavia, West Germany, Austria, Greece, and the Netherlands. I fell in love with the romanticism of Europe, with the history that underlies the castles and cathedrals that we visited and the intellectual traditions that have spanned many centuries and affected so many aspects of twentieth-century modernization. Malaysia is a relatively new country compared to Europe. Our real history began in the fifteenth century, and we have almost no buildings left from that period. I was fascinated by the beauty of age and by the splendor of the scenery in Europe. I was mesmerized by the cultures of the people, even though I was reminded time and again of the subversion of my country by European forces.

Beyond the visual and experiential overload of the trip, I felt that Europe changed my whole perspective on life. I felt liberated, free to embrace a new self. I looked at my surroundings with clearer eyes, and from a new perspective, enhanced by the greater worldview I had acquired. The changes were occurring so fast that I could hardly keep up with my emotions.

Having experienced virtually no culture shock in Canada, I thought that I had already adapted well to North American culture and was ready for American university life. I was severely disappointed, however, when I began my stay at Dartmouth College. Little did I know that I had been living a utopian existence during my two years in Canada. I was not at all prepared to face college life in the United States. I had not heard anything about Dartmouth before I arrived in Hanover, except that it was an Ivy League institution with a reputation for academic excellence. This information certainly did not prepare me for the isolation I felt during my first few days in the Dartmouth community.

I arrived at Dartmouth not knowing where to go, desperately wondering how and where to place myself, and was immediately whisked away on a freshman trip that was both physically and emotionally grueling. This trip is for many their introduction to Dartmouth. During the trip into the New Hampshire woods I felt culture shock for the first time in all its negative aspects. Because I spoke English very well, all the other freshmen on the trip assumed that I was American. People assume that if you are from a foreign country you cannot speak English very well. As I did not fit the stereotype, my classmates thought that my strange accent came from living abroad as an American, or something to that effect. In reality, I could not have felt any less American.

I had come on the trip with great expectations for this outdoor event, which everyone had told me would be a bonding experience, but all my expectations were quickly dispelled. People were talking to each other, but not communicating, not sharing. They laughed about things that I did not find funny. They impersonated characters on the television show *Saturday Night Live* and laughed at their antics; they shared common high school experiences, like playing varsity baseball or going to the high school proms, leaving me alone in my difference. There seemed to be a subtle pressure to conform, to share similar experiences, as though the similarity could somehow overshadow their feelings of alienation. The irony of that experience often returned to me later.

When they finally realized that I was not American, my trip mates were curious, but their curiosity did not extend beyond asking "Oh, where are you from?" and responding "Wow, Malaysia, that's neat!" I felt like a curiosity or a novelty. Later, the question about my country of origin was one of the most common questions that I was asked. I would have liked to answer "nowhere," which, of course, was not what my questioners expected. Nevertheless, it seems to be the answer closest to my heart. I often find myself at a loss in trying to answer that question for myself.

Despite my sense of displacement in North America, I have learned to define myself as an individual and accept the responsibility that this recognition brings. Most Americans are fervent advocates of individualism. Coming from a society that is very communal, I was interested to observe how much North Americans value personal space. People here are also more ready to express their emotions and opinions, unchained by the conventions or stifling traditions that pervade my culture. Asians' unwillingness to draw attention to ourselves, to stand out from the crowd, perhaps makes North Americans think of us as submissive or more ready to compromise. To a great extent this label is justified, as Asians are more low-key in their approach to many things, but quietness does not necessarily equal submissiveness.

One of the things I miss most when I return home is the sense of freedom I feel in North America. In Malaysia I feel I always have to conform to certain codes of behavior and adhere to hierarchical social structures, which restricts my freedom. In North America, I do not have to restrict my comments that might challenge the hierarchical structures that characterize my society. I no longer have to subjugate myself to them. I also feel more accepted for who I am in my North American home. The desire for individualism makes youths in North America separate themselves from their parents much earlier than their Asian counterparts. My freshman-year roommate at Dartmouth shocked me by proudly telling me that she had started working when she was thirteen so that she could be more independent from her parents. I never dreamed of asserting my independence at that age. My father never allowed me to work when I was in school because I was too young. He believed, as do many Asian parents, that all things must happen at the right time. My parents dictated what I was to do in my free time.

Because I have always been self-reliant, I took to the North American emphasis on individualism quite naturally. I thrive in an environment that allows me to express my opinions and feelings boldly, a marked change from the person I was, and, to a certain extent, still am when I return home. I profoundly wish that I had been able to talk easily with my parents about feelings and emotions when I was growing up, and wish that we could have been more comfortable discussing our problems instead of hiding behind a facade of ignorance or, even worse, pretending that everything was all right.

This was especially true when my father was laid off, which affected him deeply and caused tremendous upheaval in my family. In general, the man is still the breadwinner of the family, especially in a patriarchal society like Malaysia. I now realize that most of my father's behavior arose from his inability to accept that the roles in our household had reversed. My parents never talked about the situation, so as the family structure gradually changed, their relationship suffered. In my society, people do not talk about their problems, and usually "just grin and bear it." In contrast, many Americans resolve a problem by discussing it. A little more expressiveness in my family would have helped my parents iron out their differences. For this reason, I consciously try not to keep things to myself, although I inevitably fall back into the habit, which has been so deeply inculcated in my sense of values. I still am not totally comfortable in talking about my feelings, but at least now I sometimes try, though my upbringing has not made that easy.

My parents always made sure that their children were kept in their clearly defined roles, which separated parent and child. They did not believe in sharing their emotions or opinions beyond what concerned our physical well-being. Their attitude did not change when I grew older. Most activities were functional; we ate dinner without talking, and then went about our own business. One of the first things that I was attracted to in North America was the different relationship that people I knew had with their parents. I find the relative casualness and lack of hierarchical definition in their bonds quite appealing.

When frustrated with my family's lack of communication, I have felt that my family members are separated by an unbridgeable gulf. Thus, from a very young age, I began to direct my thoughts inward. I needed to find some way to develop and nurture the words that I could not utter, the thoughts that I could not express. Out of necessity, I became my own best friend. Though I am extroverted, I hide my thoughts within.

Most Chinese families are as emotionally undemonstrative as mine. Thus it is ironic that Chinese families are known for being loyal to a family member to the point of dying for a cause, and yet, they wouldn't dream of showing their feelings by hugging their children or saying "I love you." In fact, one of the first things I noticed when I came to the United States was that people say "I love you" all the time. It was a very strange feeling to hear the words I had so yearned for being uttered everywhere. Pop stars say it to their fans, mothers say it to their children, friends say it to each other. At first, I thought I had missed something important; however, I have learned since that the words do not necessarily have the intensity or meaning that I had expected.

Although I still care for my family deeply, I no longer feel totally at home when I return to Malaysia. The experience I have gained from being abroad for many years has not only shaped my perspective on things, it has also been in some ways incorporated into my being. The narrow view of the world I had before I left Malaysia is no longer sufficient to contain the experiences I have had since. I feel that I have assimilated many aspects of Western culture, and now relate to Western values and ways of being more comfortably than I relate to the ones I grew up with. In fact, I would not call the culture and values that I grew up with mine anymore, because they were never really mine, and now never will be.

There are many more elements of Western culture that I feel at home with that are alien to the social and intellectual traditions that I grew up with. Intellectual stimulation is of utmost importance for me, and I am fascinated by the European intellectual tradition. I love the ideas of Kant and Hegel; I enjoy reading Nietszche and Sartre; and I am fascinated by the ideas of Marx, whose writings are banned in Malaysia. I enjoy discussions that explore the many facets of philosophy, psychology, or English literature. I have stayed at friends' homes where I could fully explore these facets, and felt totally "at home" in supposedly foreign settings. In Malaysia, I have very few opportunities to feel as comfortable, both socially and intellectually. On a rather superficial level, I find that I like Western opera more than Chinese: Pavarotti and Freni singing a duet in Puccini's *La Boheme* sends rapturous tingles through me, whereas the shrill sounds of Chinese opera are unbearable. I would rather watch *Swan Lake* than *Tarian Lilin* (Candle Dance). When I try to place myself, I often feel lost and forlorn. My love for my family is unquestionable, and yet I constantly yearn for something more from them, something fundamentally important to me that they are unable to satisfy. I feel a stranger in my own home and in my own society.

Indeed, my view of my role in my society has changed drastically since I have lived abroad. Before being exposed to strong feminist ideas, I never questioned the custom that the women (and only women) volunteer to help the hostess with the cooking for family gatherings, while the men sit in the living room smoking or chatting at leisure. I notice now that it is always the women who serve the food, and the women who ensure that everyone has had enough to eat. My father never set foot in the kitchen, except when he felt inspired and decided to cook. In such rare instances, he needed absolute authority in the kitchen and labored for hours to produce his dish. When it was finally laid out on the dining table, all eyes had to be on his dish, which we had to compliment or he would sulk the whole day.

Strong traditions govern how men and women should act in my society. A man is expected to be the breadwinner and the head of the family. A woman, on the other hand, is supposed to take care of the children and keep a "nice and presentable" home. Nowadays, under the influence of Western values, more women are getting an education and joining the work force, but they still have to keep house and take care of the children. You want liberation? Sure, have it—but don't forget to prepare dinner, clean diapers, and wash the dishes. Women also are not supposed to interfere with their husbands' affairs. Many women know nothing about their family's bank accounts, which are controlled by their husbands. The concept of a joint account is quite novel, and 50–50 sharing of property in a divorce exists only among Westerners.

Divorce is viewed as shameful and irresponsible, especially for women, who are expected to put their children's welfare before their own, and the social pressure to preserve an unhappy marriage is very powerful. The dialogue between the disillusioned wife and her relatives and friends—and even with herself—never ends. The disgruntled wife usually ends up conceding defeat. Many parents try to keep a marriage together at all costs, not only because of their union, but also because it is the symbol of the family unit. Following Confucian values, the Chinese believe that family values are very important. Even more important, though, is honor. Breaking up the family means abandoning a fundamental part of our heritage and losing face, another situation that Chinese avoid at all costs. I saw my mother struggle with all these issues as her marriage was breaking down, but she stuck to it, for her children.

My mother devoted her life to her children, ensuring that we had the best education possible. She always wanted to go to university, but was prevented from doing so by my grandfather, who refused to support her. Instead she found a job. In her time, most women became either teachers or nurses, and she chose the latter. She was determined that her children would not be denied opportunity as she was. Despite the disappointments in her own life, she derived strength from the conviction that her perseverance would lead to great opportunities and achievements for her children. With the influence of Western values, divorce is now more common in Malaysia, but traditions still play a big role in women's lives. I have come to appreciate my mother's spirit of selflessness even more after living in a culture that is often very self-centered and individualistic. When I find myself too self-directed, thoughts of my mother's sacrifice always help me put my life back in perspective.

After the initial shock I experienced at Dartmouth, I learned to adjust better to life at college. I realized early on in my college career that I did not share the same aspirations for my four years as my classmates did. College life is such a milestone in many American teenagers' lives. It is the threshold of adulthood, and, further, it is supposed to be the "best four years of your life." There were many "activities" one was expected to participate in as part of the college experience. On weekends, all that my undergraduate advisor group wanted to do was go have a fun time at fraternities and sororities. As this scene was not exactly my preferred social option, I felt alienated from my group immediately.

I learned much later from my freshman-year roommate that they all thought I was "too worldly," that I considered myself above them, which was not true at all. I could not understand why they would not try to relate to the difference they perceived in me, but instead ostracized me because of it. My "internationalism" was considered a detriment rather than an asset. For all its unabashed support of individualism, I have found mainstream American college life quite limited and restrictive. Young college students feel compelled to conform to a certain accepted norm, and yet again, I found myself striving hard to break away from the chains of conformity. This striving helped shape my college identity and further strengthened my self-definition.

Throughout my four years at Dartmouth, I have slowly gained confidence in the knowledge that I am different. The moment I made the decision to leave my country in search of a better future, I forfeited familiarity as a source of comfort and permanence in my life. I have learned to accept that I will always feel like a foreigner at first wherever I go, which is not necessarily a bad thing. Feeling at home will only come when I have found peace within myself. As soon as I accepted that reality, I more readily found friends who shared my aspirations and interests. I have managed to establish long-lasting bonds that I know I will always keep, and which have replaced my earliest impressions of Dartmouth.

This personal discovery made the transition to my next foreign experience one of my best experiences at Dartmouth. My term on the philosophy foreign study program in Edinburgh was a decisive point in my college career. I made many good friends in Edinburgh, all of whom were either English or Scottish. Again, I found myself withdrawing from the mainstream Dartmouth group, which disheartened me with its ability to re-create Dartmouth thousands of miles from the Hanover plain. Their experience seemed to be channeled and controlled through Dartmouth lenses, everything had to be measured by Dartmouth standards. I decided that I would not be chained by this nostalgia, especially with a wealth of new experiences to explore. I immediately ventured out on my own to make friends in Edinburgh with whom I had more in common.

The quiet time I had in Edinburgh was very conducive to my spiritual awakening. I have never been religious, but feel that I am very spiritual; in Edinburgh, my spirituality finally found a chance to develop into a more powerful guiding force in my life. I never felt more at peace with who I am than during that time of self-awakening. This spiritual journey continued as I spent my next term on an internship with a voluntary organization called the Student Health and Welfare Centers Organization (SHAWCO), based in Cape Town, South Africa. It was my first time on the vast continent of Africa, and although I know my experience in South Africa does not begin to describe the richness and diversity of that continent, I felt that I left with some measure of understanding of what that diversity encompassed.

While in Cape Town, I was involved in projects run by SHAWCO: I helped in a day hospital and a child-care center based in a "colored" community; participated in a Community Health Workers' project in a black township called Khayelitsha; and worked in a mobile clinic project with medical students from the University of Cape Town Medical School. I was fortunate to be exposed to all the main groups in South Africa. I lived with a friend from Pearson, who is from an upper-middle-class white family, but worked in colored and black areas. I found the multifaceted society fascinating, and I learned by simply observing everything around me. South Africa is a country full of paradoxes and unexpected ironies. These paradoxes reminded me of my own experience in Malaysia, and helped me form a more objective idea of what my experience meant to me. I could place the anguish that I had felt at home more in perspective, and realized that although I had been discriminated against, nothing in my life could compare to what my friends in the black townships had to endure.

Coming back one year ago to the comfortable life at Dartmouth from the extremes of my South African experience was hard at first, but my friends and my newfound emotional stability helped lend continuity and a sense of belonging to my homecoming. I learned to appreciate Dartmouth more and differently after my return and felt that I had entered a new phase in my Dartmouth experience. Although I sometimes complain about the apathetic student body, or lament the lack of social options in Hanover, I have been very fortunate to have the support structure at Dartmouth that has provided me with one of the best educations I could hope to get, and made possible a host of opportunities to explore different parts of the world and a wide variety of cross-cultural experiences.

I have been through many equally trying and good times at Dartmouth. I have adjusted to a new life, dealt with my father's death midway through my studies, established newfound closeness with my family, discovered my future goals, shared special moments with close friends, and simply appreciated Dartmouth as it is. All these experiences have shaped the terrain of my life at college and helped me form a better understanding of myself and my surroundings. I finally feel comfortable in America, comfortable in who I have become and, more importantly, who I will become. Now, as I prepare to begin a new phase of my life in another part of the United States, I know that it will be easier for me to slip into life in another place, with different people.

Through my experiences abroad, I have gained a deeper understanding of how different cultures socialize their citizens. Making a break with some of the traditions I have grown up with while keeping some others intact has been, at times, an estranging experience. Sometimes I feel no attachment to home, feel detached from my past, but a conversation I had with my grandmother when I went home for the first time after spending a year in the United States added a new dimension to my feelings. My grandmother is the embodiment of Eastern tranquillity and wisdom, and I used to find her very traditional and conservative. Before I left for Canada, she told me explicitly not to come home with a Caucasian boyfriend. "They are untrustworthy," she said. Thus, she surprised me with the alacrity with which she accepted my announcement that I had a Caucasian boyfriend. She told me that my description of my friends in my letters throughout my years abroad had gradually convinced her that Caucasians are not "untrustworthy" people. I realized that her initial hesitation was because the only Caucasians she had known before she met my friends were the British colonists she knew through my grandfather's work as a station master. She could not have known them well, since she spoke no English.

She said something to me another time that again showed me that she does not fit the label that I had too readily given her. She told me that if she could relive her life, she would want to be as educated as I am, and travel around the world. She also said that if she were as educated as I am, she would not get married, but would adopt children instead.

My first reaction was absolute shock. My grandmother could embrace an idea (single parenthood) that even I did not dare entertain at that time despite my education. But, after I had time to think about what she had said, I could understand why she had such inclinations. My grandmother married at age eighteen, which her family considered late, to a man she did not know. She had eight children and dedicated herself to bringing them up, while living with my grandfather who was a very chauvinistic man, the product of a very chauvinistic society. My grandmother was not allowed to do many things she would have liked to, but she accepted her fate with strength and dignity. This quiet acceptance did not prepare me for her admission of regret at the direction her life had taken.

My grandmother's confession showed me that no matter how hard I try to break away, I will always be connected to the traditions that have shaped me and that this heritage is not necessarily bad. I should not be so quick to pass judgment on the conservatism that I see at home, and to acquiesce in defeat to the idea that things will never change. Even though my grandmother had grown up in a society where women were second-class citizens, she still could develop a more liberated outlook. Her words emancipated me, because they showed me that I could change my condition; at the same time, they reminded me that I should not abandon my past and try to exist as a disconnected Asian. I am Asian, after all, and should appreciate my heritage.

I have said that I belong nowhere, but I think it is more accurate to say that I try hard to feel that I belong everywhere. I tend to seek out what I find appealing in the different cultures that I am exposed to and gradually incorporate those qualities into my own personality. I believe that one's identity can be formed and re-formed and that who I am is constantly in flux. In that dynamic process of change, I no longer feel exclusively bound to my culture, nationality, or background.

Reliance on myself has made it easier for me to adapt to new surroundings because I am not constantly trying to define my place in relation to where I was before. Instead, I try to reconcile myself to a new home by relying only upon myself, which provides a constancy that is needed in an unfamiliar environment. Finding solace in the familiarity of oneself provides a welcome sense of permanence.

After being away from home for so long, I have learned to accept the feeling of rejection from my home country. In fact, I no longer feel connected to a "home" country, and will never feel totally at home in Malaysia again, as it has given me too many painful memories. Those experiences led me to leave the country in the first place, to look for better opportunities and a brighter future. Once I separated myself from my country of origin and began to define my autonomous identity, the pain and sense of alienation dissipated. I no longer despaired about being rejected by my own country, or felt alienated being a foreigner newly arrived in North America. I finally can confront the pain and disillusion I felt when I left home for the first time and not be overwhelmed by anger and emotions. I have learned to shape my identity outside of my home country, within myself. In myself, I feel at home.

Although I have sometimes been challenged by foreign ways and habits, I have also incorporated some aspects of them into my identity. This fusion has sometimes made me feel transient or unrooted, but I have tried to sort out the paradoxes in who I am by adopting a philosophy that at first seems alienating. I remain strong in my determination not to be connected to a particular culture, language, or background. I have found new meaning in richer and closer relationships with my friends and family, and a more defined purpose in what I do. I hope this combination will, finally, lend a sense of permanence to my life.

Battles Without/Battles Within

Frode Eilertsen
Norway

2300 hours, military time, January 4, 1997. Bourrhoz, southeastern
Lebanon, ten miles north of the Israeli border. Five of us sit in the back
of a jeep, driving along the main road in the Bekaa Valley. At a
junction, the jeep turns off from the main road, reports its position to
HQ, turns off its lights, reduces its speed, crosses the line of lights,
civilization, and safety, and starts creeping downhill toward a
neighboring canyon popularly known as Hezbollah Highway. As the
headlights flick off, we look at each other, our eyes shining in the dark.
We extend our right hands, on which we all wear Lebanese friendship
rings, to form a circle, firmly clasp hands, and whisper "One for all. All
for one."

The jeep navigates a bend and a single light appears abruptly in the
distance, about half a mile away. Bourrhoz. We each load our weapon.
Ten seconds later we jump out of the jeep, which immediately takes off
back to "safety." We are now entirely alone, and will be so for ten
hours. If trouble erupts, help is more than twenty minutes away.

We spend the first hour adjusting to the night, sometimes with the
help of our night vision goggles, with each man spread out in a
defensive perimeter, collectively covering a 360 degree view. It is
deathly quiet. No birds, no animal cries, no wind, no movement—only
looming, damp air. It is roughly 80 degrees, yet we all wear wool
underwear and experience a definite chill; the contrast from the baking
oven during the day warrants proper dressing. Every man sits silent and
motionless, alone with his thoughts.

My own thoughts this particular night are complex. On this, the night before I am to leave Lebanon, I reflect back on the six-month odyssey that has brought me from my studies at Dartmouth College back to my native Norway, then to Bosnia, and finally to Lebanon with UN forces. I think most deeply of the contrasts between Bosnia and Lebanon: Bosnia, with the effects of five years of civil war physically visible in the landscape and the buildings, but even more in people's faces and in people's deep, deep hatred for the "other." As part of a heavily armed NATO war force in Bosnia, I was a peacemaker, rather than peacekeeper. Here in southern Lebanon, however, the international presence is a UN peacekeeping force; devoid of any heavy weapons like tanks, artillery, and airplanes, we must rely just as much on respect and diplomacy as on physical force. The result? All the warring factions struggle to kill each other, completely ignoring—even laughing at—the peacekeepers.

As my mind struggles with the contradictions inherent in international relations, reality reimposes itself, and it's time for our patrol to move on. Our vision and hearing adjusted to the night, we move slowly, stealthily, with every cell in our body on alert. Mostly we attempt to stay in the bushes, using the protection of natural cover as much as possible. When we must make nerve-wracking crossings of clearings, I am overwhelmed by a mixture of intense fear, a sensational awareness of life, and a resolute focus on the mission at hand. The light-red sand makes us feel illuminated, vulnerable, fragile; it requires immense willpower and self-discipline to refrain from running off into the darkness.

At last we reach our destination—a point where we have complete control over all movements in the valley. We position ourselves, camouflaged, yet maintaining unimpeded vision. The next six hours we wait for an "enemy" we pray won't come tonight. Lying next to each other, not even daring to whisper or move, we feel an unbreakable bond. And it is this unspoken fellowship—the silent sharing of the same thoughts, hopes, and fears—that I most vividly remember from Lebanon. It was the hardship and strain during the times when nothing did happen that was the hardest, most unbearable test of character. We had to be able to lie still, suppress our fear and imagination and stay focused on the patrol mission, stifling the urge to get up and run toward the warm lights of Bourrhoz in the distance. We had to stay calm instead, appear confident and competent, and be a mental support for the person a few yards away. Whether lying still with giant bugs, tarantulas, and scorpions crawling around us, or listening intently under paralyzing pressure as we peered into the night, switching between normal vision and night vision goggles, often with no radio communication to HQ due to bad transmission conditions—we realized that this was the part no training had prepared us for and no training ever could. My earlier military training as an officer in Norway, with its stressful, physically demanding exercises, had taught me and challenged me, forcing me to grow in ways I never had before: finding my limits and recognizing a primitive egotism that insisted I hold up better than the others in my group, instead of helping the weakest and committing myself to achieving success collectively. Despite this preparation, the true experience of war was an unparalleled test of personal courage for my men.

Nothing happens that night. The only enemy is our own imagination, which we once again defeat. After six long, dark, and frightening hours, we patrol back at dawn, and at 0700 hours we are picked up again. My last, long night is over. Three hours later, I cross the border at Metullah, on my way out of Lebanon toward Tel Aviv. At dinnertime, I am at Ben Gurion Airport, boarding a flight to Oslo. I have survived hell. I land late in the evening in Oslo on January 5, and spend the night repacking at home before boarding a KLM flight for Montreal the next morning. At 11 P.M. EST, I finally arrive at my destination, back at my new home—Hanover, New Hampshire, and Dartmouth College. I am back in Heaven, exactly forty-eight hours after my last patrol in hell.

I returned to Dartmouth with an intense appreciation of life, of people, of the little everyday things we all tend to take for granted. My patrols in Lebanon forever changed me and my perspective on life. Memories of the men who gave their lives so that people like me were able to return from war, and so that civilians could be spared from further atrocities of war, will remain with me forever. Today I still wear my Lebanese friendship ring. It is a daily reminder to make the most out of each day, and also of the extremely close friends I have around the world. My experiences at war left me with a need to make sure I spend the rest of my life in a meaningful way, doing my best for society and the world. I owe it to the people of Lebanon. I owe it to the friends we left behind. And I owe it to myself.

As I returned to Dartmouth College after a year of absence, with this vow fresh in my mind, and saw again the illuminated tower of Baker Library, tears of relief and happiness rolled down my cheeks. Knowing that one day I would see Dartmouth again was what had kept me going in the past few months. And now I was back. I returned for my sophomore year harboring an exaggerated, euphoric love for this college: its rugged physical surroundings and sense of tradition and history. I loved the opportunity to learn, both from my peers and from some of the world's most brilliant scholars, as well as the bond linking Dartmouth alumni through the generations.

This love notwithstanding, my experiences in Bosnia and Lebanon forced me to look at the campus, my peers, my education, with real concern. Something had happened to my friends while I was gone. They now seemed to me tired, disillusioned, and apathetic. The naive openness, the energy, and the adventurous attitude from freshman year had disappeared, and seemed to have been replaced by a complacency and, in some cases, a surrender to cynicism. Returning from a third world, ruined nation, to this artificial, wealthy, and resourceful haven, I wanted to grab its inhabitants and scream, *"NO!* Look around you! Realize what you've got! Don't waste four unique years of life here at Dartmouth. Never again will you be surrounded by so many talented people; never again will you have so many opportunities to learn and develop; never again will you be in an environment where everything is here for your delight. For God's sake, wake up, appreciate it, take full advantage of it before it's too late!"

My life so far has been an odyssey full of contradictions, from the war-torn land of Lebanon to the peaceful countryside of Dartmouth, as well as contradictions both external and internal. Simply put, I am driven by the clashes, conflicts, and forces generated by my contradictions. First, I seek and need meaning in my life. This aspect of my personality makes me intense, passionate, and focused on making the most out of every living moment. Second, I drift from context to context, very rarely making such deep connections as I did in Lebanon. This trait has turned me into a rootless, restless person constantly seeking and needing variation, but at the same time, afraid of attachments and very protective of my own privacy. Finally, I see myself as unconventional; while I have strong values and stand by my principles, I hold a philosophy that is distinctly utilitarian. I do have a core set of values, but I will do whatever it takes to achieve the goals I set, regardless of laws, conventions, and public opinion. I support actions and principles if they are good and efficient, not because they are the norm. I have come to defy convention; as my commander in the military, a man with seventeen years of experience in the special forces, used to say against conventionality, "Sacred cows make the best burgers."

If my free spirit and my conflicting personality traits bring about the most enriching experiences in my life, then it is my upbringing in Norway that originally created this complexity of spirit. On my many ski excursions with my father and walks with my mother, I grew fond of the outdoors, gaining values and perspectives that I still hold as fundamental. Mom always emphasized the sacredness of all living creatures, the majestic beauty of nature, and the need to protect and respect the environment. She taught me all about plants, trees, birds, insects, the animals of the forests.

Since my mother didn't work outside the home, she had time to spend with me, and I think I can safely assume that it is she who's responsible for the "good" parts of who I am. My mother never shouted at me when I did something wrong. Instead, she would sit down with me and have me think about the content of my actions, so that I did what I knew deep inside was right, even if it wasn't "cool." All those times that she studied with me, read to me, and told me stories about people and events led me to see the world and my responsibility in it somewhat differently than my peers. In addition, she always encouraged me to dream, to help people unselfishly.

As a teenager in Norway, I became very involved in environmental movements, politics, and refugee work. My refugee and equal rights work brought me, through UNHCR, to refugee camps in Southeast Asia, Hong Kong, and the Philippines. My experiences in these camps forever changed me. It's hard to be indifferent after seeing refugees in Hong Kong live in worse conditions than the prisoners in the neighboring maximum security prison. Vietnamese refugees were held in a place resembling a concentration camp, with barbed wire, watchtowers, armed guards, gray cement barracks. Some had been there for more than six years, waiting to be shipped home, neglected by Western governments; many children had been born and lived their entire lives in this place—their "home" being a 6 foot by 9 foot room, separated from their neighbors by a rug hung on clotheswire.

Such an experience forces a young mind to care; this exposure has served as a motivational factor for me ever since. I am determined to try and do whatever I can to make a difference—however small—for people where it matters in the world, in accordance with the values my mother tried giving me when I was little. To a great extent, she is the one who created my desire to live a meaningful life, to make a difference.

For my restlessness, rootlessness, and unconventional, pragmatic nature, I can thank my uncle. Always an outsider, he was raised in a family of alcoholics and sexual abuse. He fled his home as often as possible, spending summers in the mountains, and taking off to be a sailor at fourteen years old. He always seems to be searching for something elusive—for new adventures, new things to experience and learn. When I was younger, I used to be afraid of him, because he seemed so stern, and almost fanatic in his ambitions. Gradually, as he took me hiking and camping, I came to understand his view on life; he was an atheist, a super-pragmatic person whose values and morals completely clashed with those of the church and the law. I believe that I filled a void for my uncle, who lacked a son, and he broadened my love for nature to include a taste for the spectacular—for the power and the adrenaline associated with experiencing extremes.

My uncle and I would go hiking and mountaineering together, often stretching ourselves to the limit. I remember especially vividly one time we were in the heartland of Norway. We had already hiked for six hours that day, when we decided to climb a peak five thousand feet above us. We dumped our main packs and took off with minimum gear. After four thousand feet we came to a six-foot-wide ridge leading to the summit, with vertical drops of more than one thousand feet on either side. The wind was raging, and we lacked sufficient gear, but adrenaline and macho stupidity kept us pushing for the top. As a result, we found ourselves completely stuck one hundred feet from the top, gazing down where we'd been. As we looked wide-eyed at one another, my uncle asked, "Are you scared?" "Yeah . . . I am shitting in my pants! And you?" "Yes." The retreat down was an unforgettable exercise—an experience I promised I would never repeat, and yet I have done so numerous times. These excursions shaped my character and fed my appetite for risk.

I constantly seek the sensation of being alive, the feeling of adventure. That is my curse and my blessing: I need variety, action, and new challenges. If something is hard, or labeled impossible, it's like a magnet for me. Those characteristics that developed through experiences with my uncle have provided me with some of the most rewarding moments in my life. The price to pay for such adventure, however, can be a constant dissatisfaction with the present, a restless searching for something new, different, better. The daredevil in me has made me an outsider who floats from context to context, making few connections as I go.

If my mother and uncle modeled behaviors and perspectives that I have incorporated into my identity, my father has modeled the antithesis of who I want to be and what I want to stand for. When I was younger and a successful athlete in cross-country running, soccer, orienteering, and karate, my father would give me rides to competition only as long as the team was doing well. It was the same thing with school; he cared about how I did only in relation to others. A typical dialogue might be: "Dad, I got a 94 percent on my test!" "Really. Not bad," he would reply, "And how did the rest of the class do?"

When people observe how I hate to lose, how I loathe not being best, I consider how my childhood environment has had an effect on my character. My ongoing search for better and bigger challenges might subconsciously be a continuation of my efforts to do something that even my father would find good enough.

In many ways, Dad showed me what I don't want to be like if I ever become a father. So many times as a little kid I huddled up in the dark with my mum and sister while dad staggered about in the house, reeking of alcohol. I remember him punching holes in doors and walls, yelling. He even denied drinking when mum confronted him. He made me feel afraid and powerless, and as I grew older, I started despising him. I hated not having control, I hated the fact that I physically feared him.

As a result of those nights spent in fear, I have always hated to feel tied or restricted. I have always wanted to have control over myself, my own situation, my own destiny. I hate to be dependent on other people, to feel bound by somebody else's words or actions. I rarely let people know who I am, and I rarely dare, or want, to attach myself to anything or anyone else. These tendencies are admirable in some ways, problematic in others.

I have even struggled with the extent to which I should feel attached to my national identity. My nationality will always be a source of pride, as well as a source of pain. I am Norwegian, and at risk of sounding dramatic, I feel there is a lot to be proud of: the country's material wealth, the clean environment and breathtaking landscape, the equal opportunity afforded women, gays, lesbians, and other minorities. More than anything, I admire how we provide all sick people with medical treatment, and the fact that our brains, not our wallets, determine our level of education. I also take pride in Norway's long and rich history and culture, which is an essential part of my identity. And, most significantly, I am proud of the Norwegian character—down-to-earth, profound, loyal, and honest. It is a character that I like to see at least in part reflected in myself.

And yet I have left Norway, for the moment, which suggests that a part of me exists independent of my national identity. Some aspects of who I am clash with Norwegian ideals. I stuck my head out too much in Norway, and that's a terrible sin in an egalitarian society founded upon the notion that we are all equal. A Norwegian author once wrote a novel about a village called Jante, centered on its foundational law: "Don't think you are worth anything; don't think you are anything special; don't think you're better than us in anything." These lines are widely quoted and ridiculed in Norway, but, ironically, people appear to live by them.

In the United States it is all right to excel; people are encouraged to pursue their dreams, to take on challenges and rise up. In Norway, the law of jealousy kicks in. In second grade, I loved math and simply couldn't get enough of it. By early November, I was done with the entire math book, meant to last us a year. Was my teacher proud of me? Did he make sure I was given further challenges? Oh, no! Instead of praising me, he reprimanded me, a terrifying experience for a well-intentioned eight-year-old. The end result was that I had to erase half of my math book. So much for excelling in Norway!

As I grew older, I felt like I was being held back, almost as if I was being restricted from being me. My Norwegian upbringing had created a need to stick out my neck and a desire to make a difference. It also ushered in my restlessness and aversion to feeling tied down and restricted. Ironically, these very traits forced me to go abroad. Norway just wasn't enough.

I came to believe that my greatest hope for expanding my experiences and my character lay in the possibility of studying abroad. Admiring education in the American undergraduate system, I applied to the most prestigious schools, which in my case meant applying to the only American colleges known in Norway. I was accepted, but the acceptance was more bitter than sweet. As a white, nonexotic European, I received financial aid from no institution. I had to defer my entrance to college by a year, in the hopes that I would be able to somehow come up with enough money to pay for four years of education in the United States.

After an aborted attempt to engage in very high-risk, high-paid military service, due to serious injury, I decided to channel my angry energy into law school. Indeed, I would most likely be a lawyer in Norway right now, save for the influence of an American Dartmouth alum whom I met at the Lillehammer Olympics. The more he described Dartmouth College, the more attractive it sounded: its relatively small, intimate setting, the focus on undergraduate education with a healthy emphasis on the big picture. And it sounded perfect for a Norwegian, in terms of climate and geography. On his urging, I applied and was accepted, this time receiving the crucial financial aid.

Unfortunately, at precisely the moment when my future began to fall into place, I was awakened one morning by a telephone call from the military: "We need you to go to Bosnia in forty-eight hours."

It was an impossible situation. Practically speaking, I couldn't go because too much had already been arranged for the coming year at Dartmouth. I had to tell the military I could not go. I felt like a traitor, since I believe wholeheartedly in peacekeeping, and was horrified by the television scenes broadcast from Bosnia. Over and over again I kept telling myself that if I, with all my expensive, specialized training, didn't go to Bosnia, then how could I expect anyone else to go? It was a moral crisis for me. For the first time in my life I had been challenged to stand by my principles and to live by the values that drove me. And I found myself unable to meet the challenge.

My freshman year at Dartmouth was a time of mingled exhilaration, from the joys and novelties of college, and guilt from not being on the battlefields. Being a carefree student in a sheltered environment, with joyous experiences from Homecoming to drinking wine and chatting about Camus in newfound friends' rooms, all subconsciously increased my feeling of bad conscience, and further intensified the pressure to make sure I made the most out of my time. The result was a very intense lifestyle, an almost desperate ferocity with which I experienced my first few terms.

I still vividly remember flying for the first time into Logan Airport in Boston, then taking the late night bus to Hanover with a peculiar tickling feeling in my stomach as we approached my new home. As I recognized the places that had previously only existed on a campus map I studied in Norway—the football stadium, Main Street, and then finally the Green with Baker Library, brightly lit up in the warm September night—I fell in love with the campus. Maybe getting here had been worth all the struggles in Norway, after all.

When I first arrived on campus, I decided that, as a way of challenging myself and "being adventurous," I would not just stick to socializing with international students, especially not just with Norwegians. I didn't come to the United States simply to seek refuge in familiar surroundings. I made a critical decision that I would be "non-Norwegian." From this moment forward, I would be "American," by aggressively forcing myself to be very outgoing. Stepping onto American soil would be a new start for me, the beginning of a new phase of my life.

I also set myself another challenge: to meet many, many people. Every time I was at a social function, I tried to get to know as many people as possible. Being a foreigner, I loved the opportunity to meet new people and learn about another culture. Rowing crew, meeting fresh faces, and experiencing the newly released energy of my peers— away from home and living free for the first time in their lives—was quite simply incredible.

In the beginning, I rode on a wave of enthusiasm and optimism I have never experienced before or since. It seemed only natural to become involved in the "Class Council," which promoted class unity by programming activities and encouraging interaction. One thing led to another, and before I knew it, I was attending nearly every sporting event and party! Ultimately, I was selected as class president. I was intoxicated by the innocence and enthusiasm of life at Dartmouth.

Gradually, though, as my freshman year progressed, I began to regain some of my perspective. I had been so concerned with not being antisocial and introverted that I found that I had become a kind of myth in my class. To men, I was a "tough" guy—one of the best rowers on the crew team and a man with "hard-core" military service. To women, I was blond, blue-eyed, and had enough of an "exotic" accent to make me attractive. Unfortunately, this attention began to feel superficial to me, and I was beset by feelings of loneliness and unhappiness. Of equal concern, I began to wonder if throwing myself into a grand social life was not simply a way for me to suppress my guilt of not being in Bosnia.

I attended fewer and fewer fraternity parties, and I grew less interested in superficial, twenty-second conversations with a thousand acquaintances in a single night. In many ways, I stopped uncritically embracing American culture and, in particular, the Dartmouth social scene. This process took place simultaneously in many different areas of my Dartmouth life. I began to take crew much more seriously, which meant less late night partying and minimal alcohol. I also lost contact with casual friends, the ones with whom I used to chat superficially at parties about classes and the latest sports game. Instead, I longed for more mature, substantial interactions with a few true friends, from whom I could learn, be challenged, and with whom I could really feel that I was building solid relationships.

Instead of finding these deep friendships, however, I started to feel more and more like an outsider, isolated by age (I am four years older than most of my peers), by my leadership position, and by my personality. As my "reputation" built up, it became even harder to engage other people in a meaningful conversation. I gradually noticed how people were intimidated by me. The best illustration of this intimidation came from my closest friend, Dave. A couple of months ago he said to me, "Frode, I know you always tell people to be honest to you and encourage them to tell the truth and criticize you. You know, everybody, including me, has been so intimidated by you, we still haven't dared to really be open and blunt with you. It wasn't until a few months ago that I finally realized that you truly mean it—that you really want your friends to be the first ones to criticize you. Regardless of what they say, people are too intimidated by you, your position, and your personality, to dare to be honest."

With this remark, which may be more true than I find easy to admit, in addition to an already superficial friendship culture I perceive at Dartmouth, I feel that my chances of making lasting, substantial friendships aren't too high. Yet I find it amusing that most people on campus would say I have hundreds of friends, while I feel that I have, at most, one person on whom I can truly rely. I believe that this paradox reflects a fundamental cultural difference. One of the greatest parts of American social culture is a sense of openness. People, at least at Dartmouth, are interested and willing to get to know others, and I've certainly met many more people on this campus than I would have ever met at University of Oslo, which is ten times larger. The problem, however, is that although I have met the majority of the student body, I hardly know anyone, and hardly anyone knows me. It strikes me that the American emphasis on individual freedom and domestic privacy seems to shape the definition of friendship. People welcome easy encounters, but do not easily expose their private lives.

However, I felt guilty during my first year of college, so, in response to a nagging conscience, I arranged to take my sophomore fall off, to do peacekeeping, first in Bosnia, and then in Lebanon, where I spent those lonely nights on patrol. My peacekeeping missions were the most meaningful application of my military training and skills. And although I can't say I found the meaning of life in peacekeeping, at least I feel that I stayed true to my ideals, my desire to make a difference. On the other hand, was war perhaps an experience that partially satisfied a subconscious need for excitement, adventure, and high tension? My peacekeeping experience provided me with a reality check, an abrupt, enforced seriousness, to which most people in the sheltered, peaceful parts of the Western world are normally never exposed. I hope that one day I will come to be grateful for this exposure, however painfully these memories may haunt me today.

I remember how, back in Hanover after returning from Lebanon, I had dinner with a senior, with whom I briefly had interacted during my first year. The conversation and company was great, and after a couple of hours, the topic turned to friendship. He looked me deep in the eyes and expressed how glad he was that we had gotten to be such incredibly good friends; in fact, he identified me as one of his three best friends on campus. I didn't know how to react to his claim. If the scale of friendship is such, there must be many lonely people in the world.

A close acquaintance of mine at Dartmouth, Mike, spent a year in high school in Norway. One time when we were having fun, cracking jokes and just goofing around, somebody asked us if we were good friends. It was really strange. We looked at each other and hesitantly said, "Yeah. Kind of. That is, in American, we're definitely good friends. In Norwegian, however, we would never call each other friends." My standards are inevitably Norwegian, so while I have several hundred "friends," I have only one real friend, my roommate, Dave.

When I had difficulty adjusting on my return from the Middle East, Dave was the only one really there for me. His loyalty, his dedication to other people, and his total honesty are all crucial strengths to me, rare in students anywhere. So many times, when I have been down; when I have been in need for someone to talk with about problems back home in Norway or when I have had conflicts, academic or personal, at Dartmouth; when I have been in need of some help or a favor, be it moving a few boxes or visiting me when I have been sick—I have experienced how people have not been there for me. Usually it's not a sacrifice to classwork, but rather to other priorities; I interpret this not being there as due to a lack of interest or a failure to keep a promise.

This is difficult to experience, not to mention to accept, as I had such high expectations of my peers. I live for my friends, and have an absolute dedication and loyalty to them. That's how my experiences have shaped me: I'll never forget the times we were transported out on patrol in Lebanon—the closeness, the words, the rings, the assurance that we'd be there, and were there, for each other. I similarly will never forget the euphoric joy of all those mornings we crossed the line back again after an uneventful night patrol. The appreciation of life and our allegiance to each other will forever be standards I apply to myself and my friends. And while the bonds formed in the military are unique, having been shaped in a short time and through very intense experiences, in which we depended on each other totally, the standard of friendship is one that I expect everywhere, unrealistic though that expectation may be in the particular context of Dartmouth.

The absence of such friendships at Dartmouth has made me feel like an outsider and an observer. To varying degrees, I feel socially, culturally, and spiritually out of place, particularly in the areas of love, alcohol, and friendship. Although I enjoy alcohol and sex, my attitudes toward each differ from that of many of my peers. I do not drink alcohol to get drunk; in fact, I hate the feeling of being drunk, as I get sick and feel I don't have any control. I most certainly do not use alcohol as an excuse for my actions. Neither do I treat women like "pieces of meat," nor do I try to get them drunk enough to take advantage of them. And I certainly do not call a hundred people my friends with the goal of having contacts for future use! In my rejection of these aspects of the Dartmouth social culture, I end up feeling marginalized.

And the funniest thing about my situation is that although I am a foreigner and feel like such an outsider at Dartmouth, my peers consider me to be as American, as mainstream, and as "inside" as possible. Since I am white and male, I am automatically seen as a WASP and associated with the dominant culture. That I come from another country with a different culture and language doesn't seem to be an issue at all; all that matters is my skin color and sex. I am white, I am male; thus, I am not considered a minority. And this ignorance, this disrespect and outright suppression of everything I and my Norwegian culture stand for, makes me feel misunderstood. I am in a melting pot, but I don't want to melt indistinguishably into a conglomerate. I am not able to blossom and fully express my individuality and my cultural identity because I "look like everybody else." This lack of understanding among my peers is hard to accept.

This ignorance about the world outside of the United States reflects a deeply ethnocentric perspective. International students are often not considered unique within the American context. Instead of grouping by culture and origin, people are grouped by their skin color or by their social and political status in the U.S. society. Culturally, my international peers and I have a hard time seeing much of a difference between a white American student, a black American student, and a Latino American student. However, the American political debate about culture and ethnicity and identity politics tends to be reduced to a debate about societal white privilege, which is a purely political and economic phenomenon, based upon skin color instead of culture or personality.

A fellow "friend" and international student in my class from South Africa, Risana, once remarked, "You know, Frode, it's funny. We see things very much the same way, and we have both experienced how incredibly cruel and horrible the world outside of the protected Western world is. However, on this campus we are put into these American categories. You are white. I am black. As if my skin color makes me have anything in common with black Americans! I have absolutely nothing in common with African Americans in this country. I am not born and raised on McDonald's. I see these people come up to Dartmouth and start to act all ghetto and stuff, and they expect me to do the same thing. I don't get it! How superficial is it possible to be?!"

Another international friend of mine, Lee from Kenya, has taken on a more pragmatic approach: "Frode, they are using me to look good on paper and in their statistics, so as to appear supportive of poor international students. I'm gonna use them. I'm going to get my education from here, I am going to take maximum advantage of them, and then I will leave and never ever come back."

As an international, white European student, it is even harder to be considered different. My skin color gives me white privileges, but it also makes me "similar" in the eyes of Americans. But I *am* different, and I have the double perspective that difference can provide, in the sense that my military and volunteer experiences and my country of origin give me the ability to approach the world at Dartmouth with a much larger perspective: to contrast, compare, and draw the big picture.

As I negotiate my own pathway through the apparently conflicting sides of my personality, attempting to develop a meaningful direction to my life, I am sensitive to the apathy of so many students around me. More and more this apathy, combined with the lack of appreciation—for the beauty of the campus and its environment, for being here, for life—concerns and bothers me. The more I think, the clearer I see some fundamental problems with the campus culture and the Dartmouth community. I feel angry that so many of my peers appear spoiled and self-centered. I am upset at the way they approach their Dartmouth experience as a right, not a privilege, and the way some students see people as objects to manipulate for their own benefit. The focus is on taking and receiving, never giving back by getting involved in school activities unless they help boost the GPA and make the résumé look good. Coming directly from a third world war zone, my perspectives are extremely different, and I have had problems coping with my peers. They seem to me to drift through college unchallenged and unexposed to the issues, problems, and responsibilities of the real world, and hence graduate uncommitted to a sense of mission or deeper vision of life.

My sophomore year, after my tour in Lebanon, I became intensely aware of aspects of college life I had ignored my first year: the drinking culture; the degrading abuse of women by many fraternity guys; superficial friendships lacking the allegiance I had known in Lebanon and even in Norway; the student focus on GPA, future jobs, and the token approach to learning. How much people take for granted their incredible luck in being at Dartmouth! I was emotionally upset, even at times alarmed, and this was clearly exacerbated by my own struggles to return and settle back into the normal world. I was struggling to accommodate visions of war with the assumed privilege of Dartmouth students.

At this time, I felt a growing desire to effect change. Especially after Lebanon, I was tired of feeling powerless; I was tired of being forced to stand on the sideline. I wanted to be in control. Together, these factors—some genuinely altruistic, others purely personal— compelled me to seek the position of student assembly president.

My work in this role has allowed me to address issues of apathy, ignorance, and of irresponsibility that have angered me. I see problems on campus: concerning human interaction, students' tenuous relationship to the outside world, and lack of deep social engagement and active citizenship. In addition, I believe there is no component of the college curriculum that instills in students a sense of responsible leadership, ethics, or awareness of the multiple dimensions of individual and cultural differences, idealism, and social and civic accountability. I find myself involved, seeking power, so that I have the opportunity to improve the current situation. That's why I sought the student assembly presidency and why I'm still working to effect change.

Though my work has been frustrating, at times overwhelming, and often disillusioning, I continue, because I feel an obligation to make the most out of my time at Dartmouth. In my eyes, the opportunity to have an impact on thousands of future shapers and movers of society—be it in areas of politics, business, social work, media, or academia–is the biggest chance I'll ever have to make a difference, and it gives me great satisfaction to be working for issues I believe in.

As my passions and drives keep pushing me forward from task to task, leading into my senior year, I am beginning to contemplate the question of where to go from here. The challenger in me wants to go higher, faster, stronger. The philosopher in me just wants to dedicate time to friends, family, and nature. The rootless adventurer in me doesn't care what I do, as long as it is new and exciting. All of these conflicting selves are bound to cause confusion and sleepless nights, as I will have to make choices, deciding on a particular path, be it science, business, politics, or social work.

However, these frictions are minor compared to the major life conflict I am dealing with right now, the conflict between my desire to do something meaningful and good for people around me, and my need to make enough money so that neither I, nor my mom, ever have to worry about money again. Right now I have no idea how to combine these two drives in me. Dave keeps asking me why—for whom or for what—I keep driving myself so intensely. He predicts I will be dead from a heart attack before I'm thirty! He may be right. I fear that my inner conflicts may be irreconcilable, though I hope for some middle road.

My challenge in the coming years will be to find a way to take advantage of the inner tensions, contradictions, and perspectives that have, ironically, helped me more than they have hindered me. My time with the UN forces and my experiences as a volunteer in Asia, as I have discussed, changed radically my outlook on life: the way I see the world and my place in it. My perspective will always be colored by thoughts of the victims of the Quana massacre in Lebanon and thoughts of the old eyes of a five-year-old Vietnamese child in a prison camp in Hong Kong. These visions accompany me every day in college, as I encounter problems that seem trivial in relation to other contexts that I have known.

I may not be able to define myself in narrow terms, or integrate the multiple aspects of myself. I may not be able to completely reconcile place with place: Lebanon with Dartmouth, Norway with America; or self with self: who I have been with, who I will be, or even the many aspects of myself that I am now. The only thing I do know for certain is that I'll always change within myself and that I'll always work for change in the world around me, no matter where I am.

Coming to Terms

Ian Sue Wing
Trinidad

Americans see me as black, though my skin is not. While I am of African descent, my name is an English bastardization of Cantonese, which forms a significant part of my ethnic heritage. My father's father was born in Canton, China, and eventually settled in Trinidad, where he married a light-skinned woman of mixed African and European descent. But I don't claim to be Chinese. I am Trinidadian. This is my cultural and experiential heritage, first and foremost. Trinidad society, with its many races, was a rich mêlée of influences that molded me for nineteen years. My father's influence was one of the most painful during these years, and I had yearned to be free of it. Without knowing it then, I was also trying to escape from myself.

I was nineteen years old. For some time I had confided in my mother that my father was making my life unbearable. He had always shouted at me, ordering me to do things the "right" way: *his* way. Stubbornly, I wanted to be independent enough to devise methods that were more efficient and with which I was more comfortable. It appeared to me that since my childhood this situation had grown steadily worse. I talked of confronting him directly. My mother countered with worn excuses, the moral benefits of turning the other cheek. He was under tremendous stress at work; he found himself at the age of fifty marking time, not knowing which direction his life would take; he was hypertensive and easily became anxious; he couldn't face the fact that his only son would be leaving home, and it was tearing him apart; above all he was a good father and I owed him respect. Yes, he was good, he provided and he loved, and that made it hurt all the more.

No matter how hard I tried to please him, I couldn't remain long in his vicinity without him lecturing me, which would rapidly escalate into him screaming at me. It was so unfair, the cutting harshness of his words, that I could never seem to stop them from wounding me, that he uttered them even in situations where he knew he was in the wrong. The way I saw it, respect meant that he, the powerful father, could take his frustrations out on me. All that I, the submissive son, could do was to sit there and take it. In that respect I would never be like him, I vowed—and I would never, ever give him my sympathy.

Worse, my father's ire was to me largely unpredictable. It was as if any word or action of mine (or lack thereof) could attract his criticism, provoking him. Afraid, I was unable to rest at home, being continually on tenterhooks, trying to read his mind, to know in advance what he expected of me, and then to do it as he wanted it done, flawlessly. Especially because I possessed neither dexterity nor great physical strength, this was a nightmare. Timid, fearful, and sensitive (especially to my father's reproach), I remained cowed in the face of his domineering, choleric personality, retreating within myself. For all the talk with my mother about confrontation, I never challenged my father in his oppression. That I knew such action in my innermost self to be just brutally proved my utter worthlessness, conclusively confirming the shameful truth of my cowardice, my weakness. Anger at my father, however, was tiny compared to that provoked by feelings of my own inadequacy. My self-perception was one of unworthiness, of vulnerability that must be hidden, defended tooth and nail against the probing eye of a cruel, uncaring, even malignant outside. I lived that confusion of emotions, all the way back from the sheltered adolescence of an only child.

Mine is a nuclear family. Wherever we lived there never seemed to be many children my own age, so I grew up mostly around adults. Circumstances conspired to isolate me, but I can't say I really recognized myself as being lonely, even though as a child I frequently played by myself at home. Through imagination, I created my own inner world and proceeded to live in it, becoming self-sufficient early on. School was pretty much the only place where I could interact socially with people at my own level, the only place I had friends. I loved school. Looking back, I can see how important school was in my life because my shyness kept me from other ways of socializing. My parents did not go out much, and that trait seemed to have been passed on to me. I don't think it helped matters.

Youthful innocence was ignorance—I knew no other existence. I could not make the comparisons that would have shown me the socially austere character of my own lifestyle. Studies came first and foremost for me. I was a cerebral boy, disliking sports because I lacked the necessary physical qualities: physique, strength, coordination. During my first years in high school, I spent my free time reading at home or playing chess in vacant classrooms with older members of my school chess club. I remember being intrigued by grandmaster Bobby Fischer's description of his opponent Anatoly Karpov—his emaciated, atrophied body, the years of study packed into a brilliant mind. Something deep inside registered this as an ideal, the triumph of the mental.

Because I was already following the model of the triumph of the mental, it was easier to continue on this road than to stop to work on the physical and social aspects of myself that had never been developed. But by the age of fourteen the outside was intruding on my world. I already sensed my own antisocial nature and knew also that I was socially graceless, awkward in meeting new people and especially in gatherings of strangers: I just didn't know how to act. Worse, I had no conception of how I would learn to get it right.

I was also by then actively exacerbating my own isolation. Academic prowess and physical weakness, combined with an utter lack of "coolness" and teenage social *savoir-faire*, made me an easy target in high school. I was seen by many as the "class brain," which automatically made me the butt of childish pranks and ridicule. It hurt, and instilled in me a hateful envy and brooding self-disgust because I most certainly was *not* a "brain." I never came first in class exams. Hell, I was almost never in the top five. My tormentors were wrong. I would read encyclopedia articles out of interest, but I was a nerd who couldn't ace a test. A fraud. The true academic stars were the same students who shone brightest on the playing fields, captains of the soccer and cricket teams: popular and sociable. True, they worked very hard, but their brilliance came naturally. I could never aspire to be like them. Having neither the brains nor the brawn, I was forever doomed to bust my arse to come tenth: above average, but not good enough. My parents' continual emphasis on standards and quality in my upbringing made me a perfectionist. I felt that because I couldn't be number one, I was dead last.

I reacted by purposefully dulling my emotional oversensitivity, almost consciously cultivating in my personality a cynical sarcasm, the weapon of the weak. The offensiveness of my off-the-wall, graphically crude self-expression (product of the fertile, vivid imagination of a teenager obsessed with sex) was perfected around that time. I tried hard to develop a cool aloofness, to become invisible and keep my foes at bay. I was labeled as disgusting, which was fine with me since it was for once a true claim to fame, and a viable defense mechanism. My world was intruding, but slowly and surely I was erecting an emotional fortress.

In retrospect, it worked all too well. Struggling to negate weakness and softness forced me to stifle emotions for, and inner feelings about, people around me. Seeking safety within my defenses, I became the outsider. At the few parties to which I went, I remember feeling acutely out of place, as if I were tagging along, not really wanted. My timid nature was a thick, transparent treacle. Fear of the humiliation that my awkwardness might invite constrained me from mingling, keeping me apart, either close to people I already knew (who were invariably male) or alone. I can see myself now, propped against a wall, trying to be invisible, looking inward at my peers. It was as if I had awoken one day, realizing to my horror that everyone else had suddenly developed, leaving me behind without a clue about how to overcome my fears and become socially at ease.

Ultimately, the most damning indication of my lopsided social development was my almost total isolation from women. In fifth form (tenth grade), most of the people I knew in school had girlfriends; by contrast I knew virtually no females my own age. Before this point, I had psyched myself into concentrating on my studies, fooling myself that I had no use for girls, confident that the inner fortress could withstand even my own hormones. Too late, I realized full well that I yearned for what I never had: contact with the opposite sex, a romantic relationship, affection. Hold on, I told myself, you'll get there. In this regard, I seem to have placed my aspirations to social fulfillment on procuring a girlfriend. I can't say when this became central to my thinking, but at some stage I knew in every fiber of my being that a sustained romantic relationship would be a pivotal point, freeing me from sterile, painful loneliness. Things would somehow be better after that.

It still amazes me that for all my book knowledge I completely failed to realize that socializing is a learned behavior, an incremental process, and that like anything else, you've got to practice to get good at it. Upper six (twelfth grade) came and found me still alone, yearning, fighting not to be swamped by the most intense academic workload I had yet experienced. It was in this condition that I finally arrived at the University of the West Indies (UWI), my first coeducational experience since primary school. Women abounded. My fellow male "freshers" (similarly repressed products of the sexually segregated Trinidad school system) went buck wild, reveling in their newfound freedom. I didn't. University was no joke. UWI was a baptism of fire, my first classes a stunning example of the ever-increasing workload of academe. It was as if the level of comprehension, of dedication, and of study expected of me had suddenly increased threefold. Ironically, this was the very first time in my life when I could actually choose to budget my time between work and socializing. But because of the cerebral ethos so ingrained in me, I didn't realize that it was virtually impossible to do all the work, that one had to work smart, making careful choices, striking a balance. My initial panic melted into resignation. It was the same old story again: Work would have to come first, without question. Dedication! I was here to work. If I really wanted to do well, the other things in life would have to be sacrificed. Sacrificing the present for a better future, why did it always have to be this way? Did this have to go on forever? An eternity of solitude! The thought was chilling. I was unhappy and afraid.

During my time at UWI, I began to seriously question the meaning of friendship. My socializing took the form of the same casual, transient relationships as in high school, hanging out with other students (all male), despite being surrounded by females my own age for the first time in years. I treated the women I met in the same manner as my male acquaintances. Inside, though, I fantasized over some of them. They were physically beautiful, desirable, yet I could never even hope to express my feelings of infatuation to them. I pictured spilling my heart out to one of these gorgeous creatures, feminine and demure, only to have her throw back her head and laugh in convulsive whoops, dark brown curls tossing in the sunlight, while I prayed with all my soul that the sky would descend upon me, crushing me into nothingness. As such a late starter in what was obviously a game, it seemed that everyone was out of my league.

I remember watching those peers who were experienced in the relationship/sex game, and being mystified at their free and easy manner, their smug self-assurance, talking their amorous talk to three, four, five girls at a time. I wondered about their thoughts, their innermost feelings. There was a seriousness, a dedication in their pursuit, yet it was never apparent. This led me to question my own perceptibly serious demeanor, and the importance that I attached to matters of the heart. I did not flirt; I couldn't. Didn't know how to. The few times I tried I'm sure it was too tame to be noticeable. I was almost certain that trying harder would cause me to make an ass of myself, provoking the ridicule that I so feared.

Games. Being a horrible player, I have never liked them. So much so that I've remained a nonparticipant. It galled me: Not one of the many women that surrounded me displayed any interest in me, or seemed even curious about what lay beyond my emotional defenses. Had I nothing attractive about me—nothing that I could offer that women would want? I couldn't tell. No matter how hard I tried to learn by observation, I never trusted that I could correctly interpret the subtle cues of nonverbal romantic language.

To be wanted sexually, physically, emotionally! This was my dream, the culmination of my desires, the way to boost my sense of self-worth. I would jump at the chance, without hesitation. It's acutely embarrassing, the readiness with which I would accept a submissive role, further revealing my ineffectual nature. Was the male not supposed to be confident and strong, the "dominant" partner? Such emasculation represented the only easy way out of the contradictions of my weakness, sparing me having to endure the many hard knocks of romantic and sexual emergence. Confronting my fears meant exposing my inner self, dismantling hostile emotional ramparts of a don't-care, leave-me-how-you-found-me posture directed against the outside world. I had meticulously constructed them in response to years of pain: How could I withstand any more? I was eighteen years old, for God's sake; my innocence would be met with derision! The whole world expected that sex and love should no longer be a mystery.

After a year of persistent, concentrated effort only to achieve second-class academic honors, I was fed up with UWI. I had intended to transfer to the Faculty of Engineering in my second year; instead I withdrew—I had been accepted to Dartmouth, and I would do engineering there. My uncle (who I barely knew) had been encouraging me to come. An established dramatist and respected playwright with a doctorate from Yale, he was now retired after living in the States for twenty years and teaching in the drama department at Dartmouth. I had brains. If I applied, I would get in with his help. Such an opportunity. Apply, my mother nagged me, even though I was already settled at UWI. What the hell, it was worth a try. I applied. I was accepted. I came. No choice; I had to get away before home drove me mad. Now it was Dartmouth's turn.

Freshman Week came in early September. Gangs of newly arrived men and women roamed the campus nightly, searching for the next party, the next drink, the next fuck. I'd sit in my room, preparing for tests that could enable me to be placed in courses above introductory level. Credit on intros meant fewer courses required for graduation, which meant less time enrolled, which meant less money for my parents to spend. The equation was simple. Revising differential calculus, I'd hear their drunken, carousing voices—gaiety right outside my window, intruding upon my focused consciousness. Opportunity. Dedication. I hadn't come here to party, to waste my parents' money. It seemed everyone here was rich. I, decidedly middle-class at home, was now impoverished by international exchange rates. My parents were eating into years of carefully hoarded savings so that I could enjoy this four-year "joyride." For me this was the chance of a lifetime. I would show them all.

Yet even as I cloistered myself, those voices called to me. Having escaped to a new world, I was on my own, to do as I pleased. Freedom! Socializing! Women! Ah, yes, sex: the S word. I forced myself to shut them out, chained by timidity, my anguished soul wishing that I could be anything other than naive and shy. You got problems, Ian: no self-esteem. Knowing that I was older than most of the people in my class; that most of them were probably just as screwed up inside as myself (but they, in their element, never seemed to let it bother them); knowing the stigma of my social immaturity and the depths of my shame; knowing my lust for physical and emotional intimacy with the opposite sex: none of this helped me. Analytic knowledge—it brought me no closer to myself or what I felt. Agonizing over my sorry state, my mind was awash with self-pity while my heart burned with anger. Between knowledge and feeling there stretched an abyss of self-doubt, the monstrous maw of despair.

Bitter frustration: I had more important things to do than lust over these bitches, like even one of them would ever feel anything for me! I was more alone than ever. So stay that way, then, and to hell with everything around me. Dedication. Self-denial was the only way. Work. Sacrifice. Ian, prove to yourself for once in your miserable life that you are strong! The pain was more than I could stand. I headed for the door, voices beckoning me out into the warm, welcoming night.

"Hi, I just love your accent. Where are you from?"

Contact. The pasty-faced blonde reeked of alcohol. Freshman, like myself. A complete stranger, sporting what I now know to be a southern twang. No baby, I thought, you get no stars for the introduction. Middle of the night and she just came up to me in the middle of the street. Where I come from, we call such presumptuousness "fast and out of place." Be nice, I told myself, you're in the white people country now.

"Trinidad."

My answer must have exuded infinite patience.

"Wow! That's so cool. Isn't that near Saudi Arabia?"

"Sorry, love, wrong hemisphere." I had to keep myself from laughing. So they were like this (the appalling geographical ignorance of the Americans). I just walked away, leaving her there. My youthful naiveté. Astonishing, in my desperation it never even crossed my mind that this random female might have been interested in me, and trying in vain to express it. More than likely she was just making drunken conversation, trying to be nice. I would never know. As before, I was blind to the possibility of the romance, the sexual encounter that I so craved. But now things were worse, as I couldn't even discern friendly advances on the part of others. Confusion reigned. The plunge into the alienation of American society amplified it. Having finally acknowledged the existence of my inner needs, I knew I had to do something to address them. However, I was damned if I even knew how to begin. I was confronted with a bewildering new array of behavioral variables to assimilate, interpret, judge, and to which to respond. My sheltered psyche, hopelessly unaccustomed to interpreting social signals even within the context of my own culture, was overwhelmed. This was but symptomatic of the larger problem of alienation on a human level. I didn't regard this woman (or anyone in the crowds of pleasure-seekers) as quite human. They were oddities to me, strangely two-dimensional, their blank, inebriated smiles and bubbly voices nameless, devoid of identity, of meaning. I doubt they saw me very differently. My dress, actions, speech all betrayed me as being a fresh-off-the-boat, hot-pepper-eating, "Interesting/Unusual West Indian Prototype."

The first thing that struck me about Dartmouth was the number of white people. I had never seen so many in the same place at the same time. Even the blacks were utterly alien. Their experiences throughout a history of slavery appeared so different from the British colonialism of my homeland. Their self-expression, mannerisms, convenient identification with an indistinct, long-lost cultural heritage in starving Africa while believing wholeheartedly in American acquisitiveness— all made them an enigma. For the first time I experienced the concept of "The Cause," and was actively questioned by African American students as to whether I was down with it or not, whether I was to assert my cultural and political identity, devote time and energy and money (and if need be myself) to benefit persons of African descent both in America and throughout the world. For them, the focus of activities on campus was the AAm, the African and African American society. It was a confusing time. I was barely African and certainly *not* American, and had neither the precedent nor the basis to identify with the likes of Malcolm X, with whom they were so enamored. Then, I had known virtually nothing of his life.

The behavior of the whites was initially striking. I detected a subtle, pervasive mindlessness, a superficiality in their attitude, annoying in its vacuousness and seemingly inextricably linked to the propensity to get drunk at the drop of a hat. More lengthy personal interaction with these natives invariably exposed the gung-ho sociopolitical mores rife in the land of the free and the home of the brave: America is number one, we are mighty, and might equals right— love it or leave it. My good old "Trini" crap detector made it impossible for me to stomach the myths that the locals confused with reality. I thought of the pernicious cultural penetration of satellite television and the Voice of America at home, feeding my people the "strike out and get yours with a pioneering spirit" American Dream so widely favored at Dartmouth (especially among the rich, who already had theirs). These Yankees just want to impose their ways on countries like my own, I thought, and of course they want me to believe in those same ways and congratulate them for their cleverness.

There seemed to be this constant, oppressive expectation that I, a lowly foreigner from a third world country, should unquestioningly embrace things American. At the same time, all that I encountered was transient curiosity in my heritage or traditions, in my difference. Patronizing curiosity all too often thinly veiled the need to confirm the superiority of their culture, traditions, and society. Ian, I told myself, you have to fight against this. In the eyes of these people (and not just my fellow students, either) the rest of the world really didn't count. Christ, this was *Ivy League!* It was these parochial ignoramuses who were assumed to be the pinnacle of the educated class, whose opinions on matters of import would be deferred to by the rest of the world! In my first year alone, I was confronted with several glaring instances of, I shall be charitable, "cultural insensitivity."

Popular culture ("the mainstream") was evidence enough for me that the whites were just plain barbarians inside. Observing the intense, seemingly unbridled hedonism of Freshman Week was a cultural shock wave that intensified the crushing pressure of my difference, my aloneness. Still I went out, the nonparticipant, a spectator, looking inward through the impervious, transparent wall of an overly self-conscious, antisocial personality. Dormitory parties abounded. Furniture was pushed back, the fridge stocked with booze, music turned up, and doors thrown open wide—an instant fête as people gathered.

It takes two to make a thing go right . . .

Youthful voices chanted hoarsely over the resonant bass of rap music. Loud. The stereo was expensive—you couldn't even buy systems like that at home. Vivid memories of a white girl in high heels, miniskirt, and bra gyrating atop a desk in someone's room, half-empty quart bottle of peach schnapps in her outstretched arm. Desire. She looked so young and small and vulnerable. And drunk. Yet looking back I remember no real attraction, only diffuse lust. Outside, through the open window I could see one of my "peers," being helped by a friend. He was bent over, hands propped on his knees, vomiting profusely onto the lawn. You could smell the alcohol.

Early on I observed this time-honored tradition of imbibing until one threw up. I made my first visits to fraternity basements. Alcohol is no big deal to me. I like its taste, but I knew how it felt to be drunk—and I hated it. Over the course of the last night I sipped three beers. In full control of my faculties, my alien eye went to work, dissecting the scene, taking it all in. The atmosphere, the drinking games, the exaggerated gesticulations, the speech getting louder and more slurred, the antics of the crowd (predominantly white males) as the intoxicant took hold. One I recognized, a sophomore living in my dormitory. He had been doing shots of tequila. Drunk off his arse, he didn't even see me. Didn't see the last three steps of the stairway either. Missed them, falling face first. Hard. Broke his jaw. I saw him for the next three months with his mouth wired shut. That night he didn't even feel it. Was *this* the scene that had historically dominated social life at Dartmouth? Repulsed, I left, never to return. If this was social life here then I wanted no part.

I withdrew inward, immersing myself in academics. The first month was a whirlwind. Early September and I had never lived away from home before. I played it by the straight and narrow, falling back on the disciplining influences of my upbringing. It was no accident, my father had seen to that. The war we'd waged on the battlefield of my adolescent mind had been lost before it started, had been won in the womb. His influence lived within me—luckily for me, because I was busier than I had ever been in my entire life. No longer having my parents' help with the responsibilities and chores of living meant that seeing to my own day-to-day personal business was a full-time occupation. In addition, massive financial aid (the only reason I could afford to be at Dartmouth) required me to have a job on campus. That meant at least ten hours less free time each week.

A Monday morning in October. Jesus, it was winter! Already the first snowfall. I was awake at 6:30. Language drill at 7:45 A.M., and my throat felt like red-hot barbed wire. For two weeks I'd seen tiny crystals airborne, diamond hard as they struck my face on the frigid wind. Flurries, they called them. This was the first time I had ever seen snow; the colder it got was the coldest temperature I had ever felt in my life. Why couldn't this damn school be in the tropics?

Huddled in my robe, I ran down the hallway toward the bathroom and morning shower. White outside. It was freezing. My room on the ground floor of the dorm was last on the steam line of the entire building. The thermostat was on the third floor, perpetually warmed by the rising heat from the two stories of shivering bodies below. By the time upstairs cooled off enough for the heat to kick in I had to wear a down jacket just to stay in my room. By the time the steam got to the room it had largely condensed to water, and most of its useful heat content was gone. Cold. It had got inside of me. At least I could take scalding hot showers, hopefully warming up some. It was all I could do to face the day.

IAN YOU'RE DEAD!

This bit of morning cheer greeted me as I entered the shower stall, scrawled on the nasty gray-tiled wall in shaving cream. Some joker trying to be funny, I thought, dismissing it. Four of my hallmates proceeded to dump a dustbin full of snow over my naked body. I didn't fight back, try to get away, even scream—I just stood there and took it. Inside, where it counted, I was already numb. The hot water helped, as did their leaving, trailing whoops of laughter at their prank. I wished I'd had the balls to curse, throw a punch, do *something*, but as weak and thin as I was, I could easily see them team up on me, beating my arse. Consequences. I coughed convulsively. *Fuckers!* I said to myself, watching my own blood swirl in the vortex of my bathwater, going down the drain. Just like my life.

At last! Away from home, here was the freedom I so craved, that beautiful, wretched dream. Astronaut's horror, vertigo of the first spacewalk, looking down and seeing galactic emptiness between your feet, where there should be a floor. I felt as a child, magically popped into the cockpit of a jet fighter doing a victory roll only a hundred feet above the ground. I was now in full control. I alone had to, would, make this work. Now, I longed for a return to dependence, the primordial urge to cling to my mother's bosom, eyes shut tight. As much as I thought their presence stifled me before, I loved my parents then, needed them deep inside, an instinctive realization spawned by loss. I was sure I'd have gladly endured an eternity of my father's own specially tailored hell. The safety net was gone.

That "initiation" of snow was but a mere beginning. I was to have bronchitis for the next four months. Trips to the student clinic saw the doctors prescribe everything from lozenges to plenty of liquids to cough syrup to antibiotics. Drugs did little to affect the symptoms. They did not even come close to approaching what I knew to be the root illness—winter. My first. During my morning coughing fits I would wonder whether it was the bitter bile of phlegm or really the acrid taste of homesickness that filled my mouth. I knew then that I would never make America my home.

What am I doing here?

I asked myself this more times than I can remember. Why did I ever come? Wasn't I happy enough in Trinidad? Carnival Monday morning, *J'ouvert*,* late February, people fêting since 4:00 A.M., one million naked bodies prancing through the streets, gyrations well greased with alcohol and the deafening din of steelbands and calypso in what has been dubbed the greatest show on earth. I imagined the blazing tropical dawn as I, 4500 miles to the north, ran huddled to a physics exam, groggy, with chills and fever. Outside was a freezer, ten below zero with the wind chill, and barely light at seven A.M. I cried, tears barely an inch down my cheeks before they froze on my face. Why? I knew the answer: Opportunity.

Above all, academics—what I came for—meant *work.* Although possessed of no real aptitude in science and mathematics, the course of study I pursued was engineering sciences, reputedly the most difficult major on campus. I chose the hard road. Gone was the British educational system to which I was so accustomed, where everything depended on performance in final exams at the end of year long courses. Instead it seemed that the same material was now packed into ten-week terms, with a new topic covered almost every day I went to class. Before, examinations had meant periods of stress-filled dread. Dartmouth was like shock therapy: With most science courses having two midterms and a final exam, I was taking tests virtually every three weeks! If I passed, good; if I failed, I tried to control the damage. Above all, I kept studying to get a handle on new material to pass the next test, because they just kept on coming. Thank God for UWI! I never thought that I'd have said it, but that one year of university life proved invaluable. The experience had already introduced me to university-level work and study habits, which was a precious head start on my peers. I was, nevertheless, desperately afraid of failure, and fought not to be overwhelmed by Dartmouth's furious pace, regularly returning from my studies in the wee hours of the morning. You're in college now, Ian, it's time you abandoned childish luxuries like sleep.

Living at home had enabled me to take for granted another luxury: privacy—being able to physically withdraw to your own surroundings. No longer. For the nine months of my freshman year I had two roommates. We were all squeezed into a dormitory accommodation of

---

*Creole corruption of the French *jour ouvert* ("day opens" or "daybreak"), denoting the commencement of Carnival festivities.

two rooms and annexed bath (toilet and sink). I was relieved when that experience was over. They were both white and middle class: *P.* from Oregon, *R.* from Colorado. Culture shock continued in a big way, as this was my very first experience living in close quarters with strangers, let alone strangers with experiences alien to my entire world. For the first time, inward retreat was difficult, as I had to separate myself from room life, from *them.*

I mostly returned to the room to catch a few hours of shut-eye. *R.* regularly woke me, though, staggering in stone drunk at 6:00 A.M. He'd crash for the rest of the day, emerging in the evening, only to sally forth once more. I doubt he made it to any more than half of his classes as a freshman. After not attending lectures for the entire term he'd sit with a stack of borrowed notes and a beer, turn up the rock 'n' roll in his headphones to toxic levels, and read, plowing through page after page of raw knowledge all night before a final exam. No work and he maintained a B+ average. Granted, classes were easier freshman year, but this was nothing short of remarkable. Comparing this with my no-play A– average, I burned with bitter envy at the injustice of it.

Brilliance. More than ever before, Dartmouth taught me not to take it for granted. These same drunken, nasty specimens were the embodiment of pure talent. *P.* had it, a basketballer recruited to play on the varsity team. Throughout the year he trained religiously virtually every day, even through injury, continually honing his ability. *R.* certainly had it. Accepted in the previous year, he deferred entry to go to Malaysia on a Rotary exchange, living with a family there and learning to speak the language fluently. An accomplished swimmer, he also played viola and cello in a youth orchestra and had performed on a tour in Europe.

I paled in comparison to them. I had, though, one attribute that they seemed to lack: a *work ethic.* A dogged, go-for-broke resolve to achieve academic excellence, an affliction peculiarly common to foreign students from third world countries. I didn't see myself having such intensity at all. I just worked like a demon, acutely feeling the handicap of my lack of raw talent. Academic inferiority, coupled with social and sexual frustration, was a white-hot inner wellspring of rage. Tangible fury, I could take hold of it and lash out, driven, throwing myself body and soul into my work. Academics was the one thing in my miserable life that was truly mine, the only endeavor in which I could ever hope to achieve excellence. I was nothing without it. But for all the effort and the hours I put in, my performance was never good enough, never number one. I knew that I was light-years away from the perfection that I expected of myself.

Even so, the work in which I was engaged did hold an attraction: the joy of understanding, that rush upon coming to the solution of a difficult problem through the sheer effort of my own mind. It was as if I actually felt the barriers of my dark ignorance being pushed back, the light of knowledge illuminating just a little bit more of the universe. Triumphs of the mental thus sustained my flagging sense of self-worth, challenging me to further endeavor. Such flashes of wisdom punctuated my career in the liberal arts environment at Dartmouth, especially where curriculum or student activities enabled exploration of subjects completely new to me. Learning Chinese was one such experience.

My grandfather's life, which had begun in a turn-of the-century village outside Guangzhou (Canton), ended with a slow death, his emaciated frame no more than skin and bone, confined to bed for the last year of his life. Learning Chinese was a way to connect with that part of my background. Until that last year, I always saw my grandfather as a permanent human fixture. His memory lives on within my mind: the way he forever slumped in a cloth beach chair, reading novels from the Mainland, their rows of neat, incomprehensible characters marching down the page from right to left. He lived with my aunt, whom I visited infrequently. An introverted fifteen-year-old, I felt no sadness at his passing, only a strange, distant loss as I saw my father's tears. I touched the body barely an hour after it happened, the wrinkled, loose skin of his hollowed cheeks. Cold. The eternal chill of death.

Loss was later to crystallize into anger. Waste, missed opportunity, the realization of all that I could have learned from him. A vital part of my culture gone forever. I vowed to atone: if ever I was able, somehow, somewhere to learn about that lost part of myself, if the opportunity presented itself, I had to take it. I owed it to my grandfather's memory to do so. I found the opportunity at Dartmouth, where Chinese language was offered. I enrolled without hesitation in the introductory course sequence freshman year, and continued on, spending the following summer on a foreign study program in Beijing.

I saw my search for cultural completeness as distinguishing me from most Americans, whose society contained particularly corrosive and soporific influences that were constantly trying to racially and culturally define me. My own identity, self-knowledge, and cultural integrity were the only defense against this insidious process. For instance, at home people call me "red man" if they look at the color of my skin, or "half-Chinese" (funny, they never mention what the other half is) if they look at my features; once, somebody even called me "white boy," which I am *not*. But in this land of overwhelming whiteness, because I was not white, I was automatically considered black. As a Caribbean man, a large part of my heritage is indeed African, but I have red-brown skin and a Chinese name. I do not believe the narrow American mind-set that I encountered was equipped to deal with such diversity in one human being. I was a living contradiction. "Black" was a device for them to simplify me, thereby subsuming both my individuality and ethnicity.

This made for the first awakenings of political awareness within me. Immersing myself in academics and my perceived inferiority, I initially eschewed political activity. However, in the midst of culture shock and recoiling against the excesses of the mainstream, I actively tried to define myself as being culturally alien (and proud of it) by speaking in dialect. My Trini accent, seemingly never strong at home, was to me close to Standard English, born of my middle-class status, privilege, my insulation from any real poverty. Needless to say, at Dartmouth it was strong and immediately noticeable, differentiating me from African Americans, and forcing people, I believe, to deal with me on an additional basis other than color. This presentation of what I thought a cultural stance (a decidedly political act, on reflection) failed miserably. I dropped into true Standard English after about a month because no one could understand anything I said.

If fighting to be an individual and to maintain my own cultural integrity made me politically left wing, then by God I was a Marxist! Continuing to reject the distinction between culture and politics, I became active in the International Students' Association. ISA's mandate was to facilitate meaningful cultural exchange and to impress upon the campus alternative (i.e., non-American) viewpoints on international events. I saw this almost as a moral obligation on the part of the foreign (and particularly the third world) minority: justly counteracting the ignorance of a conspiratorial mainstream that threatened to absorb and culturally sterilize us. The resistance I encountered in achieving this end was an introduction to Dartmouth's polarized politics, and its activism. Campus life seemed largely apolitical for the average white American, the majority of students appearing by choice to remain ignorant of the implications of international issues. The rural isolation of the college helped, enabling escape from a reality filled with gross, and to me very tangible, injustice. It was appalling: Even such a prestigious education couldn't instill in them the capacity to think critically, even encouraging them to remain complacent in the universal rightness of their myths, of their own society and privilege. They seemed to swallow the conventional wisdom fed them by the American media, churlishly regurgitating the same tired rhetoric when their world view was challenged.

This amorphous mass of humanity seemed to perceive me as being representative of "third world peoples," a perception that I used to advantage. Adopting third world peoples as my constituency, I tried to impress upon them that their continued profligacy contributed to deprivation and suffering in underdeveloped countries like my own. Mainstream consciousness was both ideological battleground and spoils of victory for the ISA. Student organizations like ours represented the "progressives," identifying collectively with the cause of the "voiceless oppressed," instigating change by opening the minds of those insulated by privilege. Defending that myopia were the conservative groups, the most infamous being the *Dartmouth Review*. They represented the historical oppressor, seeking to maintain power and perpetuate their own supremacy. Whereas we stood for redress, revolution, and equality, they stood for discrimination, the status quo, and even a reactionary return to traditional white American values. We were the liberals, the communists, the freedom fighters, the anarchic, rabble-rousing "febrile left." They were the right wing, the fascists. With battle lines drawn in stereotypes, the war was fought with protests and pamphlets, speeches and editorials, and constant lobbying of the college administration. The front stretched on and on, from environmental and social responsibility in Dartmouth's investments to the status of women on campus to gay and lesbian rights to international student enrollment to racism to multicultural education, encompassing every possible issue.

None of which should be taken too seriously. The romantic aura of activist, radical campus politics is compelling. I believe it is easy to fool yourself into actually believing the rhetoric of the speeches and propaganda and that by "being radical" you're actually achieving something. In my final year at Dartmouth, I'm still fooling myself, which is good—I suppose my political idealism has not completely atrophied. However, I remain very cynical about the extent to which our actions could make any difference at all. We left-wing activists were all to an extent hypocrites: Our identifying with the cause of the oppressed didn't mean shit in the cosmic scheme of things. Didn't we ourselves enjoy the benefits of the very social, economic, and political injustices we found so abhorrent? Were we not privileged to belong to that tiny constituency able to afford such an education? Were any of us really ready (or even willing) to sacrifice ourselves to aid the oppressed in their plight? It all seemed so futile, our pathetic little mock battles, conducted for the sole purpose of assuaging our guilt. No matter how hard we tried, we were still part of the problem, not the solution.

Nevertheless, fulfilling my inner need to do something about the injustices of the world was quite useful, even cathartic, and gave me channel for my visceral anger. In addition, having to define my own identity forced me to reconcile my experiences and emotions in America with those at home, and analyze my "self" in different contexts. Somehow, without knowing it, instead of simply being introverted I was now actively looking inward. Such self-discovery was the first stage of becoming more at ease with myself, the biggest single step that I took toward maturity. Much of this was the result of my experiences in training for the martial art of aiki-jitsu, beginning in the spring of my freshman year.

With aiki-jitsu, I got much, much more than I bargained for. As a total beginner in the martial arts, I wanted to compensate for my neglect of the physical within myself, to develop strength, coordination, and mental discipline, and at the same time learn self-defense. Training was indeed very physical: Repetitive practice of the fighting movements and constant attention to technique, plain hard labor to drill the body to respond in the way of the art. However, what most attracted me was the philosophical basis of the art, which had its foundation in Zen Buddhism.

Benevolence, politeness, courage, justice, honor, veracity, loyalty. The principles by which I trained were these, the Seven Virtues of *Bushido*, the "way of the warrior." Our instructor (a six-foot-five, white ex-marine) continually exhorted students to reflect upon how each of us as an individual defined ourselves. These were principles to live by, aiki-jitsu being merely an avenue through which we strove to attain awareness, a higher plane of existence, a more human state of being, in harmony with the rest of the universe. Any endeavor could be a ladder—patience, diligence, commitment, and compassion, *that* was the climb. I saw, then, that achievement in the art was secondary, only a goal. Especially lacking in strength and coordination, disheartened by my lack of progress, I drove myself to overcome my physical deficiencies, training hard. On the rare occasions that I tested successfully and achieved a new belt, which meant a higher rank in the art, I realized the transient nature of my triumphs, immediately moving on to even more challenging techniques.

Over time this enabled me to make the connection: Life continued regardless, always bringing with it a new ladder to climb, new goals in an infinite succession. My unhappiness, anger, frustration, and bitterness—all were bound to my hopes and fears, to my dreams and aspirations. Did I not suffer as a direct result of investing my self-worth in achieving them? Academic and physical standards to which I thought I had to conform, emotional and social targets I never felt man enough to attain, what did they mean? Within the fortress, had anything about my inner self really changed? Did anything matter at all?

But I knew that my efforts to achieve had not been in vain. Through them I learned much about the world around me, and, most importantly, about myself. Realizing this revealed what is to me a fundamental truth. It was the *process* that was important, coming to terms with myself through endeavor, continually striving for self-improvement. Blindly caught up in my own mind, I had followed that road all along. Nevertheless, my sufferings were completely necessary. Reflecting upon the tumult of my emotions gave me the power to question and ultimately to understand the nature of my passage through life, my interaction with the rest of the universe, the character of my own soul. From the very beginning I had questioned, but that questioning had come primarily out of the habit of being hard on myself and of allowing my fears to drive me. Exacting perfection by being my own slave driver was futile: No matter how I tried, I couldn't make myself into what I was not. I was not at one with my true self but I could never escape from that self. This created enormous tension that fueled the fires of anger within, warping my capacity for introspection.

Things were different now. All I had was myself. Standards I set for myself had nothing to do with the outside world. Instead, they demanded that I be honest with myself about my own feelings and desires, and that I look inward, critically assessing my own ego and behavioral responses to interactions with the outside world. Questioning was merely the beginning; through observation and reflection I would learn from myself *about* myself. It was no accident that I loved revelation: Understanding was what gave me *purpose*. In the final analysis the most important thing was to understand my own development as it unfolded before me: a reconciliation, coming to terms with myself. In this, the ultimate endeavor, I would not invest my ego or self-esteem in success. Calmly, with focused passion, I would simply do my best. Any more was impossible—any less, unthinkable.

Afterword
Mervyn Morris

I feel a certain kinship with these essayists. I too have been an "international student"–not in the United States, however, but in the United Kingdom (from 1958 to 1961). I even wrote an essay–one of a number by African, Asian, and West Indian students "on their attitudes to the colour problem," assembled in a book called *Disappointed Guests*. The title still makes me uncomfortable, for I was not disappointed. Like the authors in *Crossing Customs* (neatly named), I saw my experience as positive though I identified some problems. Like the essayists in this book, I sketched where I was coming from and examined my responses to my new encounter; I tried to construct an evolving version of myself.

So of course I like this book. I observe with sympathy the concern to register uniqueness. Autobiography implies, however fleetingly, that there is no other individual quite like the person writing it. Listening to these voices, I hear many personal circumstances–often related to intra family dynamics– which the authors present as more crucially important to their formation than the broader cultural context of growing up in Bulgaria rather than Trinidad, or Nigeria rather than Norway. Each of us has multiple (mobile) identities, provisionally defined. To place these essayists as international students is to name one aspect of their complex realities. These are individual persons telling us who they are; admitting us, often, to a process that they know will never end ("who I am," writes Lai Heng Foong, "is constantly in flux"). The essayists give specifics: of affection, conflict, ambiguity, pain; of the ongoing development of students who, in personality, temperament and experience, significantly differ not only from their hosts but also from each other.

To respect individuality is to acknowledge difference (or differences). Acknowledge, not insist upon–few people wish to be invariably defined by the same one category of difference. Aassia Haroon remarks with irony: "As an international student, I am seen as inhabiting a space separate from other students–a space entirely individual, because of the absence of family and community, and yet collectively representative of the curiosities of culture, history, and geography." Devyani Sharma finds among international students "the unspoken understanding that we have . . . come to terms with being isolated." But, responding to a contrary pressure, Ian Sue Wing notes: "There seemed to be this constant, oppressive expectation that I . . . should unquestioningly embrace things American." Misun Kim is one of those who recognizes the pull in both directions: She writes as "a person who struggles to escape her stereotyped identity, while struggling even harder to keep her 'difference' in order to define who she is." Yu Chen similarly, embarrassed not to have understood the instruction to bring quarters to the washing machine, reflects: "I quite often met people who either assumed there was nothing in China or assumed that people lived in the same way as in America, neither of which made me comfortable." This collection vividly illustrates diversity among international students. That is one of its strengths.

There are some things, all the same, on which many of the essayists agree. For example, many have been disturbed by Americans who know little about the world outside the United States. On the evidence of this book, the problem is not so much ignorance as the confident unconcern among students in an inordinately powerful nation. The essayists–some no doubt older and more experienced than their American counterparts–also find the general run of students noticeably immature, especially with regard to alcohol, relationships, and a pernicious connection between the two. Though the student assembly president argues for greater emphasis on moral education, the faculty and facilities get generally excellent reviews. The international students in this collection know why they have come to study in the United States, and, though they have not all been happy all the time, they know they have developed usefully in various ways. ("Here, in America," says one of them, "I am free to chase my goal of growing endlessly.") Having gone away, some think they see their homelands more objectively. Some will return home strengthened. For some, drawn into American life, it may be difficult to return. As Stephen

Kobourov says, "People gradually become more objective in judging their home countries and lose their objectivity toward the countries they are living in."

This is a fine collection because it presents so many interesting people reflecting on their experiences. "You cannot let yourself be perceived through the eyes of others," writes Aassia Haroon. At least, not only through those eyes. With frequent qualification and many nuances, our authors write for us how they have seen themselves.

About the Contributors

Yu Chen, twenty-six, was born in the east coast province of Jiangsu, China. After completing high school, she attended military school for one year and went on to attend Beijing University in 1990, where she earned a degree in Burmese. In 1993 she came to the United States and has since returned to China twice, both times conducting research on issues related to girls' development. After graduating from Dartmouth College in 1997, she entered law school at Boston University. This essay was written in her junior year at Dartmouth.

"Devneesh" is a pseudonym for a male contributor from India.

Frode Eilertsen, twenty-five, was born and raised near Oslo, Norway. He served his required military service upon graduating from high school and completed both officer and specialized training. He gained subsequent military experience through participation in peacekeeping missions in Bosnia-Herzegovina (IFOR) and Lebanon (UNIFIL). After completing his service, Frode was awarded his bachelor's degree at the University of Oslo in Russian area studies and philosophy and pursued post graduate studies in law. He is currently president of the Student Assembly at Dartmouth, where he will earn a bachelor of engineering degree and a bachelor of arts degree in 1999. His essay was written in his junior year at Dartmouth.

Lai Heng Foong, a senior at the time of writing, was a pre-med student majoring in philosophy, with a minor in chemistry. She spent fall of her junior year on a philosophy foreign exchange program in Edinburgh, and later worked with a voluntary organization in black townships in Cape Town, South Africa. After Dartmouth, she did her master's in public health at Johns Hopkins University, with a focus on refugee health and primary health care. Her studies culminated in a practicum with the American Red Cross in Phnom Penh, Cambodia, where she assisted the Ministry of Social Affairs National Task Force in conducting a situational assessment of disabled persons in Cambodia. She then went to Australia to start the first graduate medical course in the country. She is now based at the Royal Darwin Hospital and hopes to return to Cambodia to gain some experience in trauma surgery.

Georgina Gemmill was born in Johannesburg, South Africa. She spent her early childhood as a tomboy known as George, in Lidgetton, a small farming community in Kwa-Zulu Natal. At age six, however, her family returned to Johannesburg, and she spent the remainder of her secondary education in private girls' schools. A postgraduate year at the Hotchkiss School in Lakeville, CT, introduced her to the ideals of a liberal arts education, and she decided to attend Dartmouth, where she pursued a degree in history and graduated in 1996. Today, she works for a consulting firm in Boston and is an active volunteer at an area battered women's shelter. She looks forward to returning home to South Africa in the near future.

Aassia Haroon was born in Hong Kong. She moved to Karachi, Pakistan at the age of twelve, attending the Karachi Grammar School and completing A levels in history, literature, and art. She entered Dartmouth College as a member of the class of 1996, pursuing a degree in government, concentrating in International Relations. Her junior year was spent at the London School of Economics and Political Science, and after returning to Dartmouth, Aassia pursued an extended creative writing project. For the past two years, Aassia has been an Editorial Assistant at Newsline Magazine in Karachi, but has just gone freelance in order to pursue writing for other international and local publications and consultancies for local organizations. Her essay was written during her sophomore year.

Almin Hodzic, twenty-one, was born in the village of Rakovcani (in Bosnia and Herzegovina). His family was forced to leave their country in April 1992, after barely avoiding execution at the hands of Serbian soldiers occupying their village. They spent twenty days in the Trnopolje concentration camp in extremely adverse conditions, at times without food and water, before escaping to Croatia. Sponsored by the

Connecticut Friends of Bosnia, Almin's family subsequently arrived in Greenwich, CT, where he studied at Greenwich High School for three years. Currently Almin is a sophomore at Dartmouth, pursuing a major in psychology and a Russian minor; he is a member of the Dartmouth rowing team. His essay was written in his sophomore year.

"James" is a pseudonym for a male contributor from Nigeria.

"Misun Kim" is a pseudonym for a female contributor from South Korea.

Stephen Kobourov was born in Sofia, Bulgaria. He graduated from Dartmouth *summa cum laude* in 1995 with majors in computer science and mathematics and a minor in classical studies. He received his master's degree in computer science from Johns Hopkins University in 1997, and is currently working on his doctorate. Stephen now lives in Baltimore, Maryland, with his wife, Jennifer, also a Dartmouth graduate. They are anticipating an extensive trip around the world before settling down, with a planned visit to Russia, Greece, and Italy, and Stephen's home in Bulgaria. Stephen wrote this essay during his junior year at Dartmouth.

Maria Popova, twenty-three, was born in Sofia, Bulgaria. She recalls a childhood greatly influenced and enriched by her parents, brother, and grandparents. With her parents' encouragement, she developed a knowledge of English and math as well as a love for reading at a very young age. The confidence and ambition they inspired led her to the National School for Gifted Children, where she received her education prior to commencing her studies at Dartmouth. She graduated from college in 1997, married her high school sweetheart, and is currently pursuing a doctoral degree in government at Harvard University. This essay was written during her sophomore year.

Devyani Sharma, Indian by birth, spent her childhood and adolescence attending a series of schools in various countries, traveling in accordance with her father's job as a diplomat. Upon completion of high school in Geneva, she pursued a one-year art degree in London and began a program in visual communication in Berlin. Changing academic aspirations led her to Dartmouth, where she double-majored in anthropology/linguistics and art. She then spent a year in California, working as a graphic designer, before deciding to explore her interest in linguistics. She is currently pursuing a Ph.D. in linguistics at Stanford University, where art remains a meaningful, private activity in her life. Devyani's essay was written in her first year at Dartmouth.

Ian Sue Wing was born and raised in Trinidad, West Indies. After completing his secondary education at Fatima College and taking classes at the University of the West Indies in Trinidad, he enrolled at Dartmouth in the class of 1993. There, he pursued a degree in engineering sciences and environmental studies, and graduated magna cum laude before going on to complete the bachelor of engineering at Dartmouth's Thayer School. In 1994 Ian was awarded the Commonwealth Caribbean Rhodes Scholarship, and attended Mansfield College at Oxford, where he read for the master's degree in economics for development. He is currently a doctoral student in technology, management, and policy at the Massachusetts Institute of Technology, researching the economics and policy ramifications of global climate change. His essay was written during his junior year at Dartmouth.

About the Editors, and the Foreword and Afterword Writers

Andrew Garrod, a Canadian citizen and graduate of Oxford and Harvard, is associate professor of education and chair of the department at Dartmouth, where he teaches courses in adolescence, moral development, and educational psychology. As an assistant professor at the University of Victoria, he worked in a teacher preparation program for Gitskan and Carrier natives in northern British Columbia, and at Dartmouth he works closely with international students. His recent publications include the co-edited casebook *Adolescent Portraits: Identity, Relationships and Challenges*, the co-authored volume *Preparing for Citizenship: Teaching Youth to Live Democratically*, and a co-edited collection of essays by Native American college graduates, *First Person, First Peoples*. For the past few years, he has spent time conducting moral development research in India, the country of his birth and childhood. In 1991, he was awarded Dartmouth College's Distinguished Teaching Award.

Jay Davis was born to English teacher parents in Katete, Zambia, in 1968, and studied and worked in Spain and France while attending Dartmouth College. After graduating in 1990, Jay tutored international students at the college, and developed an abiding interest in teaching, the experience of outsiders, and helping students find their voice. He has worked closely with Andrew Garrod on numerous book projects, and co-authored a teacher's guide to a collection of Canadian short stories on adolescence. He received a master's in arts and teaching from Brown University, and has taught at a rural boarding school, a school for learning disabled students, and in a school district in Providence, RI, where seventy-eight languages were spoken. He currently teaches English and French at the Richmond Middle School in Hanover, New Hampshire.

Marianne Hirsch is Distinguished Research Professor in the Humanities and Chair of the Comparative Literature Program at Dartmouth College. Having emigrated from Rumania as an adolescent, Hirsch completed her undergraduate and graduate work at Brown University. She has edited or co-edited several feminist collections including *The Voyage In: Fictions of Female Development* (1983), *Conflicts in Feminism* (1991), *Ecritures De Femmes: Nouvelles Cartographies* (1996), and *The Familial Gaze* (1999). She is the author of *The Mother/Daughter Plot: Narrative, Psychoanalysis, Feminism* (1989), and *Family Frames: Photography, Narrative and Postmemory* (1997). Currently she is working on the second-generation memory of the Holocaust and the relationship of memory and trauma.

Mervyn Morris is Professor of Creative Writing and West Indian Literature in the Department of Literatures in English at the University of the West Indies in Jamaica. Drawing on his experience as a Rhodes scholar at Oxford University from 1958 to 1961, Morris wrote the award-winning essay in *Disappointed Guests*, a book of essays by African, Asian, and West Indies students in Britain that served as the inspiration for this book. His volumes of poetry include *The Pond, Shadowboxing, Examination Centre*, and *On Holy Week*. The Institute of Jamaica awarded him a Silver Musgrave Medal in 1976. In Autumn 1992 he was a United Kingdom Arts Council Writer in Residence at the South Bank Centre, London. In 1993 and 1994 he directed the poetry workshop at the University of Miami Summer Institute for Caribbean Creative Writing.